S0-CQS-991

SPECULATIVE PHILOSOPHY

SPECULATIVE PHILOSOPHY

A Study of Its Nature Types and Uses

by

Andrew J. Reck

Albuquerque

UNIVERSITY OF NEW MEXICO PRESS

Manufactured in the United States of America
Library of Congress Catalog Card No. 72-80751
First Edition

TO THE MEMORY OF
DON MICHELE MANGIARACINA
(1856–1940)

ACKNOWLEDGMENTS

I wish to thank the Tulane Research Council for a grant which enabled me to take a leave of absence during the 1967–1968 academic year to work on this book.

Chapter II was presented as colloquia papers at Florida State University, Vanderbilt University, and Johns Hopkins University. Early versions of Chapter VII were presented as lectures at St. Mary's College and St. Theresa's College in Winona, Minnesota; as colloquia papers at Rice University, the University of Delaware, and Northern Illinois University; as Thomasfest Lecture at Xavier University in Cincinnati, Ohio; and as Suarez Lecture at Spring Hill College in Alabama. I am grateful to the philosophy students and faculty of these institutions for permitting me to ventilate my views.

Andrew J. Reck

CONTENTS

INTRODUCTION

Alfred North Whitehead drew a distinction between "the Reason of Ulysses" and "the Reason of Plato." The import of Whitehead's distinction is unmistakable. It exposes the role of reason not simply in philosophy but in civilization.

The Reason of Ulysses is exclusively practical, and Ulysses "shares it with the foxes."[1] Despite its much vaunted practicality, however, Ulysses' reason rarely solves real problems. Pressed by interminable exigencies, it adopts a strategy of evasion. Even when Ulysses, at his best, restricts reason to solving problems, one relentlessly following upon the heels of another, he has reduced reason to mere methodology; and finally weighted with fatigue, he loses his wiliness. Preoccupation with methods and means blinds the wholly practical man to the nature of goals and ends, so that mechanism no longer subserves but rather supplants final causation in the conduct of life. Thus futility and doom are the fate of Ulysses, and as Whitehead remarked: "the bones of his companions are strewn on many a reef and many an isle."[2]

The Reason of Plato is theoretical, and Plato shares it with the gods. Plato's reason seeks to understand "the Universe, or at least factors in it, . . . in their character of exemplifying a theoretical system."[3] It is "enthroned above the practical tasks of the world. . . . It seeks with disinterested curiosity an understanding of the world."[4] It reaches from partial to complete understanding, providing life with a vision of what is possible and investing it with a new dynamism. "Speculative reason" is Whitehead's term for theoretical reason in its proper sense. By means of the adjective "speculative," Whitehead sought to distinguish Plato's reason not only from practical reason in its usual senses but also from methodological reason, a species of practical reason operative in the special sciences. Looking beyond means to ends, beyond mechanism to possible goals, beyond efficient causation to final causation, speculative reason is, Whitehead affirmed, "in its essence untrammelled by method. Its function is to pierce into the general reasons beyond limited reasons, to understand all methods as coordinated in a nature of things only to be grasped by transcending all method."[5] Although Whitehead admitted that "the bounded intelligence of mankind" can never attain the "infinite ideal" of speculative reason, he nonetheless held that "what distinguishes men from the animals, some humans from other humans, is the inclusion in their natures, waveringly and dimly, of a disturbing element, which is the flight after the unattainable."[6]

The "flight after the unattainable" characterizes the unique condition of man. It is manifest in his greatest cultural achievements—social institutions, religion, art, and science. Nowhere is it more conspicuous than in speculative reason's first fruit—speculative philosophy. Nearly all the great philosophers from Thales to Whitehead have been speculative, except perhaps such leaders in the empirical tradition as John Locke and David Hume, although even they display some qualities of the speculative philosopher.

Speculative philosophy is *systematic*. The speculative philosopher seeks to define a group of ultimate categories which are consistent with one another, mutually support one another, and are applicable to all subject-matters. These ultimate categories, or basic concepts, may of course be supplemented by secondary categories as special subject-matters require.

Speculative philosophy is *comprehensive*. The speculative philosopher seeks a system of concepts which claims to be capable of explaining whatever is or may be. This claim sometimes necessitates that new items presented in experience be interpreted in extraordinary ways so that they may fit into the system.

Speculative philosophy is *metaphysical*. The ultimate categories on which speculative philosophers concentrate are invariably concepts of being or knowing—whether substance, process, mind, or what not.

Speculative philosophy is *explanatory*. Speculative philosophers may disagree about the nature of explanation, as they would about other essential characteristics of speculative philosophy. On the whole, however, each would maintain that his set of ultimate categories subsumes, describes, or in some fundamental sense illuminates every part of experience and reality. Speculative philosophy, then, is said to furnish knowledge about things whereby they are really known or understood.

Finally, speculative philosophy is *conjectural*. However dogmatic a speculative philosopher may be about the certainty of his set of ultimate categories, there should be no doubt that the categories he offers extend beyond the contexts of knowledge and experience from which they originally arose. If they are extended to embrace all experience and reality, the ultimate categories proposed by a given speculative philosopher may, when successful, elevate him to a position of astonishing vision.

At least philosophy, it might seem, would remain essentially speculative. Yet the foxes have invaded the philosophical vineyard in such large numbers that, with few exceptions, the fruits of speculation have been devoured before they could ripen. Although speculative philosophy has persisted, nourished by the themes set by the classic American philosophers and extended in the works of contemporary thinkers,[7] the plight of twentieth-century philosophy in America attests to the prevalence of the foxes.

The century opened with the birth of pragmatism, and before 1925 John Dewey was widely regarded as the leading pragmatist and even the American philosopher *par excellence*. Dewey had little enthusiasm for traditional metaphysics with its flights of speculation. He attacked any philosophy which evaded the problems of men by seeking security in a table of experience-transcending categories.

Then in the 1930s logical positivism seemed to join hands with pragmatism in the repudiation of speculative metaphysics. Whereas pragmatists asserted that metaphysical speculation was a useless escape from the problems of men, the logical positivists vigorously denied that metaphysics was cognitively meaningful. It is impossible to underestimate the damage which the logical positivists and their followers have done to philosophy in the United States. No doubt, logical positivism attracted many young students because of the simplicity of its position. Peremptorily it dismissed the whole history of philosophy before 1922, the year when Wittgenstein's *Tractatus Logico-Philosophicus* was published. It also applauded science, or rather promoted a restrictive conception of scientific knowledge, and so claimed credit that belonged to science. Professional pressures of a political type, however, cannot be discounted. When I was in my first year as a graduate student in the late 1940s, a visiting professor of philosophy at the university where I was studying told me: "Become a logical positivist, or you will have no future."

Later the analytic philosophy of ordinary language was to have its negative impact on speculative metaphysics in America. The linguistic analysts ruled out "the craving for generality" characteristic of speculative metaphysics. They were inclined to reduce the meaning of a term to its uses in various contexts and sought, instead of the principles of reality, the language rules governing these uses. When they conceded that metaphysical statements afford insight, they contended that the kind of insight furnished was of the same type as that the psychoanalyst seeks.

Hence pragmatism, logical positivism, and linguistic analysis, all three very powerful tendencies in American philosophy during mid-century, induced many young philosophers to turn away from speculative metaphysics. Manley Thompson in his survey of metaphysics in the United States from 1930 to 1960 has prophesied a dim future for speculation. While he is unwilling to assert that "speculative metaphysics in the grand manner . . . will disappear altogether," he deems it "safe to say" that such enterprises "have about run their course."[8]

Yet speculative philosophy has not perished. Indeed, one feature of contemporary thought has been its resurgence. During the high tide of logical positivism in the United States, in 1947, Paul Weiss founded *The Review of Metaphysics,* and in 1950 he established the Metaphysical Society of America.[9]

Weiss, who was temporary chairman of the first meeting of the Metaphysical Society held on April 15, 1950, at Yale University, presented an address entitled "The Four-Fold Art of Avoiding Questions." Dismayed by the antimetaphysical tendencies then prevailing, Weiss denounced any philosophical method which denies, as he declared,

> . . . the importance or meaningfulness of anything which lies beyond its scope or power. But we have been given no assurance by fact or dialectic that the mysteries which beset us are to be solved in only one way. We need not one but many methods, not one but hundreds of schools—or better, we must avoid prescribed methods, limitative schools or programs, and instead invite a host of independent inquirers to submit to one another's criticism the products of honest thought. No man or school has mastered all the ways by which we can learn all that we should.[10]

Invoking the name of Peirce, whose writings he had coedited with Charles Hartshorne, Weiss called for a community of inquirers. These inquirers, he exhorted, should face root questions and speculatively propose answers. They should display "humility in the attitude, . . . freedom from provincialism, . . . catholicity of spirit, some courage too," and while they would rely in part upon "the insight and wisdom of others," they should never merely repeat what has already been said.[11] Weiss emphasized: "The one great intellectual crime, C. S. Peirce observed, is the crime of blocking the road of inquiry."[12]

Weiss's exhortation has proved effective, if one is to judge by the numbers of thinkers who have participated in the Metaphysical Society of America and who have published in *The Review of Metaphysics* during the past quarter of a century. Hence the time has come to study speculative philosophy itself. For so far as this enterprise has been investigated in recent decades, the investigation has mainly been conducted by those thinkers who are antipathetic to the nature and function of speculative metaphysics. The present work, therefore, is offered as a new attempt, in the face of felt needs, to define speculative philosophy, specify its types, and delineate its uses.

Now a presupposition of the present work is that the sort of attempt it makes may be expected to succeed only if due attention is paid to the history of philosophy. Too often in current philosophical literature metaphilosophical theses about the nature and course of philosophies are advanced without the presentation of sufficient evidence of what has actually been thought in philosophy. Of course the history of philosophy is no substitute for philosophy proper, nor even for metaphilosophy. Considerations of structure and of types involving complex criteriological decisions, should here take precedence over considerations of mere sequential development. Thus the history of philosophy cannot be ignored, but it is utilized in the present work primarily for philosophical rather than historical purposes.

Chapters I and II are concerned to define what speculative philosophy is. Further, Chapter II seeks to ascertain the principle (or principles) from which the major types of speculative philosophy spring. Chapters III through VI treat, respectively, the four major types: realism, materialism, idealism, and process philosophy. Chapter VII delineates the uses of speculative philosophy—theoretical, religious, aesthetic, moral, social, and psychological. This last chapter is most appropriate at a time when every study is confronted with the demand to be relevant. Nonetheless, speculative philosophy is, in the last analysis, intrinsically "useless." It is "useless" in the classic sense, according to which a liberal science exists not for the sake of anything else but for its own sake. Indeed, everything else may be for its sake, too! Hence the "uses" of speculative philosophy are extrinsic only.

Still the practical import of speculative philosophy should never be underestimated. The fox alone is death, as the disarray of contemporary civilization testifies. The recovery of a rational and humane order is contingent upon the resumption by speculative reason of its function in furnishing comprehensive visions of the things that are and of the things that are possible. One way or other, these visions affect our lives in their most intimate recesses, and their authors are ultimately our governors. It is impossible to state the point better than Whitehead did in the closing sentences of *Science and the Modern World:* "The great conquerors, from Alexander to Caesar, and from Caesar to Napoleon, influenced profoundly the lives of subsequent generations. But the total effect of this influence shrinks to insignificance, if compared to the entire transformation of human habits and human mentality produced by a long line of men of thought from Thales to the present day, men individually powerless, but ultimately the rulers of the world."[13]

I

THE NATURE OF SPECULATIVE PHILOSOPHY

The term "speculative philosophy," like the terms "man" or "novel" or "city," is a class term with existential reference; there are many speculative philosophies, just as there are many men, novels, and cities. The common meaning in the different uses of the term may be discerned, if discerned at all, through consideration of the particular cases. It would serve no purpose, save perhaps the exposition of one's own private meanings, to stipulate a definition which had no applications in the history of thought. An understanding of the meaning of "speculative philosophy" is correct to the extent that it is consonant with the conceptions held by the great speculative philosophers.

CLASSICAL VIEWS

A first step in the elucidation of the term "speculative philosophy" is an examination of its component words. The word "philosophy" is a compound originally formed in the Greek language from two words, *philos* and *sophia,* the first translatable into English as "love" and the second as "wisdom"; it literally means "the love of wisdom." In the Greek language, the compound term, with appropriate endings, could denote either a person or an activity. There was, moreover, no settled meaning for the term *sophia:* it signified the exercise of intelligence in business, conduct, or the skilled crafts. Plato (429–347 B.C.), following Pythagoras (fl. 570 B.C.), converted wisdom from exclusive practical concern with human life to the speculative quest for the vision of the whole truth.

In *The Republic* Plato considered wisdom to be the virtue which makes knowledge possible, including knowledge of the good and so of right conduct. In the ideal state wisdom is the virtue resident in the ruling class. Explicitly distinguished from correct opinion, which guides the skilled crafts, wisdom is evident in the policy which governs the state. In the good man wisdom is the virtue operative in the rational part of his soul, an excellence which is manifest in sound character and conduct; it involves rational control of his entire person, of his will and his appetites. The speculative nature of wisdom is heightened by Plato's interpretation of the conditions requisite to the actualization of the ideal state.

At first Socrates, Plato's spokesman in the dialogue, evaded Glaucon's challenge to show that the ideal state may be realized; he remarked that an ideal is not any less an ideal because of its lack of actuality. Presently, however, Socrates succumbed to pressure and pronounced, in a moment of supreme irony, the celebrated dictum that the ideal state will be realized when philosophers become kings and kings, philosophers. This dictum, though expressing a remote possibility, opened a new line of discussion, seeking the definition of the philosopher, with the attendant digression on epistemology and metaphysics in Books V and VI of *The Republic*. Unlike those who love perceptions and opinions, the philosophers are "lovers of the vision of truth." [1] They "only are able to grasp the eternal and unchangeable." [2] In quest of truth, the philosopher seeks knowledge, that is to say, certain cognition which has as its object immutable and perfect being—the universal forms. For love of wisdom the philosopher yearns for a vision of purely intelligible being—an absolute and independent world of universal forms (or Ideas) embraced by the form of the Good.

The Platonic conception of philosophy, at least as it has been construed by the tradition, is tantamount to the equation of philosophy with speculation. Now etymologically the term "speculation" has its origin in the Latin verb, *speculari,* meaning "to spy, to observe." A cognate is the Latin noun, *specula,* signifying "a watch tower." *The Oxford English Dictionary* offers, among the various definitions of speculation, several applicable to philosophy. Two are worthy of citation: 1) "The contemplation, consideration, or profound study *of* some subject;" and 2) "Contemplation of a profound, far-reaching, or subtle character; abstract or hypothetical reasoning on subjects of a deep, abstruse, or conjectural nature." [3] In Baldwin's *Dictionary of Philosophy and Psychology,* the article on speculation in philosophy, written by John Dewey, supplies three definitions, two of which restate the formulae quoted above: 1) "Meditation or reflection of the mind upon itself, or upon spiritual things"; and 2) "A form of theorizing which goes beyond verifiable observation and reflection, characterized by loose and venturesome hypotheses (popular use)." [4] Whereas these definitions of speculation convey the sense that its subject is fundamental, profound, ultimate, they also connote that it is abstruse, conjectural, hypothetical. The finality of its subject-matter is matched by the uncertainty of its method. How far these definitions deviate from the classic conceptions may be estimated as the sketch of the history of those conceptions is resumed.

Aristotle (384–322 B.C.) carried on the Platonic tradition in speculative philosophy. Like Plato, he divided philosophical statements into three kinds: ethical, physical and logical. He radically revised this classification, however, when he propounded his own definition of knowledge into theoretical, practical, and poetic. Without adhering rigidly to this division, Aristotle held that knowledge is either pursued for its own sake, for the sake of action, or for the sake of making things. Theoretical knowledge is, by definition, knowledge pursued for its own sake; it includes first philosophy, physics and mathematics. Yet inasmuch as physics and mathematics may also be sought as poetic knowledge—i.e., for the sake of making things, it follows that first philosophy, whatever it may be, is the only kind of knowledge exclusively theoretical.

Aristotle's conception of first philosophy is by no means easy to ascertain. Adronicus of Rhodes, who edited Aristotle's writings circa 70 B.C., decided to place the treatises dealing with first philosophy after the physics, with the result that the term "metaphysics," meaning "after the physics," came into being as the synonym for first philosophy. Despite this humble etymology, the term "metaphysics" signifies many things. Thus, in standard philosophical usage, it refers to the theory of knowledge (epistemology) and/or the theory of being (ontology); and in ordinary usage, it connotes that which is beyond nature (supernatural) and/or beyond experience (mystical, transcendental). Further, the term "metaphysics" denotes ambiguously a subject-matter and/or a method.

As subject-matter, metaphysics may be studied by any method, including the critical and analytic methods; as a method, however, metaphysics has traditionally been speculative. In recent discussions analytic philosophers have drawn a distinction between descriptive metaphysics and revisionary metaphysics. The descriptive metaphysician attempts to lay bare the most general features of our conceptual structure; he seeks to describe the actual structure of our thought about the world as language reveals it.[5] Descriptive metaphysics may be traced back to Aristotle's *Categories,* where Aristotle defines ten ways things are meant in ordinary language: substance, quantity, quality, relation, place, date, posture, possession, action, and passion. Revisionary metaphysics is "an attempt to re-order or to reorganize the set of ideas with which we think about the world; assimilating to one another some things which we customarily distinguish, distinguishing others which we normally assimilate; promoting some ideas to key positions, downgrading or dismissing others . . . a re-drawing of the map of thought—or parts of it—on a new plan."[6]

Aristotle's *Metaphysics,* while it contains much descriptive metaphysics, is a leading specimen of revisionary metaphysics. Whereas descriptive metaphysics is inherently analytic, and whereas revisionary metaphysics should be analytic in part, it is evident that, because of its innovative function, revisionary metaphysics is essentially speculative. While it is correct to acknowledge that metaphysics need not be speculative, it is equally correct to admit that metaphysics has been, and may properly remain, speculative. At any rate, speculative philosophies are usually metaphysical systems, so that the present study of speculative philosophy is inevitably a study of metaphysics. No doubt, the ambiguities of the term "metaphysics" hark back to Aristotle's discussions of first philosophy.

One point on which Aristotle seems clear is that first philosophy is Wisdom. He seems clear, too, on the distinguishing characteristics of the wise man: 1) that he knows all things, although not in detail; 2) that he knows things which are difficult to learn (and so are not perceived by the senses); 3) that he is exact in his knowledge; 4) that he is able to teach his knowledge; 5) that he possesses knowledge for its own sake; and 6) that he is superior and should command others who in turn ought to obey him.

Aristotle, however, was not clear concerning the subject-matter of first philosophy. In the *Metaphysics* he presented at least four, perhaps incompatible, conceptions of this subject-matter. Early in Book I Aristotle defined first philosophy as the science of first principles, and the remainder of the book he devoted to the first principles construed as the four causes constitutive of physical realities: the efficient, the material, the formal, and the final causes. Initially the subject-matter of first philosophy is nature, and metaphysics is a speculative extension of physics. A variation on this conception of first philosophy occurs when the first principles are equated with the principles of logic. Then metaphysics concentrates on the justification of the first principles of logic, the so-called laws of thought, and in particular, on the principle of contradiction.

On the other hand, Aristotle distinguished first philosophy from the other theoretical sciences of physics and mathematics by contending that whereas physics studies substances which exist separately but are not immovable and mathematics studies substances which are immovable but do not exist separately, first philosophy studies substances which both exist separately and are immovable. As the study of the separate immovable substances, first philosophy is tantamount to theology—in Aristotle's sense, the science of the pure actualities which sustain and rule the physical world of change. Aristotle also defined first philosophy "as a science which investigates being as being and the attributes which belong to this in virtue of its own nature."[7] As the study of being *qua* being, first philosophy is ontology. Fortunately, it is not necessary to decide between the rival conceptions of first philosophy in Aristotle or to demonstrate that they are reconcilable.[8] Suffice it to remark that these conceptions pervade the post-Aristotelian developments of speculative philosophy, spawning rival Aristotelianisms.

On the whole, the schools of philosophy that flourished in the Hellenistic period subordinated philosophical speculation to moral considerations. Stoicism, epicureanism, skepticism, and mysticism were the main philosophical traditions in the Graeco-Roman world. Although stoicism and epicureanism contained metaphysics, the stoics building on the flux philosophy of Heraclitus (530–470 B.C.) and the epicureans on the atomism of Democritus (460–360 B.C.), these systems sought essentially to define the good life for men, the life of virtue or the life of pleasure, and to enunciate those practical rules, recommending either passionlessness or withdrawal from involvement in institutional affairs, which, if followed, would enable men to attain the good life.

Similarly, skepticism and mysticism exhibited the primacy of the concern with the practical prevalent in the Graeco-Roman world. By subjecting the possibility of knowledge to irresoluble doubt, skepticism foreclosed speculative philosophy, while it expected, by means of the universal suspension of judgment, not only to save men from error but also to gain for them at last that peace of mind which formerly had been imputed to strict adhesion to fixed beliefs. As regards speculation, mysticism was more tolerant than skepticism. In the case of Plotinus (A.D. 205–270), mysticism projected a major system of psychology, ontology, and cosmology, a system which, despite its neo-Platonic appellation, owes as much to Aristotle and others as to Plato, and is unquestionably original in form. Nevertheless, mysticism, too, was overlaid with a practical, indeed a religious, intention: to save men from deficiency of being for communion with the One by means of the mystical method of dialectic and intuition—"the flight of the alone to the alone."[9]

In due time the new religions which invaded the Roman Empire from its eastern borders superseded the ethico-religious systems of late antiquity, and these religions in turn surrendered the field to a triumphant Christianity. The moral preoccupations of philosophy were absorbed in the religious yearning for salvation. Philosophy did not perish, although it was hard pressed by the hostility of such Church Fathers as Tertullian (A.D. 155–220).

The role of philosophy in life and civilization was, however, radically altered. Inquiry untrammeled by authority and tradition yielded before the supremacy of religion as expressed in Sacred Scriptures and backed by the institutions of the Church. Philosophy was required to adjust itself to faith, a requirement which inspired one of the crucial themes of Christian thought—namely, the relation of reason and faith. Existing within the context of faith, speculative philosophy was constantly checked by revealed theology, which was a complex blend of Sacred Scriptures, traditional interpretations supported by the officialdom of the Church, and mysteries acknowledged by her most famous theologians. In sum, philosophy, including speculation, was the handmaiden of theology, and whatever the place accorded natural or rational theology, highest honor went to revealed theology.

MODERN CONCEPTIONS

The recovery of speculative philosophy did not occur until the advent of rationalism in modern thought. René Descartes (1596–1650) established the rationalist ideal of speculative philosophy. His aim, superbly expressed in the first of his *Meditations on First Philosophy* (1642), was to discover the secure basis upon which science and philosophy could be erected. In his *Discourse on Method* (1637) he presented as the rules for all rational inquiry the same rules which, he believed, he had employed when he invented analytic geometry and which he uncovered when he reflected on the procedures he had followed in his mathematical researches. These rules are four: 1) Never accept anything as true except what is recognized as true by the clarity and distinctness of its conceptions; 2) divide up the difficulties of any problem into as many simple parts as possible and as are requisite for its solution; 3) proceed in due order from the simplest and easiest to understand to the more complex and more difficult; and 4) review the steps taken in the investigation to ascertain that nothing has been omitted.[10]

In effect, what Descartes recommended was the reconstruction of philosophy in accord with his conception of the mathematical model. Henceforth all philosophy would begin with self-evident principles, indubitable axioms, consisting of clear and distinct conceptions explicitly defined. Then by rigorous deductions from these axioms the philosopher would proceed to establish certain theories concerning the existence of the self, God, the external material world, and all other knowledgeable matters. While Descartes subscribed to the axiomatic-deductive method of seventeenth-century mathematics as the sole valid method of inquiry, he insisted upon the unity of the sciences and, with equal emphasis, upon their foundation in metaphysics. In the Preface to the *Principles of Philosophy* Descartes resorted to the Biblical tree of knowledge to symbolize his interpretation of the system of the sciences. "All philosophy," he wrote, "is like a tree, whose roots are metaphysics, whose trunk is physics, and whose branches springing out of this trunk are all the other sciences, which reduce to the three principal ones—that is, Medicine, Mechanics, and Morality." [11]

Baruch de Spinoza (1632–1677) realized the rationalist ideal in speculative philosophy more perfectly than Descartes had done. Achieving what Descartes had merely approached, Spinoza not only presented Cartesian philosophy in geometrical form in his *Principles of Descartes' Philosophy* (1663); he also absorbed practical concerns within the compass of speculative thought. Although Descartes had, in the concluding clauses of the tree-of-knowledge passage cited above, described the science of morality as "the highest and most perfect morality, which, presupposing total knowledge of all the other sciences, is the last degree of Wisdom," [12] the morality he did formulate was provisional only. Hence Descartes claimed, as in the synopsis of his *Meditations,* that the truth he explained is exclusively theoretical. By contrast, Spinoza conceived the unity of the theoretical and the practical to be so intimate that he could allow no separation. Human happiness, he remarked in his *Treatise on the Improvement of the Understanding* (1677), depends wholly on the quality of the object which we love. Only an infinite and eternal object is worthy of the kind of love that is blessed with happiness;

such an object must be God, for God is, according to Spinoza's conception, Substance absolutely infinite and eternal, or Nature creative and created.

Spinoza's *Ethics* (1677), with its axioms, definitions, and demonstrated theorems, is the most conspicuous exemplification of the rationalist ideal in speculative philosophy; and it encompasses religious and moral themes in its rigorous deductive argument, culminating in the intellectual love of God in which alone true happiness is found. As Spinoza wrote in the concluding paragraph of the *Ethics,* "the wise man, in so far as he is considered as such, is scarcely ever moved in his mind, but being conscious by a certain eternal necessity of himself, of God, and of things, never ceases to be, and always enjoys true peace of soul." [13]

The rationalist ideal of speculative philosophy is, no doubt, intoxicating. Among recent philosophers, John McTaggart (1866–1925) has succumbed to its fascination. In his major work, *The Nature of Existence* (1921–1927), he endeavored to construct an entire metaphysical system on self-evident premises from which he claimed to deduce a total theory of reality. Into this rationalistic structure McTaggart poured an idealistic content. Further, the idealism is pluralistic, deriving more from Gottfried Wilhelm Leibniz (1646–1716) than from the monist Spinoza.

The rationalist ideal in speculative philosophy, however exhilarating, has been betrayed by its own adherents. As Charles Sanders Peirce (1839–1914) has contended, the method of establishing beliefs by appeal to a priori principles and self-evident axioms reduces merely to individual taste, each philosopher exploiting those notions that appeal to him. The appeal to clear and distinct ideas is, despite its pretension, scarcely logical, but is rather nothing more than the acceptance of familiar notions, whether or not they are intrinsically clear or operationally definable. Subjective feeling therefore invades the rationalist ideal, so that the rationalist's philosophy more readily reflects his own temperament than the world. Cognizant of this consequence, William James (1842–1910) has dubbed rationality a sentiment, and has even gone so far as to classify philosophies according to the tough-mindedness and tender-mindedness of the philosophers. At any rate, the rationalist ideal in speculative philosophy degenerated into several incompatible systems, three of which have been historically prominent: the dualism of Descartes, the monism of Spinoza, and the pluralism of Leibniz. To safeguard his own system against the challenging alternatives, each rationalist resorts to dogmatism.

The empiricists, through an examination of human knowledge, undermined the rationalist ideal. The rationalists employed the mathematical model in speculative philosophy because they believed in innate knowledge and considered it legitimate to try to spin the structure and content of an entire knowledge of the world out of a finite set of basic human concepts. On the other hand, the empiricists, when consistent, maintained that all knowledge originates in experience. For the general scheme of the world in which men live, the empiricists looked to Sir Isaac Newton (1642–1727), whose commitment to the priority of fact over theory is summed up in the declaration: "Hypotheses non fingo." What remained for the empirical philosophers was to explain how knowledge of nature along Newtonian lines is gained. John Locke (1632–1704) set the tone for the empiricists when he styled himself "an under-labourer" in the field of science and philosophy,[14] and his statement of purpose in the Introduction to his *Essay Concerning Human Understanding* (1690) prescribed their work as well as his own: "to inquire into the original, certainty, and extent of *human knowledge,* together with the grounds and degrees of *belief, opinion,* and *assent.*"[15] Since, according to Locke, human understanding cannot fathom the depths of "the vast ocean of Being,"[16] it is incapable of a comprehensive, profound grasp of reality; it cannot apprehend the nature of substance in general, nor the relation between mind and matter, nor finally the real essences of things. Although Locke was consoled by the pragmatic thought that "our business here is not to know all things, but those which concern our conduct,"[17] he shut the door to speculative philosophy.

The empiricists in effect relegated the study of nature to the physicists, then called natural philosophers. What remained for study, as David Hume (1711–1776) saw, was man himself. Hume proposed to study man by means of the same experimental method which had proved effective in the natural sciences. But the germ of skepticism in Locke's philosophy was contagious, and despite the efforts of George Berkeley (1685–1753), it spread from Locke's denial of the possibility of knowledge concerning substance in general and real essences to Hume's conception of human reason itself. Reason, according to Hume, could not even validate such basic principles of reasoning as the principle of causation; these had to be explained psychologically as natural beliefs, products of experience and mental dispositions. Consequently, the conclusion to Hume's *Enquiry Concerning the Human Understanding* (1748) is not surprising. On his theory, since all theology or speculative metaphysics consists neither in abstract reasoning concerning quantity and number, nor in experimental reasoning concerning matters of fact, it should be committed to "the flames, for it can contain nothing but sophistry and illusion."[18]

Traditional rationalism led to dogmatism in speculative philosophy, and traditional empiricism to skepticism. As Immanuel Kant (1724–1804) surveyed the field in his *Prolegomena to Any Future Metaphysics* (1783), this impasse blocked metaphysics from becoming a science. Were metaphysics a science, it would be a peculiar sort of knowledge: first, its sources would be wholly nonempirical; second, its principles would lie beyond experience; and third, it would be wholly a priori, coming from pure understanding and pure reason.

To establish metaphysics as a science, Kant proposed a new method in philosophy—the critical method. He critically examined the knowledge furnished by the mathematical and the natural sciences to educe the a priori forms, categories, principles, and cognitive faculties which these sciences presuppose. Hence metaphysics becomes science when it becomes critique—that is, when it systematically presents, analyzes, and justifies the a priori elements in all our knowledge.

Kant's method resolved Hume's skepticism, for it revealed an a priori which has its source in pure understanding and pure reason. The category of cause, for example, is seen to be an a priori category of the understanding. It springs not from man's habits and empirical observations, but from his rational faculty, and it prevails universally in experience and nature. Experience is structured by man's rational faculty, which imposes upon sense-data the a priori categories. Reason legislates for experience, and since nature is another term for experience, for nature as well. Thus Kant's critical philosophy culminates in transcendental idealism. The percepts, upon which empiricism rested its philosophy exclusively, are blind without concepts. On the other hand, the pure concepts are agents of synthesis; they unify the data of experience, and have no epistemological function except in relation to these data. By maintaining that sense-experience conditions all human knowledge, Kant avoided rationalist dogmatism.

Kant's attitudes toward metaphysics were influenced by the leading eighteenth-century German philosophers, Christian Wolff (1679–1754) and A. G. Baumgarten (1714–1762). A dogmatic rationalist who expounded Leibnizian doctrines, Wolff had defined philosophy as "the science of the possibles insofar as they can be."[19] In his classification of the parts of philosophy, he defined metaphysics as "the science of being, of the world in general, and of spirits."[20] Ordered according to the priority of their principles, the parts of metaphysics are: ontology, cosmology, psychology, and theology. Wolff equated ontology with "first philosophy" and defined it "as the science of being in general, or insofar as it is being."[21] Baumgarten, whose *Metaphysics* (1739) Kant adopted as a textbook, was a disciple of Wolff. Kant dropped ontology from his system, and put metaphysics as critique in its place. Analyzing, systematizing and justifying the concepts and principles of knowledge, Kant formulated a table of forms and categories which, while inapplicable to being in itself, comprises the conditions of human experience. The two forms of sensibility are space and time; and the twelve categories of understanding are unity, plurality, totality, reality, negation, limitation, substance, causality, reciprocity, possibility, existence, and necessity. This list Kant regarded as absolute and final.

Kant's critical method also uncovered three Ideas of Reason—of the Self, of the Cosmos, and of God. From these Ideas, he contended, sprang the three branches of speculative metaphysics: 1) rational psychology, which studies the human mind, self, or soul; 2) rational cosmology, which studies nature and its supernatural conditions; and 3) rational theology, which studies God, especially by constructing proofs of his existence. An unavoidable undertaking of human reason, speculative metaphysics is, in regard to knowledge, doomed to failure. As Kant said: "There exists . . . a natural and unavoidable dialectic of pure reason—not one in which a bungler might entangle himself through lack of knowledge, or one which some sophist has artificially invented to confuse thinking people, but one inseparable from human reason, and which, even after its deceptiveness has been exposed, will not cease to play tricks with reason and continually entrap it into momentary aberrations ever and again calling for correction." [22]

Despite the pretensions of speculative metaphysics to afford knowledge which transcends human experience and reaches absolute being, Kant's critique is intended to show that all genuine human knowledge is bounded by experience—indeed, conditioned by sensibility. In the case of each branch of speculative metaphysics, Kant argued that the attempt to win knowledge transcending (and thrusting into the unconditioned conditions of) nature and experience either depends on fundamental fallacies in conception or results in antinomies, i.e., apparent contradictions. The correction of these fallacies and the resolution of these antinomies, effectuated by the application of the critical method, impel reason to retreat from speculation. As Kant declared: "Critique, therefore, and critique alone contains in itself the whole well-proved and well-tested plan, and even all the means, required to establish metaphysics as a science; by other ways and means it is impossible." [23]

RECENT PERSPECTIVES

In the history of philosophy Kant's establishment of metaphysics as critique has been revolutionary. Yet once the critical method had been introduced, its surgery has proved to be more extensive than Kant, who used it simply to cut speculative metaphysics out of the body of sound knowledge, had anticipated. R. G. Collingwood (1889–1943) recognized that Kant's a priori was not as universal and necessary as Kant esteemed it to be. Collingwood believed that metaphysics is analysis, "the analysis which detects absolute presuppositions."[24] He defined metaphysics as "the science of absolute presuppositions."[25] In addition, he defined absolute presupposition as an assumption which, while it is not a true or false proposition, is logically prior to a body of knowledge. As Collingwood said, "Metaphysics is the attempt to find out what absolute presuppositions have been made by this or that person or group of persons, on this or that occasion or group of occasions, in the course of this or that piece of thinking."[26] According to Collingwood, Kant's a priori principles are absolute presuppositions, but—and this is Collingwood's original thrust—they are all bound up in the historical development of science. Despite the allegation of eternal validity, Kant's categories "can be read as a history of the absolute presuppositions of natural science from Galileo to Kant himself."[27] Hence for Collingwood, metaphysics is a branch of history: "All metaphysical questions are historical questions, and all metaphysical propositions are historical propositions."[28]

Nevertheless, speculative philosophy has not died. After Kant, in fact, it found renewal in both reason and experience. G. W. F. Hegel (1770–1831) best represents the reinvigoration of speculation from the standpoint of reason; Henri Bergson (1859–1941), from the standpoint of experience.

Hegel considered Kant's philosophy to be a philosophy of the understanding rather than a philosophy of reason. Kant checked reason whenever concepts, extended beyond experience, led to contradiction. The philosophy of reason, Hegel held, regards contradiction not as a stopping place but as a starting point for speculation. Overcoming the contradictions dialectically, reason assimilates the original opposites in a higher synthesis. For Hegel, therefore, a philosophy of reason is inveterately speculative; it is also panlogical. Under logic Hegel subsumed all the branches of metaphysics: ontology, rational psychology, rational cosmology, and rational theology. The course of thought and of the world unfolds dialectically in pure concepts, culminating in an Absolute which is both substance and subject. The truth is a whole to which all the special sciences contribute; further, the whole is more than its parts. As Hegel said:

> The relation of speculative science to the other sciences may be stated in the following terms. It does not in the least neglect the empirical facts contained in the several sciences, but recognizes and adopts them: it appreciates and applies towards its own structure the universal element in these sciences, their laws and classifications: but besides all this, into the categories of science it introduces, and gives currency to, other categories.[29]

The thesis that speculation introduces categories into the empirical sciences, categories acquired independently of experience, and by means of dialectic alone, aroused grave objections to Hegel's system. On this score F. H. Bradley (1846–1924) and A. E. Taylor (1869–1945), both Hegelians, concur in opposing Hegel. Although they accepted as the task of metaphysics the resolution of the contradictions of seeming and being, appearance and reality, they repudiated the dialectical method and disavowed speculation. Bradley's position is overlaid with irony, conspicuous in his oft-cited aphorisms—for example, "Metaphysics is the finding of bad reasons for what we believe upon instinct, but to find these reasons is no less an instinct." [30] In contrast, A. E. Taylor presented his position with simplicity. For A. E. Taylor, metaphysics rises from the contradictions between appearance and reality, contradictions which are encountered in experience and in thought; it "sets itself, more systematically and universally than any other sciences, to ask what, after all, is meant by being *real*." [31] So far, Taylor and Hegel agree. But then Taylor described the method of metaphysics as analytical, critical, nonempirical, noninductive, and constructive. These adjectives clearly do not connote speculation in Hegel's sense. Even the description of metaphysics as constructive signifies merely that, like any science, it produces in the individual a certain intellectual attitude toward the world. Thus for Taylor metaphysics is essentially analytical and critical—i.e., "directed to the detection and removal of contradictions in the categories of thought." [32]

While Hegel's followers withdrew from speculation to criticism, philosophers who invoked experience rather than reason revived speculative metaphysics. Superbly illustrating this tack in philosophy, Bergson appealed to intuition, in order to go beyond the abstract concepts of reason and to penetrate the concrete flux of experience. Resembling the mystic's drive for immediate communion with being, Bergsonian intuition, however, grasps no fixed structure of unchanging reality; it grasps duration. In his *Introduction to Metaphysics* (1903), Bergson equated metaphysics with the movement of intuition between two extreme limits. At one extreme is the "pure homogeneous," the "pure repetition" which circumscribes materiality, and which is reached as intuition regresses "toward a duration more and more scattered, whose palpitations, more rapid than ours, dividing our simple sensation, dilute its quality into quantity."[33] At the other extreme intuition grasps a "duration which stretches, tightens, and becomes more and more intensified; at the limit would be eternity."[34] This eternity, Bergson insisted, is "an eternity of life. It would be a living and consequently a still moving eternity where our own duration would find itself like the vibrations in light, and which would be the concretion of all duration as materiality is its dispersion."[35] On the basis of the intuition of duration Bergson erected a speculative philosophy of creative evolution. Needless to say, the critics pounced upon it. Notwithstanding his rejection of concepts on the grounds that they distort the flux, Bergson used them to render his thought systematic and coherent. Bergson's philosophy was confronted with a serious dilemma: adhere to intuition, and no theory is possible; or construct a theory, and intuition must be surpassed.

Other philosophers took their stand on experience, with various reverberations for philosophical speculation. From the start, traditional empiricism has been skeptical of speculation, and since the nineteenth century, it has been toughened up as positivism. Nevertheless, after Kant a conception of experience quite different from the traditional view came to be accepted, if not universally, at least widely. Both traditional rationalists and traditional empiricists had conceived experience to be a collection or sequence of discrete sense data devoid of genuine relatedness; indeed, that is why Kant invoked a priori reason to provide sense data their relatedness. However, some post-Kantian philosophers came to regard experience as an integrated and moving whole of qualities and relations. William James termed the new approach "radical empiricism." Accordingly, experience is a stream in which relations and qualities are both immediate.[36] Adopting James's concept of experience, John Dewey (1859–1952) added the characteristics of objectivity and sociality. For Dewey experience serves as the foundation of a metaphysics; it furnishes the clues to the generic traits of existence.[37] Nevertheless, Dewey had no enthusiasm for a philosophy which found security in a table of categories and evaded the problems of men; he attacked the traditional metaphysician for his transcendent flights of speculation.

WHITEHEAD'S THEORY

Few among twentieth-century philosophers equal Alfred North Whitehead (1861–1947) in fundamental contributions to speculative philosophy. Whitehead's conception of speculative philosophy reconciles the claims of both reason and experience; it meets the legitimate demands of both rationalism and empiricism. Whitehead offered his conception of speculative philosophy in Chapter I, Part I, of *Process and Reality* (1929), and again in Chapter XV, Part II, of *Adventures of Ideas* (1933). "Speculative philosophy," he said, "is the endeavour to frame a coherent, logical, necessary system of general ideas in terms of which every element of our experience can be interpreted."[38] According to this definition, speculative philosophy is both rational and empirical: rational because of its internal criteria of coherence, logic, and necessity; and empirical because of the external criterion of interpreting every element of our experience.

Whitehead nodded to rationalism with the requirement that the speculative system be coherent and logical. If the system is consistent, violating no rule of inference, and consisting of determinable basic concepts, it is deemed logical. The coherence of the system signifies more; it means "that the fundamental ideas, in terms of which the scheme is developed, presuppose each other so that in isolation they are meaningless."[39] Here Whitehead leaned on the side of Hegelian idealism with its doctrine of internal relations, which he extended beyond the conceptual elements to all elements in the system. He declared that it is "the business of speculative philosophy to exhibit this truth" that "no entity can be conceived in complete abstraction from the system of the universe."[40] Further, the necessity of the speculative system is, for Whitehead, equivalent to the universality of its fundamental concepts. In expressing this requirement, Whitehead radically modified rationalism. The necessity of the system means, he wrote, "that there is an essence to the universe which forbids relationships beyond itself, as a violation of its rationality. Speculative philosophy seeks that essence."[41] In still other ways Whitehead departed from traditional rationalism. Explicitly he repudiated the rationalistic contention that the fundamental principles could be clear and distinct axioms from which by deductive methods alone the rest of philosophy could be inferred.

Whitehead's commitment to empiricism in speculative philosophy is evident in his acknowledgment of experience as the origin and the test of philosophical principles. After all, he held that the system of general ideas must be able to interpret "every element of our experience." By "interpretation" he meant "that everything of which we are conscious, as enjoyed, perceived, willed, or thought, shall have the character of a particular instance of the general scheme."[42] Thus he made explicit the external criteria for an acceptable system of speculative philosophy: the interpretation should be "applicable" and "adequate" to experience. Whitehead, in fact, put major emphasis on the empirical side of speculative philosophy. He said, "Our datum is the actual world, including ourselves; and this actual world spreads itself for observation in the guise of the topic of our immediate experience. The elucidation of immediate experience is the sole justification of any thought."[43]

In attending to experience, speculative philosophy must be descriptive; at the same time, it must generalize. In Whitehead's words, "the primary method of philosophy is descriptive generalization."[44] Rooted in experience, generalization takes observed and analyzed elements of immediate experience as the clues to the nature and structure of remote experience, since it proceeds solely from the awareness of difference, and beyond. Unfortunately empirical observation is limited. Whitehead playfully illustrates this limitation: "Sometimes we see an elephant, and sometimes we do not. The result is that an elephant, when present, is noticed."[45] Observation does not suffice for generalization, because just those elements of experience which are most pervasive and hence most useful for valid generalization are the most difficult, if not impossible, to observe. To supply the requisite difference, "imaginative generalization" supplements observation. Whitehead has compared this method to the flight of an airplane. "It starts from the ground of particular observation; it makes a flight in the thin air of imaginative generalization; and it again lands for renewed observation rendered acute by rational interpretation."[46]

The method of generalization, therefore, utilizes "specific notions, applying to a restricted group of facts, for the divination of the generic notions which apply to all facts."[47] This guarantees that the empirical requirement that the system apply at least to experience and that the items of experience be interpreted in terms of the general conceptions of the system. After selecting a specific set of notions and generalizing them into the basic conceptions of the system, the method of generalization must proceed in "unflinching pursuit of the two rationalistic ideals, coherence and logical perfection."[48]

Because rationalism has led historically to dogmatic yet false systems, Whitehead maintained that the coherence of the generic notions should not take precedence over the interpretation of experience, and that the generic notions, once achieved, should never be held as dogmatically certain. "Metaphysical categories," he asserted, "are not dogmatic statements of the obvious; they are tentative formulations of the utmost generalities."[49] Thus the logician's alternative of true or false cannot readily be applied to the basic categorial scheme, and if applied, "the answer must be that the scheme is false."[50] Whatever truth the scheme possesses is dependent on "unformulated qualifications, exceptions, limitations, and new interpretations in terms of more general notions."[51]

As Professor W. Mays has said, "The method of philosophical construction put forward by Whitehead resembles the hypothetico-deductive method used by the scientist and the mathematician."[52] Speculative philosophy, in Whitehead's words, "embodies the method of the 'working hypothesis'. . . . Such an hypothesis directs observation, and decides upon the mutual relevance of various types of evidence. In short, it prescribes method."[53] The resemblance between speculative philosophy and science should not, however, be mistaken as identity. The first step in the construction of a philosophical system, already mentioned as imaginative generalization, involves "philosophic intuitions," so much so that on one occasion Whitehead described philosophic system "as an attempt to coordinate all such intuitions."[54]

Another difference between philosophy and science comes to the fore, one which is supportive rather than divisive. Speculative philosophy, Whitehead wrote,

> seeks those generalities which characterize the complete reality of fact, and apart from which any fact must sink into an abstraction. But science makes the abstraction, and is content to understand the complete fact in respect to only some of its essential aspects. Science and Philosophy mutually criticize each other, and provide imaginative material for each other. A philosophic system should present an elucidation of concrete fact from which the sciences abstract. Also the sciences should find their principles in the concrete facts which a philosophic system presents.[55]

Whereas the sciences offer specialized theories, speculative philosophy presents a comprehensive working hypothesis: "to coordinate the current expressions of human experience, in common speech, in social institutions, in actions, in the principles of the various special sciences, elucidating harmony and exposing discrepancies."[56]

Whitehead pointed to one resemblance between philosophical and scientific systems that is usually ignored. As every student knows, the history of Western thought is strewn with the wreckage of philosophical systems. This predicament of speculative metaphysics Kant had cited in contrast with the apparent achievements of the natural sciences, particularly of physics and of mathematics, in formulating basic conceptions upon which lasting knowledge could be built. But as Whitehead demonstrated, Kant's contrast of certain science with uncertain philosophy is mistaken. As the career of Newtonian physics has testified in the present century, science, no less than speculative philosophy, undergoes radical revisions of its ultimate categories. Whitehead, however, did not despair of attaining truth in science and philosophy; the quest for true principles, he held, is unrelenting. Borrowing a term from mathematics, he described this approach to truth in both science and philosophy as "asymptotic."[57] Accordingly, the systems of philosophy and of science can never be closed; they must remain open for revision, addition, and alteration. As Whitehead said: "The proper test is not that of finality, but of progress."[58]

Whitehead's definition of speculative philosophy as a coherent and adequate scheme of basic categories, capable of interpreting all items of experience, yet tentative and open to further revision, is most attractive. It manifests affinity with the openness to truth evident in the thought of Plato and of Aristotle. It combines the methodological virtues of rationalism and empiricism. It submits to the discipline of self-criticism as the critical philosophy demands. It even retrieves by its own hypothetico-deductive method of imaginative and descriptive generalization much of the content of Hegelian idealism. Having located science itself in the development of philosophy, Whitehead succeeded in stating the case for speculative philosophy in a scientific age.

II

TYPES OF SPECULATIVE PHILOSOPHY

Speculative philosophy promises to provide the scheme of basic categories which comprehend all the elements of reality and experience in a coherent system. Yet speculative philosophy has encountered a disarray of its own making—the multiplicity of its own types. As the history of philosophy testifies, speculative philosophers have been exceptionally fertile, so fertile that students who have consulted philosophy in quest of a single truth have been disheartened to find, instead, a seeming warfare of incompatible doctrines. Speculative philosophy, which claims to explain all, is alleged to weaken its claim when it disintegrates into rival and even opposing systems. The explainer is itself in need of explanation.

As philosophers have advanced in sophistication, they have addressed themselves to the task of explaining philosophies. The philosophical investigation of philosophy is, to use a technical word, metaphilosophy. The subject-matter of metaphilosophy is philosophy itself. Metaphilosophy resembles the history of philosophy, since both disciplines have philosophy as their subject-matter. But the resemblance is not complete. The metaphilosopher is primarily a philosopher. His interest is systematic and critical: to order the materials which the various philosophies supply and to offer an explanation of them. The historian of philosophy has more in common with the historian in general; he is not required to explain so much as to describe the rich manifold of man's intellectual developments and to trace connections in the whole without questioning the whole as such. The paths of metaphilosophy and the history of philosophy crisscross. Without a competent knowledge of the history of philosophy, the metaphilosopher is prone to concoct arid theories, devoid of exemplification.

As a recognizable branch of philosophy, metaphilosophy is of recent vintage. Only in the past generation have philosophical scholars devoted their intellectual energies to metaphilosophical questions. Ideally the metaphilosopher is neutral regarding the philosophies with which he deals. He should, unquestionably, be critical; but the criteria of criticism he adopts must apply equally to all philosophies, and must have their justification equally in all. The achievements of metaphilosophy have been most conspicuous in the subbranches of meta-ethics and meta-logic. Less well-recognized, although certainly well-cultivated, is the branch of metaphilosophy which concentrates on speculative philosophy. It is appropriate here to examine some leading metaphilosophical theories of speculative philosophy.

ROYCE'S THEORY

Josiah Royce (1855–1916) presented, in the first volume of his work, *The World and the Individual* (1899), an explicitly metaphysical metaphilosophy. Royce was not a neutral; he was a dialectician bent on establishing his own metaphysics of absolute idealism. According to Royce, metaphysics embraces two disciplines, ontology and epistemology, each indispensable to the other. Ontology is the study of being, and epistemology of knowing. *The World and the Individual* pivots on the mutual, the reciprocal involvement of being and knowing.

Royce sought to define being. Although his primary concern was religion, he considered ontology to be prerequisite to philosophy of religion. Royce said: "I shall dwell upon the nature of Being, because to assert that God is, or that the World is, or even, with Descartes, that I am, implies that one knows what it is to be, or in other words, what the so-called existential predicate itself involves."[1] To define being, Royce resorted to the analysis of language. By means of this analysis, he proceeded to formulate a classification of the major conceptions of Being.

First, to delimit the field of ontology Royce attended to language and its principal uses. He observed that verbs, adjectives, and other expressions implicate language in assertions concerning *what* things are or do, and that still other expressions implicate language in assertions *that* things are or are not. Noting that this distinction in linguistic function corresponds to the traditional metaphysical distinction between essence and existence, Royce circumscribed ontology proper to the study of the *that,* of existence.

Second, Royce detected in ordinary language three classes of expressions which are germane to the definition of being. The expressions in the first class declare that "their object is *to be seen,* or is *at hand,* or can be *found,* or is *marked,* or is *plain,* or *stands out,* or is *there,* or, as the Germans also say, is *vorhanden;* while the unreal has *no standing,* or is *not at hand,* or is *not to be found,* or is *not there.*"[2] According to the first class of expressions, to be is to be immediate. By contrast, a second class of expressions "declares that an object is real, not by virtue of its mere presence or obviousness, but in so far as it is *deeper* than what is visible, or in so far as it has *foundation, solidity, permanence, interior constitution, profundity* of meaning."[3] According to the second class of expressions, to be is to be well-founded—i.e., to be independent. A third class of expressions designates unreality as "an *appearance,* a *delusion,* a *sham,* a *myth,* a *fraud,* a *phantasm,* an *imitation,* a *lie,*" and it designates the real as "what you can *depend upon.* It [the real] is *genuine,* no mere *imitation.* It is true."[4] According to the third class of expressions, to be is to be genuine and true—i.e., to be valid.

On Royce's analysis, ordinary language offers "hints, so to speak, of our various more technical conceptions of Being."[5] Each class of expressions corresponds to a type of ontology, or major conception of Being. For Mysticism, Being is the immediate; for Realism, Being is the independent; and for Critical Rationalism, Being is validity. Since ordinary language suggests three conflicting, even contradictory, conceptions of being, its expressions do not display Royce's own conception. This conception of Being is constructive idealism: "*To be . . .* means to fulfil a purpose, in fact, to fulfil in final individual expression, the *only* purpose, namely, the Absolute purpose."[6] The correct path to the true ontology, therefore, is not the analysis of language, but the theory of knowledge—epistemology. The problem of being, the "worldknot" as Royce termed it, finds its solution in epistemology. As Royce said: "I am one of those who hold that when you ask the question: What is an Idea? and: How can Ideas stand in any true relation to Reality? you attack the worldknot in the way that promises most for the untying of its meshes."[7]

A brief review of Royce's treatment of the four conceptions of Being should illuminate his theory of the types of speculative philosophy.

Realism conceives the real to be what "is simply *independent* of the mere ideas that relate or that may relate to it. For this view, what is, is not only external to our ideas of it, but absolutely and independently decides as to the validity of such ideas."[8] Realism posits a realm of independent beings, of possible objects of knowledge to which knowledge makes no difference. Nevertheless, the realist, in defining being as independent, fails to untie the worldknot. When beings are independent of one another in the ultimate sense that independence is the essence of their being, it is impossible to relate them. Consequently, realism is torn between monism and pluralism, between a Realm of One, independent yet needing no relation because there is no other, and a Realm of Many, each independent and unrelated because independence precludes relatedness. The impossibility of relating independent real beings, according to Royce, renders knowledge impossible. Knowledge requires the relation of an idea to its object, so that for realism knowledge is impossible, since the idea as being and the object as being cannot be related. Neither One nor Many, neither knowing nor known, Being realistically conceived turns out to be "the realm of absolutely nothing."[9]

Mysticism is "the logically precise and symmetrical correspondent of realism."[10] Mysticism insists upon the immediacy of being: "that is real which is absolutely and finally *Immediate*."[11] "*To be* means to quench thought in the presence of a final immediacy which completely satisfies all ideas."[12] Despite the apparent oppositeness of realism and mysticism, with realism stressing independence and mysticism stressing immediacy, their dialectical outcome at the hands of Royce is the same. Mysticism cancels the subjective consciousness in the absolute immediacy; hence mysticism "loses all finite outlines, lapses into pure immediacy, quenches thought, becomes ineffable, satisfies even by turning into what ordinary Realism would call a mere naught."[13] As Royce concluded, realism and mysticism finally agree: "Each in the end defines Nothing whatever."[14]

Critical rationalism equates the real with the valid. "To be real now means primarily, *to be valid, to be true, to be in essence the standard for ideas.*"[15] According to Royce, this conception of being is a singular attempt "to define the Real as explicitly and only the Universal."[16] Plato, Thomas Aquinas, and Kant are cited as exponents of this type of ontology. Royce subjected the third conception of being to his dialectic. He questioned the definition of being as validity. He asked: "The truth is, indeed, valid; but is it *only* valid? Can the realm of validity remain *merely* a realm of validity?"[17] He sought his answers in two directions: first, in consciousness, and second, in objective reality. The upshot of Royce's dialectic was the rejection of critical rationalism as an incomplete system, and the proposal in its place of constructive idealism.

Royce presented his fourth conception of being, constructive idealism, as a synthesizing ontology. With realism, it posits an Other distinct from and authoritative over the finite idea. With mysticism, it identifies Being with the fulfillment of purpose. With critical rationalism, it "asserts that Being essentially involves what gives the validity to ideas."[18] But, as Royce emphasized, constructive idealism offers its own definition of being. The real is, therefore, that "which finally presents in a completed experience the whole meaning of a System of Ideas."[19] "To be means simply to express, to embody the complete internal meaning of a certain absolute system of ideas."[20]

Royce's arguments for this fourth conception of being are manifold, but metaphysical to the core. The ontological strand of his argument has to do with the problem of the One and the Many as interpreted in the absolute idealist context of relating the finite individual to the Absolute; it involves the doctrine of the concrete universal, which will be considered in Chapter V. The epistemological strand of Royce's argument merits consideration here; it has to do with the relation of an idea to its object.

Royce defined "idea" to be "any state of consciousness, whether simple or complex, which, when present, is then and there viewed as at least the partial expression or embodiment of a single conscious purpose."[21] Royce called this purpose the internal meaning of the idea. In addition, the idea has a reference; it points to an object, a real being, which would fulfill its purpose. This Royce termed the external meaning of the idea. The duality of internal meaning and external meaning corresponds to the problem of relating the idea to its object. Briefly, Royce solved this problem by treating the internal meaning of the idea as an intent which selects its object, and by considering the external meaning to be the object thus intended. Idea corresponds to Being in that its own felt purpose, impelling it from a condition of insufficiency and finitude and even error, is realized and fulfilled in Absolute Being.

Royce's metaphilosophy is susceptible to criticism. Particular conceptions of being—e.g., critical rationalism—are not clearly presented; indeed, in the case of the definition of being as validity, doubt may be raised as to whether the philosophers, such as Plato and Kant, whom Royce mentioned, have even advocated it. The scheme of these four conceptions also lacks adequacy; it fails to include all major conceptions of being. Conspicuous throughout Royce's discussion is his bias. His metaphilosophy culminates in absolute idealism, because it is implacably partisan. Royce did not trouble himself to be neutral.

SPAULDING'S THEORY

Historically Josiah Royce has had his opposite in the American neorealist, Edward Gleason Spaulding (1873–1940). Spaulding's major contribution to metaphilosophy is *The New Rationalism* (1918); it is a formidable treatise in which the case for realism is constructed on the basis of modern logic and science, and it proceeds through the criticism of opposed philosophical systems. Philosophical systems, according to Spaulding, conform to the formal model of hypothetico-deductive science. A system of philosophy is like a system of geometry; it consists of a set of postulates from which all other propositions within the system are deduced. Spaulding recognized that most philosophers, influenced by tradition or by their own emotional dispositions, have been unconscious in choosing their postulates, although this psychological fact should not obscure the logic involved. Thus he proposed to make these implicit postulates explicit and to elucidate the structures of the historically important types of philosophical systems. Not content to record merely the opinions of past philosophers, Spaulding examined the logic of philosophies. His intention is constantly proclaimed: to affirm philosophical realism as the sole true philosophy. As Spaulding wrote: "Realism is that constructive philosophical position which is derived by an empirical and critical examination of other philosophies, most of which are found to presuppose, or to contain, explicitly or implicitly, positions and principles that are to be accepted as true." [22]

The key to the various systems of philosophy is the theory of relations which each presupposes or affirms. The old logic, which stems from Aristotle, presents a theory of internal relations. Upon this theory are grounded all the false philosophies opposed to realism. The new logic proposes a theory of external relations. The direct denial of this theory is the theory of internal relations. Upon the theory of external relations the whole true philosophy, realism, is founded.

Spaulding expressed the theory of external relations symbolically as $\underline{a}/R/\underline{b}$. The formula means

> (1) that, if two terms are related, neither term influences the other, (2) that the absence of either term would be *without effect* on the other, (3) that either term may come into being and into relation with the other term without affecting it, (4) that, accordingly, no term is *complex* by virtue of being related, and (5) that no third term, $\underline{u}$, underlying $\underline{a}R\underline{b}$ in the sense of $\underbrace{\underline{a}\ R\ \underline{b}}_{U}$, is necessary in order to medi-

ate the relationship between $\underline{a}$ and $\underline{b}$. Briefly, the theory of external relations is, that *relatedness and independence are quite compatible.*[23]

As the direct denial of the above, the theory of internal relations assumes two forms: the modification theory and the underlying or transcendent reality theory. Spaulding expressed the modification theory by the symbolic formula: $\overset{\longrightarrow}{\underset{\longleftarrow}{\underline{a}_b\ R\ \underline{b}_a}}$. The formula means that, "if two terms are related, (1) each term *influences* the other, (2) that related terms are *complex,* (3) that either term out of relation with the other would be different from what it is in relation to that other, (4) that terms are *what they are by virtue of being related to other terms* (the organic view)."[24] Further, Spaulding expressed the underlying reality theory of relations by the symbolic formula $\underbrace{\underline{a}\,R\,\underline{b}}_{U}$. The formula means that "if two terms are related, and whether they modify each other or not, there is an *underlying* or *transcendent* reality, U, to mediate this relation, indeed to make it possible at all."[25]

The modification theory and the underlying reality theory allegedly initiated the traditional concept of causation and the traditional concept of substance, respectively. False philosophies are classified according to their foundation in one theory or the other, the so-called causation philosophies on the modification theory and the so-called substance philosophies on the underlying or transcendent reality theory. Spaulding listed among the main causation philosophies: phenomenalism, subjective idealism, positivism, naturalism, and pragmatism; and he identified as the supreme substance philosophy: objective idealism. Spaulding's discussion of these various philosophies is a closely reasoned, systematic analysis of the postulates and principles which characterize each type. In the examination of causation philosophies Spaulding was careful to show that logically prior (though not necessarily chronologically prior) types lead to logically posterior types. Thus phenomenalism, by the alteration or elimination of a minimum of basic postulates and principles, logically entails subjective idealism; subjective idealism, in turn, entails positivism; and so on. Spaulding also sought to demonstrate that each type is inconsistent. That is, each type implicitly presupposes principles which are incompatible with its main contention—principles which reveal, in fact, a latent realistic philosophy at the base of all other systems.

Spaulding's metaphilosophy, the opposite of Royce's, culminates in realism. Objective idealism, grounded in the underlying or transcendent theory of internal relations, is repudiated as a substance philosophy which reduces all beings to attributes of one absolute whole. In its place Spaulding proposed a philosophy of function—realism. The foundation of realism is the theory of external relations. This theory is vindicated in epistemology. For Royce the failure of realism had been epistemological: realism was allegedly unable to relate the idea in the mind of the knower to the object existing independently of the knower. For Spaulding, however, no such failure occurs. As an external relation, knowledge may relate the knower to his object without impairing the ontological independence of either. An external relation may relate terms that exist independently, and the knowledge relation is such an external relation. The knower is, no doubt, affected by the knowledge relation; the cognitive content of his mind is advanced; yet his mind is not therefore causally affected, but rather is functionally affected. Knowing neither alters the object known, nor requires an underlying or transcendent reality to mediate the knower and his object.

Spaulding's claim that the outcome of entire philosophical systems rests upon the theories of relations which these systems uphold has a contemporary ring. True or false, it is an interesting thesis which merits consideration. Whether theories of relations determine systems, or systems theories of relations, may be a moot point. Spaulding's judgment that the theories of relations are the determinants falls short of demonstration. In making the judgment Spaulding may, indeed, have been inconsistent. If true, Spaulding's judgment supposes that any theory of relations is internally related to its system, but not in the sense that the system underlies or modifies the relations, since that would mean that the system determines the relations and not otherwise. Rather, if Spaulding is correct, the parts of the system are modified by the relations which relate them, or the relations underlie or transcend the system, or both. But then Spaulding's theory of external relations is false. Further, Spaulding's conception of philosophical systems as wholly conforming to the formal model of geometrical systems illustrates the rationalist ideal in speculative philosophy. This ideal, discussed in Chapter I, does not do justice to the factor of experience in the construction of philosophical systems. Finally, Spaulding's metaphilosophy, like Royce's, exhibits too little neutrality. His adherence to the theory of external relations, particularly in regard to the knowledge relation, guaranteed in advance of argument and evidence that realism would prove triumphant. The dogmatic tone of Spaulding's work, despite the penetrating analyses it contains, has militated against its acceptance. Certainly, it has not deterred individual idealists from proposing their favorite doctrines.

HOCKING'S THEORY

William Ernest Hocking (1873–1966) carried on the idealist tradition which Royce, his teacher, had espoused. Although Royce had pursued his inquiry into metaphilosophy by combining ontology and epistemology, Hocking, however, in his *Types of Philosophy* (1929), separated the two. Some types of philosophy are primarily metaphysical (ontological), others are primarily epistemological, and still other types intertwine both philosophical disciplines. Thus Hocking sought to escape the assault launched against idealism by those realists who, having distinguished ontology from epistemology and having placed primary emphasis on the former, regarded the knowledge relation as an external relation which did not affect the independent ontological existence of the terms related. Regardless of the outcome of the controversy raging in epistemology, Hocking was enabled to espouse idealism.

Other differences between Royce's metaphilosophy and Hocking's are discernible. Royce defined only four types of philosophical systems; Hocking detected seven types. There is, according to Hocking, an *ur*-philosophy which is the primitive form of all philosophizing: spiritualism. The first explicit type of philosophy is naturalism. It is the naive yet critical opposite of spiritualism, critical in that it negates claims of spiritualism concerning the existence of God and of the afterlife, naive in that it does not examine the methods and criteria of its own knowledge. The purely metaphysical types, spiritualism and naturalism, yield before two purely epistemological types: pragmatism and intuitionism; and these two, in their turn, give place to the four most sophisticated types: dualism, idealism, realism, and mysticism.

The heightened irenicism of Hocking's metaphilosophy best distinguishes it from Royce's and from Spaulding's. Royce and Spaulding agree that all types but one are false; they disagree over what the one true type is. By contrast, the structure of Hocking's philosophy, though admittedly idealistic, contains all the other types as well. While Royce rejected mysticism and realism, Hocking embraced them both within his idealism. Mysticism, he insisted, is realistic when properly conceived; and realism mystical. He wrote:

> The real cannot be either the absolute One of the mystic or the absolute Many revealed by realistic analysis. The Mystic and the Realist, each being guided in what he sees by his practical preoccupation, and believing final what he most effectively deals with, each grasps *half of the truth* about the world. Each therefore supplements and corrects the other. Both realism and mysticism thus appear as aspects of an idealistic world-view, which explains and places them both; while they, in turn, make clearer the practical necessity of rhythm or alternation.[26]

Hocking proposed a synthesis of the types although his conception of synthesis is idiosyncratic. He actually exhorted others to formulate their own individual philosophies. Since eclecticism is the method of combining into a more or less coherent whole the principal conceptions of several systems, he recognized eclecticism to be a significant preliminary step in thinking through one's own position. Eclecticism, however, proves to be ultimately inadequate. One's own philosophy "will necessarily correspond, in part, with one or more of these types; for they present, on fundamental questions, the possible alternatives."[27] This does not mean that one's own philosophy is a mere replica of one of the constant types. On the contrary, one's own philosophy, according to Hocking, is a product of one's own intuition of the world—unique yet universal. As for Hocking, his personal intuition of the world was inveterately idealistic. He, like Royce, maintained that "there is some kind of mental life at the core of reality." [28] As Hocking declared in his final chapter, *Confessio fidei,* "I believe that idealism is not so much a separate type of philosophy as the essence of all philosophy, an assumption whether recognized or unrecognized of the philosophic enterprise. I take idealism, then, so far as this argument carries us, as the centre of my metaphysics." [29]

Although Hocking claimed that synthesis is an achievement of dialectic, personal intuition rather than dialectic holds sway. But personal intuition varies with the temperament of the philosopher. Hence the synthesis is easily split up into many different systems, systems so much at odds with one another that both Royce and Spaulding agreed that only one is true. Philosophers disagree—that is the scandal of philosophy. The fact of disagreement, among philosophers, as well as the fact of conflict and contradiction among philosophies, becomes a problem with which metaphilosophy must cope.

SHELDON'S THEORY

Wilmon H. Sheldon has made the fact of conflict among philosophies, "the strife of systems" as he called it, the crux of his own investigations. Sheldon is unequivocally opposed to the stratagem of adopting a partisan position and refuting alternatives from its standpoint. In *The Strife of Systems and Productive Duality* (1918), Sheldon asked: "If all schools of thought but one are fundamentally in error—as nearly everybody thinks in every age—would it not be a miracle that one should escape the common lot?" [30] Instead of being partisan, Sheldon has sought to understand the strife and to find within it the principle which makes a synthesis of systems possible. Sheldon's enterprise has been sustained by three convictions: that since philosophy exhibits an array of recurrent types of system, these systems must in some sense be true; that their contradictions can be mollified; and that the source of the strife, if detected, bears forth an unknown yet fundamental character of reality.

Sheldon's list of the recurrent philosophical types has undergone revision. In *The Strife of Systems,* Sheldon explored a dialectical progression of systems. First comes subjectivism, then its counterpart, objectivism. Their opposition is resolved in the "solvent" of "pure experience." The system of pure experience is superseded by "great" subjectivism, which is then locked in conflict with "great" objectivism. The conflict is succeeded by the irrationalist group of philosophies: intellectualism, pragmatism, and intuitionism. These philosophies are next set against the rationalistic synthesis of Hegel and his British disciples. The rationalistic synthesis, in its turn, is opposed to the practical synthesis—Thomism. Subsequently, Sheldon has recognized recent trends in existentialism as forms of irrationalism, while he has also added Process Philosophy to his list. In *God and Polarity* (1954), Sheldon wrote: "Our list of the more fundamental issues is now: idealism or spiritualism vs. materialism, each and both vs. dualism, rationalism vs. irrationalism, Thomism vs. Process, and within idealism, monism and pluralism or personalism"; [31] or as these topics are organized to shape up the chapters of *God and Polarity:* "idealism, monistic or pluralistic, materialism, Thomism, Process, and irrationalism." [32]

Each type of system is designed to meet a different human craving; hence it is unavoidable. Monistic idealism insists on the objective rationality of the universe and the identification of the universe with value, personalist idealism focuses on the irreducible reality of finite conscious minds, and materialism vaunts the values of the body and corporeal nature. Synthesizing materialism and idealism, the Thomistic philosophy reconciles their values in an eternal hierarchy of substances rising from a base of corporeal elements, reaching through a variegated domain of hylomorphic creatures, and culminating in a heaven of purely spiritual beings dominated by an absolute Creator. Contrasted with Thomism stands Process Philosophy, still vague in detail, yet definite enough in outline, to disclose that it "takes time seriously," adjusting the static vertical structure of the Thomistic levels of being to the horizontal dynamics of temporal development. Existentialist irrationalism, revolting against the rationalism of the other types, calls attention to the category of crisis and the primacy of the human condition in the construction of theory. Thus each philosophy is right in emphasizing a given set of values neglected by the other philosophies. Insofar as it is positive, it is true. Its truth is verified in the living experience of its adherents.

Each philosophy is true in what it affirms, false in what it denies of the others. In *The Strife of Systems,* Sheldon ascribed the interminable controversy of philosophies to a logical predicament which constrains them to contradict each other. In *God and Polarity,* he traced the genesis of disagreement back even beyond this logical germ to its source in the philosophers' loves and valuations, to their passionate worship of some exclusive category and their consequent blindness to others. He declared: "Disagreement is due to disvaluing."[33]

In *The Strife of Systems,* Sheldon sought to show that contradiction is inevitable as long as philosophy is a congeries of systems each short of the total truth. Two principles govern our thought: the principle of internal relations and the principle of external relations. They contradict each other, constituting the "disease-germ which had poisoned all human philosophy."[34] According to the principle of externality, "there are entities which are the same in all environments, independent of the relations in which they enter, and ultimate."[35] Every system in opting for the ultimacy of its category—matter, mind, and so forth—acknowledges the principles of externality in respect to this category. Yet each system, in striving to understand what lies on the other side of its favored category, employs the principle of internality. It must, in other words, reduce all other categories to its own or to some relation of its own: materialism, for instance, defines mind as relations of matter. "It is as if each category said of its counterpart, 'I am ultimate and you are not, for you are only a relation in me.'"[36] Each system, then, applies externality to its own basic category, and internality to its counter-category. Can the conflict of systems be resolved by eliminating one or the other principle of relations? Both Royce and

Spaulding would have answered this question affirmatively, although each would have eliminated the other's principle. Sheldon, however, answered the question negatively. Without internality, he insisted, the universe could never be understood as a single whole. Without externality no category could be singled out as an object of belief or experience.

In *The Strife of Systems,* Sheldon attended to the logical form of the contradiction between philosophical systems. He expected a new interpretation of logic, a new theory of negation, to mollify this contradiction. He wrote:

> That little word "not" . . . contains just enough of ambiguity to misdirect the intelligence. For we use that one word to mean now the relation of otherness between terms, now the denial of a suggested judgment. . . . *Otherness* is a very different concept from *opposition* or denial; unfortunately the negative of human language has not indicated the difference.[37]

Hence each system of philosophy is true when it asserts its ultimate category; it goes wrong when it infers from this assertion that it must deny the ultimate categories of the other systems. For Sheldon, a fundamental misinterpretation of the nature of negation is responsible for the denials and for the contradictions between philosophical systems. The strife of systems can be remedied if it is recognized that in the philosophical context negation means "*otherness* rather than *removal* of what is negated."[38]

The resolution of the strife of systems is in keeping with the character of the real world which has itself harmonized basic antagonisms. Sheldon said: "The deepest trait of reality, in short, that which makes it the moving, productive thing it is, is just this marriage of two principles whose apparent hostility has constituted the continual frustration of man's effort to map the universe."[39] *Polarity* is Sheldon's term for this positive principle. Pervading all that is, polarity is defined as

> one or another phase, aspect, relation, event or entity and *its* counterpart; the two opposite as it were in direction, in way of acting, yet each capable of fruitful cooperation with the other, also of opposing,

> denying or frustrating it, having thus a degree of independence and a being of its own, and between the two a trend or lure of cooperation in which one of the partners takes the initiative and the other responds, yet each freely; the relation has a certain asymmetry.[40]

As the deepest trait of reality, then, polarity accounts for the rise and progression of different philosophical systems. When misunderstood, it accounts for the strife of systems. When understood properly, it makes possible the synthesis of systems.

"Synthesis," declares Sheldon, "is the life-blood of philosophy."[41] True synthesis must be systematic without annulling the categories it comprehends. On this score Sheldon judged monistic idealism to be unsatisfactory since it derogates the reality of all beings except the Whole. On the other hand, he has praised Thomism as "the fullest synthesis as yet offered to thinking man."[42] Nevertheless, he has found Thomism defective because of an excessive intellectualism which subordinates the active phase of man's life to the contemplative. This defect Sheldon sought to rectify by making action "coordinate with intellect and intelligibility."[43] Hence Thomism is to assimilate the positive dynamism of Process Philosophy. As Sheldon said:

> The Thomist *can* admit the "new logic," as we call it, of self-alteration or self-expansion, and to high degree has already taught it. The opposition between the ultimate reality of substance, and that of becoming, is needless. . . . Substance is essentially dynamic.[44]

In sum, Sheldon has sought to synthesize Thomism with Process Philosophy.

Process Philosophy is, according to Sheldon, a new philosophy; it is America's own progressive philosophy.[45] Thomism, also according to Sheldon, is the greatest philosophical synthesis so far attained, the fulfillment of the best traditions in ancient and medieval philosophies. The synthesis of Process Philosophy and Thomism would, indeed, be a supreme achievement.

Whether or not Sheldon has succeeded in effectuating this synthesis is not a topic to be discussed in depth here.[46] Process philosophers would certainly object to his granting Thomism the position of priority and primacy in the synthesis. Viewed critically, Sheldon's synthesis may well illustrate the hazards of trying to combine artificially rival philosophical systems. Eclecticism, in bringing together principles and categories from various systems to be parts in a new whole, imposes a unity on the whole which often compels distortions in the parts. Thus the parts are no longer recognizable for what they were; and the whole, by parity of reasoning, is not the whole of the parts it was intended to be.

PEPPER'S THEORY

Stephen Pepper has, among recent metaphilosophers, been most firm in opposing eclecticism. For Pepper each philosophical system is autonomous, in that it determines what constitutes truth, evidence, and proof within itself. Thus he has declared: "Eclecticism is confusing."[47]

Better than any of the foregoing thinkers, Pepper has attained neutrality in the presentation of his metaphilosophy. A philosophical system is a "world hypothesis"; it is a specific kind of belief which attempts to embrace and organize all facts within a coherent system. It is not a question for Pepper, as it was for Royce, Spaulding, Hocking, and Sheldon, to investigate philosophies as preliminary to the defense or construction of one's own system. Like Spaulding, Pepper approaches the various philosophies with his eye fixed on their logic and their method of proof. Whereas Spaulding saw philosophical systems as types of formal systems, *more geometrico,* Pepper sees them, in consonance with the formula A. N. Whitehead fashioned, as comprehensive and coherent theories which, like the hypothetico-mathematical sciences, interweave both formal and empirical factors. At the same time Pepper's approach is not exclusively dominated by logico-methodological considerations. In part, it is influenced by his aesthetic sensitivity, attuned here to the way the human mind functions in theory construction. Pepper accounts for philosophies by means of what he calls "root metaphors." There is an area of commonsense fact or experience in terms of which a philosopher undertakes to interpret all other areas of fact and of experience. This original area is, in Pepper's words, the "basic analogy or root metaphor" of the world hypothesis.

Pepper classifies and describes world hypotheses by their root metaphors. After dismissing as inadequate such philosophies as the Ionian substance philosophy and mysticism, Pepper concentrates on four principal world hypotheses: formism, mechanism, organicism, and contextualism. *Formism* is the sort of philosophical realism associated with Plato, Aristotle, the medieval scholastics, and their contemporary heirs; it takes its root metaphor from the common experience of similarity. *Mechanism,* commonly called "naturalism" or "empiricism," is associated with Democritus, Lucretius, Thomas Hobbes, John Locke, George Berkeley, and David Hume; its root metaphor is the machine. *Organicism,* commonly called "absolute idealism," is associated with Schelling, Hegel, T. H. Green, F. H. Bradley, Bernard Bosanquet, and Josiah Royce; its root metaphor, often confused with the biological organism, is identified with the historic event, provided that the integration and not the duration of this event be taken as primary. *Contextualism,* commonly called "pragmatism," is associated with Charles Peirce, William James, Henri Bergson, John Dewey, and George Herbert Mead; it shares with organicism the same root metaphor: the historic event, but it stresses the temporal actuality of the event, i.e., the act in its context.

Pepper weighs the relative claims of each of the major world hypotheses, and concludes that all four are equally adequate, although each suffers weaknesses. Because of their autonomy, already mentioned, no world hypothesis may disprove the others. Already mentioned, too, is Pepper's thesis that the rival world hypotheses cannot be synthesized, that, in other words, eclecticism will not work, because it is confusing. In this connection, Pepper even cited Whitehead's philosophy as an example of eclecticism and the failure it produces. Whitehead, he charged, had mixed the root metaphors, concocting an illegitimate fusion of mechanism and formism.[48] On this score, Pepper has since switched his position; he now concedes that Whitehead was groping for a new root metaphor. Indeed, he has translated Whitehead's concept of "the actual occasion" into one of his own—"the purposive act," and he takes the purposive act to be the root metaphor by means of which he constructs a new world hypothesis. Pepper asserts that "in the description of purposive action, almost alone in the whole expanse of nature, we have both a highly articulated qualitative description and a highly articulated conceptual description which refer to exactly the same actual process."[49] In offering a new world hypothesis, one which he calls "selectivism,"[50] Pepper abandons neutrality.

STALLKNECHT AND BRUMBAUGH'S THEORY

The influence of Pepper's metaphilosophy is evident in the work of Newton P. Stallknecht and Robert S. Brumbaugh. They, like Pepper, offer a fourfold classification of philosophies. The Stallknecht-Brumbaugh classification is mechanism, formalism, vitalism, and creationism. Each type expresses a way of thought which stems from subphilosophical "regulative themes or notions that preside over and guide the development of philosophical thinking."[51] These notions orient the thinker in relation to his world; and as Stallknecht and Brumbaugh indicate, the orientation is not exclusively theoretical, it is practical as well.

Mechanism expresses the viewpoint of the technician or the engineer; formalism, that of the mathematician; vitalism, that of the naturalist—i.e., the biologist; and creationism, that of the artist, critic, or art lover. The first three types are manifest in the great historical traditions in philosophy: 1) mechanism in materialism and sensationalism, originating with the Milesians and continuing in British empirical thought; (2) formalism in the Platonic tradition; and (3) vitalism in the Aristotelian tradition. The fourth type—creationism—is exhibited in the philosophies of Bergson, Whitehead, and the existentialists. Each type of speculative thought is, furthermore, "essentially comparative or analogical."[52] Mechanism takes its model from the machine; it analyzes reality downward into atoms, atoms of matter or of sensation. Vitalism, or naturalism, takes as its model the notion of the organism or the specimen. Holding fast to the notion of organic structure, it strives descriptively to provide an anatomy of all that is. Formalism takes the diagram as its starting point. The formalist concentrates on the notion of field: he initially encounters the notion of field when he observes "celestial designs marked out by points of light," which suggest to him that "the basic structure of nature is a sort of expanse or continuum within which determining points of some kind set limits and form patterns."[53] The fourth type is less definite as regards its model and its structure. Although it contains vestiges of idealism, it is aligned with existentialism, and most obviously, it is a type of Process Philosophy—in particular a variant of Whitehead's.

In one respect the Stallknecht-Brumbaugh scheme is unsatisfactory. It is guilty of a glaring omission—it pays no attention to absolute idealism. Creationism, of course, makes passing concessions to idealism, but that may be because it lacks definiteness. A modicum of dubiety surely attaches to any philosophical type for which the claim is made that it spans process cosmology and existentialism. In another respect, the Stallknecht-Brumbaugh scheme lacks clarity of viewpoint. On the one hand, it appears to be as neutral as Pepper's metaphilosophy. Certainly it is devoid of the polemics to be found in the works of Royce and Spaulding. Yet, on the other hand, Stallknecht and Brumbaugh refuse to retreat from the issue of deciding between the types, and unlike Pepper, who at the last has felt it necessary to invent a new philosophy, they seem to fall back on creationism. Stallknecht and Brumbaugh, then, follow Bergson, who recommended the method of intuition, to decide between the rival philosophical systems. For them, as for Bergson, "intuition is essentially a vision of reality."[54] They do, however, disavow the anti-intellectualism of Bergson, and recommend that intuition be used rationally. Otherwise any claim in philosophy would carry equal weight with any other claim, and there would be no point to seeking a true position. By means of intuition, then, Stallknecht and Brumbaugh appear to espouse a Whiteheadian variant of creationism.

CONCLUDING OBSERVATIONS

It is germane to observe that intuition has been employed rationally by other philosophers to justify systems alternative to creationism. Jacques Maritain, the French neo-Thomist, has contended that intuition is the proper cognition with which valid metaphysics begins; he has emphasized that the object of intuition is being. Of intuition Maritain has written:

> It is a very simple sight, superior to any discursive reasoning of demonstration, because it is the source of demonstration. It is a sight whose content and implications no words of human speech can exhaust or adequately express and in which in a moment of decisive emotion, as it were, of spiritual conflagration, the soul is in contact, a living, penetrating and illuminating contact, with a reality which it touches and which takes hold of it. Now what I want to emphasize is that it is being more than anything else which produces such an intuition.[55]

The notion of being which intuition reveals to Maritain is the notion which St. Thomas Aquinas has elaborated in his philosophy. It is a notion different from the notion of creative process which intuition reveals to Bergson, to Whitehead, to Brumbaugh and Stallknecht.

It is also germane to observe that Hocking used intuition to justify one's construction of a philosophy. But he did not rely on intuition absolutely; he made use of eclecticism and dialectic. Royce, who heavily influenced Hocking, employed dialectic almost exclusively. Spaulding, Royce's opposite, resorted to logical analysis. Sheldon was wholly eclectic, although the compass of the synthesis may have been his ultimate criterion, the wider the compass the better. Pepper, in viewing philosophical systems as world hypotheses, actually restated Whitehead's definition of speculative philosophy, a definition which, in some sense, incorporates all the methods considered in this chapter but which, as we have seen in Chapter I, marks a new, and at present the best available, viewpoint on the nature of speculative philosophy. Whitehead's definition is worth repeating here:

"Speculative philosophy is the endeavor to frame a coherent, logical, necessary system of general ideas in terms of which every element of our experience can be interpreted."[56]

A survey of the writings of the metaphilosophers discussed in the present chapter easily brings to the fore the major types of systems which illustrate more or less adequately, more or less precisely, the Whiteheadian definition of speculative philosophy. These types may be named as follows:

1. Realism,
2. Materialism,
3. Idealism, and
4: Process Philosophy.

Remarkably each type corresponds to a particular conception (or rational intuition) of being. Realism holds that whatever is in any sense is real; idealism that mind and its content alone are real; materialism that matter and its patterns alone are real; and process philosophy that process and the factors in process are real.

Our classification may be compared with the various classifications discussed in the present chapter. Royce recognized realism and idealism, but he had no place for materialism, except so far as he subsumed it under realism, and he neglected process philosophy, perhaps because this type of philosophy had not yet loomed brightly on the philosophical horizon. Spaulding recognized all the types in our classification and more, although in conceiving realism as a philosophy of function and not of substance, he equated it with process philosophy. Hocking, too, recognized all the types in our classification and more, partly, no doubt, because he granted the methods of intuition and of pragmatism the status of major philosophical systems. Sheldon recognized all the types in our classification as well, but Sheldon elevated realism (Thomism) and process philosophy to the special rank of being the ultimate synthesis that had to be synthesized. Were Sheldon's method correct, all the types of philosophy would be absorbed in his one master type. Stallknecht and Brumbaugh completely overlook one major type: idealism. Possibly this is due to the fact that, writing in the middle of the twentieth century, they could reduce idealism to a subjective form of sensationalism which they accommodated to atomism (a species of materialism), and they could also disregard absolute idealism with relative impunity because it has so few adherents. Our classification approximates Pepper's most closely; realism corresponds to formism, idealism to organicism, materialism to mechanism, and process philosophy to contextualism. But it is not tied down to the root metaphor theory, a theory which induced Pepper to treat Berkeley, for example, as a mechanist, hence as a materialist in some truncated sense.

Our theory is most faithful to the conceptions of being which philosophical systems express. Here, then, is our advance on Whitehead's definition of speculative philosophy. There is an *ur*-principle, an ultimate, which consciously or unconsciously the philosopher, in constructing his system of basic concepts adequate to experience, seeks to be true to; that is his conception of what is really real, the conception of being. Perhaps Willard Quine hit the same point when he said that one's ontology is basic to one's conceptual scheme, but if so, Quine's point should be liberated from its logico-mathematical context, and his conception of ontology should be supplemented, as E. W. Hall has suggested, by the categorial contributions of epistemology and axiology.[57]

In one sense, our advance on Whitehead is a return to Royce, but without Royce's partisanship. In another sense it demonstrates that partisanship in philosophy is inescapable. No matter how much a philosopher may strive for neutrality, his test for the true philosophy is always predicated on the assumptions that his conception of being presents being as it is and that the conceptions of being his rivals uphold are partial or false. Recognition of one's own bias in regard to first principles is the first step to a judicious perspective on the available types of speculative philosophy.

III
REALISM

Realism in philosophy has two meanings. It signifies (1) the scholastic doctrine of the objective existence of universals, and (2) the belief that there exists an objective world independent of the mind that knows it. In the first sense, realism is an ontological theory. In the second sense, realism is an epistemological theory.

Ontological realism is opposed to nominalism and conceptualism. Nominalism maintains that only particulars exist in reality and that universals are words merely. Conceptualism concurs with nominalism on granting sole existence to particulars in objective reality, but it allows that universals exist as concepts in the mind. Although ontological realism and its alternatives became explicit doctrines during the Middle Ages, they were present in ancient Greek thought, and flourish even today.

Epistemological realism is opposed to idealism. Whereas epistemological realism affirms the existence of things apart from minds, idealism maintains that things exist only in mind. Epistemological realism, too, may be traced back to ancient Greek thought, although it became an explicit doctrine only as late as the eighteenth century. Tacit epistemological realism is the most widely held philosophy; it may rightly claim the plain man of common sense in all ages and climes as its adherent.

Ontological realism and epistemological realism may be affirmed in independence of each other—occasionally, indeed, to one's exclusion of the other. Epistemological realism may hold that objects exist in reality independent of minds, while denying that universals are such objects. Ontological realism, in affirming the existence of universals apart from the mind that knows them, seems necessarily to embrace epistemological realism; however, some ontological realists have proceeded to locate these universals in the mind of God or the Absolute. Despite the variations on the realistic themes that unfold in the history of philosophy, it would appear that—at least—in the major systems of realism the two senses are conjoined. There appears, in fact, to be a core from which all realisms radiate—the thesis that while cognition relates knowing minds and the objects known or knowable, they may and do exist apart. This thesis has generated a series of dualisms. Inasmuch as cognition may be analyzed into perception and conception, ontological dualism has risen separating the perceptual objects from the conceptual objects—viz., Plato. In addition, two other dualisms have developed in the history of realistic philosophies. Arthur O. Lovejoy (1873–1963) has aptly named them "epistemological dualism" and "psychophysical dualism."[1] Both dualisms are to be found in the philosophy of Descartes. Epistemological dualism distinguishes mental elements—sense-data, percepts, ideas—from external objects. Psychophysical dualism distinguishes mind, which is the locus of mental elements and acts, from material objects, including one's own body.

PLATO

Plato set the stage for later realistic philosophies in his famous Divided Line passage in the *Republic*.[2] Here Plato drew a line to represent the gradations of being and the types of mental or cognitive acts appropriate to each grade of being—to picture, in sum, the hierarchy of being and knowing.

Plato's line is divided into two unequal sections, one segment representing the domain of intelligible substances, the other the domain of sensible substances. The diagram below will help us imagine Plato's line.

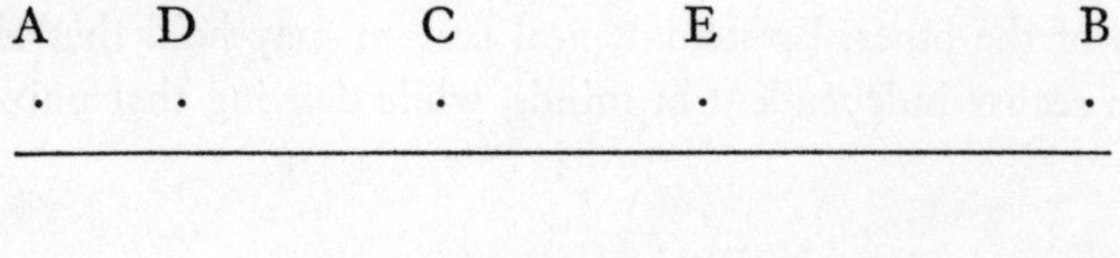

A D C E B

. . . . .

The line AB has as its first major division AC and CB. In regard to reality, AC stands for the entire class of sensible substances—i.e., becoming; CB for the class of intelligible substances—i.e., being. Each letter on the line represents a different degree of substance. A denotes the class of images, D the class of particular things (physical and manufactured objects), E the mathematical principles, and B the universals (Forms). The line is noteworthy in another significant respect. Its parts refer not only to distinct types of substances, but also to distinct faculties of apprehension and knowing. AC represents opinion; CB knowledge. A denotes imagination—i.e., the faculty of apprehending or fabricating images; D the faculty of belief; E the faculty of understanding; and B the faculty of knowing, of rational intellection. Thus just as the line marks an ontological ascent from the least substantial entities to the most substantial, each level of entity approximating truth to a certain degree, it marks also an epistemological ascent from imagination to rational intellection, each faculty ordered as higher or lower to the degree of clearness with which it apprehends its object. The inequality of the segments of the line, moreover, symbolizes the unequal approximations of each grade of substance to perfect substance, or of each faculty to truth.

The lowest level of the line, AD, treats images (εἰκόνες) and imagination (εἰκᾱσία). The class of images includes: 1) shadows, 2) reflections in water or on smooth surfaces, and 3) the contents of dreams. Imagination is the faculty of apprehending or fabricating images. It covers the sense-perception of present images, the recall of past images, and, as in dreams, the fabrication of new images. Whether imagined or perceived, each image is simply what appears; it is a phenomenon. As appearance, an image is at least in the rudimentary sense of being; at the same time, it is not—at least it is not that of which it is the image, or from which it is derived. The being of the image has a paradoxical status; it *is* in the sense that it is *about* something which it *is not*. Ontologically the image indicates a higher, more substantial type of realities which it copies or which produces it.

The next segment of the line, DC, deals with the things which produce the images. These things are the concrete individuals encountered in ordinary experience—the living animals, the vegetable organisms, the inorganic singulars such as rock formations or artefacts. Each of these things is more real than its image; each persists for a while longer than the image and each enjoys a measure of independent being, of sufficiency, greater than that possessed by the image. To this extent each thing is more perfect than the image of it. No thing, however, is absolutely perfect. All have causes, so that none is self-complete or self-existent. None is unalterable, immutable, or everlastingly persistent in its present state. Each thing becomes; it is and is not. It *is* what it is at the moment; it *is not* now what it has been and what it will become. The being of the thing that becomes is understood in two ways. In one way, the thing consists of universal Forms; it is a concatenation of universals. In another way, the thing is understood to consist also of materiality; it is composed of the basic material elements: Earth, Fire, Water, and Air, which in turn derive from the Receptacle. Thus the constitution of the thing is mixed, with quality and relation coming from the Forms and spatio-temporal structure and materiality coming from the Receptacle.

Appropriate cognitive acts and operations correspond to the things that populate the domain of Becoming. In the *Timaeus,* Plato spoke of a special mode of cognition to grasp the Receptacle. All the changing things that play upon the surface of phenomenal existence are stripped away in imagination, and a "bastard intuition" apprehends the Receptacle as an ultimate and persistent substrate. In the *Republic,* where Plato had not yet formulated a theory of the Receptacle underlying the world of becoming, he placed becoming between being and nothing. Sophistically perhaps, he designated ignorance as the "cognitive act" of knowing nothing. Furthermore, as the Divided Line indicates, belief (πίστις) is the mode of cognition appropriate to things. Belief is a species of opinion (δόξα). As a grade of knowing, belief rises above mere image making, but falls short of knowledge in the proper sense (ἐπιστήμη). For belief is infected with the transience, the instability, the changeableness of the objects toward which it is directed. Belief is therefore never certain, never really true; rather, it is probable only; it *seems* to be true. As Plato intimated in the *Timaeus,* beliefs about the physical world of changing things are at best probable tales.[3] Statements in natural science, including the most general beliefs about the natural world, belong as much to myth as to science. No wonder that Plato's cosmology, as expounded in the *Timaeus,* is an arresting mixture of science and mythology, a mixture so thorough that it is not easy to separate the one from the other.

C marks the basic division in the line. On one side ranges opinion with its objects of becoming; on the other side, knowledge with its objects of being. The segment CE is the first on the side of knowledge and of being. It represents the domain of mathematical entities and the relevant cognitive act. That Plato accorded mathematical entities an ontological status according to which they exist apart from mental concepts and linguistic symbols cannot be gainsaid. Indeed, for Plato, mathematical entities assume the characteristics of substances. In this respect Plato was profoundly indebted to the Pythagorean metaphysics, which defined Substance as Number, and which he applied when he unfolded his theory of the natural elements. What is at issue among Plato's interpreters, however, is whether mathematical entities belong to the domain of the Forms or whether they are intermediate between Forms and things. The Divided Line passage grants mathematical entities a status within the domain of being; they belong to the same general type as the Forms, and are marked off from the domain of becoming, where things dwell. On the other hand, they are known by a mode of cognition different from the mode appropriate to the Forms. That a distinct mode of cognition is requisite for mathematical entities, just as one was requisite for images, suggests the existence of a separate kind of being.

Understanding (διάνοιᾰ) apprehends the mathematical entities. It is a mode of knowing inferior to the mode appropriate to the Forms. It is inferior for two reasons. First, it employs visible images, such as the diagrams geometers construct, which possess the imperfections characteristic of sensible things. Second, it rests upon assumed hypotheses. Understanding makes certain deductions from its given assumptions; but its results are uncertain since they rest on assumptions which are, within the mathematical framework, mere assumptions.

At last the highest level of being and knowing is attained, represented by the segment EB of the Divided Line. This is the level of the Forms (εἶδος, ἰδέα), and of knowledge in the strictest sense (νόησις).

Forms are the most substantial entities in Plato's ontology. They *are,* and do not *become.* Since they do not become, they are not subject to motion, and since time is the measure of motion, they are timeless. Since they are in themselves, apart from the distorting feature of the Receptacle, they are not restricted to a fixed spatial location. Each Form *is* and is *one;* each is an Individual, an indivisible simple. Yet each Form is a universal, a One of Many, since each Form is the norm or model which time-bound, space-materialized singular things imitate or in which they participate. Each Form, therefore, is a perfect value, a being which lacks nothing to be eternally. Finally, each Form is wholly intelligible; it is free of the mutable material factors that cause sensations and may be grasped by intellectual intuition at the end of a dialectical inquiry. Hence, for Plato, a Form is a perfect intelligible being, a timeless, nonspatial, universal individual.

Dialectic achieves knowledge of the Forms. It proceeds from ideas through ideas to ideas. It finds its rest in the intuitive grasp of an unhypothetical principle which supports the entire subordinate structure of ideas or ideal Forms. This principle embraces all genuine knowledge; it is the absolute source from which all the sciences deductively flow.

Stated throughout his writings, Plato's arguments for the Forms are several. The process of defining general concepts is one which terminates in a formula which refers to a Form. The classification of particular things, moreover, pivots on the recognition of common properties, of an essence which is the same in many instances; and that essence is a Form. Communication by means of language presupposes that words, on Plato's theory, refer to meanings which different minds may entertain; and these meanings are Forms.

Knowledge, by definition, is certain; it is universal, necessary, immutable. Knowledge, however, can possess these properties only if its objects are universal, necessary, immutable; and the objects which possess these properties are Forms. Particular things do not qualify as the proper objects of knowledge in the strict sense, since these things change. But in changing, things exhibit qualities and relations which remain self-identical in many different contexts. These self-same entities are Forms. Logic, language, knowledge, reality supply evidence for the Platonic theory of the Forms. Further support for the doctrine is rendered by morality. Plato attributed the corrosion of Greek individual and institutional morality in his own day to the popular acceptance of ethical relativism. For him, the doctrine of the Forms furnished the absolute values to ground the moral life. The Forms serve as ideals to inspire conduct; they also serve as standards of criticism and for guidance.

Plato, moreover, ascribed to the Forms a cosmic function. In the cosmology presented in the *Timaeus,* Plato invoked three coeval principles to account for the world of becoming.[4] One principle is the Demiurge, the master craftsman who creates the visible world out of the material he is given. The second principle is the Receptacle, the material given which the Demiurge shapes into the visible world. The third and highest principle is the domain of the Forms, the immutable pattern which inspires the Demiurge, which indeed the Demiurge copies, as he molds the material into the visible world.

The doctrine of the Forms, despite the philosophical purposes it has served in promising a rationally unified cosmos and the integration of the several spheres of experience, has entailed problems which have troubled thinkers ever since Plato. One set of problems has to do with the relation of the Forms to each other. Another set has to do with the relation of the Forms to particular things. Plato himself recognized their severity. In the first part of his dialogue, *Parmenides,* Plato anticipated the major objections which have since been raised against his doctrine.

The first criticism of the Forms deals with the range of Forms. Proponents of the doctrine of Forms never doubted that likeness and unlikeness, unity and plurality, rightness, beauty, goodness are

Forms. Nor did they doubt that there are Forms of motion and of rest. Wavering first occurs with respect to the Forms of the natural species—e.g., man, oak tree—and of the natural elements—e.g., fire, water, and so forth. It spreads to the artefacts—e.g., chair, bed. Parmenides, cast by Plato in the role of interrogator and critic, pressed Socrates concerning "things of which the mention may provoke a smile . . . such things as hair, mud, dirt, or anything else which is vile and paltry."[5] Socrates, who was reluctant to admit that there are Forms of such objects, is admonished by Parmenides. It is suggested that when philosophy has matured Socrates sufficiently, Socrates will come to acknowledge such Forms. Plainly, Parmenides' criticism may be extended to the question whether there are Forms of negative things and of disvalues—of Nothing, of Evil, of Ugliness.

The next line of criticism touches on the problem of how things, from which the Forms are separate, participate in the Forms. In the *Phaedo,* Plato taught that things partake of the Forms.[6] In the *Parmenides,* this teaching is revealed to entail a serious dilemma.[7] Each thing that partakes of a Form receives as its share either the whole of the Form or a part of it, and the Form, being One in Many, is divided from itself, and its unity is destroyed. On the one hand, if the same Form is wholly present in a number of particular things, then the same Form may be to the right of itself or the left of itself, depending on the location of the things which partake of it. On the other hand, if the Form is only partially in the particular thing, then the things have unequal parts of the Forms, and this is paradoxical. Consider, for example, the Form of Largeness. Each thing that is large is large by virtue of having a part of this Form, so that each thing is large by having a part smaller than the whole of largeness, and some things are large though they have larger or smaller parts of largeness than other large things have.

Parmenides then took up what is often called "the third man argument." This argument proceeds from the acceptable assumption that a Form may be posited whenever things exhibit a single character and so constitute a single class. The Form is that character, held to subsist apart from the things. But then the Form and the things also share or exhibit a single common character. Thus the positing of a second Form follows from the presence of the single character in the plurality of the Form and the things. The regress continues to infinity, a situation the Greek mind considered irrational.

The theory that things participate in the Forms encounters grave objections, most of which focus on the shattering of the simple unity of the Form. In addition to, if not in place of, the theory of participation, Plato maintained the theory of imitation. According to this theory, the Form is a model, the things are copies. Thus the Form may be one; its imitations many. Parmenides, however, subjected even this theory to critique. The relation of imitation depends upon the Form of likeness. The thing is like the Form. But likeness is a symmetrical relation. Consequently, the Form is like the thing, if the thing is like the Form. Which is copy, which is model, is disputable given the logic of the relation of likeness. Besides, the likeness of Form and thing constitutes a second Form, which is also like the first Form and the thing, and this new relation of likeness constitutes a third form, ad infinitum.

So far the criticisms of the doctrine of the Forms implicit in Parmenides' questions bear on the relations to things and to one another. Parmenides also brought into question the relation of the Forms to the knowing mind. He entertained and rejected the conceptualistic thesis that each Form is a thought existing in a mind. If the Form is a thought in the mind, it cannot be a character of the things as they exist outside of the mind. The consequence is that Forms lose their cognitive value as well as their ontological status if they do not apply to objective things. On the other hand, if the Form is a thought in the mind and yet constitutes things, then things must be minds. Neither of these alternatives seemed plausible.

Finally, Parmenides objected to the doctrine of the Forms on the grounds that it leads to skepticism. The division of Forms from things establishes two levels of being and knowing, each with its own relations exclusively within it. Thus the relation of the Form of master and the Form of slave will itself be a Form, but the relation of a naturally existing master and a naturally existing slave will be a naturally existing relation. No relation connects both levels, and the consequence for knowledge is devastating. The Form of Knowledge and the actual knowledge we exercise are two wholly distinct and unrelated entities. The actual knowledge we exercise is confined to the natural things to which it is related, so that we are prevented from ever knowing the Forms. Similarly, since God's knowledge, being perfect, is the Form of Knowledge, and since the relations of Forms are themselves Forms, God can know only Forms, and so is unable to know things. As long, therefore, as the Forms and the things are conceived as belonging to two wholly separate domains, knowledge is blocked.

In his various dialogues, Plato threw out the numerous suggestions relating the Forms to each other and to things. In the *Republic,* for example, he presented the Form of the Good as that ultimate principle which generates and illuminates the entire domain of Forms.[8] So fundamental did he consider the Form of the Good that, refusing to define it, he esteemed it the source of all being and all knowing, though itself beyond being and beyond knowing. In the *Sophist,* he considered participation as the relation that holds between the Forms.[9] Diversity participates in Identity, and conversely. In the *Timaeus,* Plato revived the doctrine of imitation, but in a new cosmological context. He resorted to the spiritual principle of the Demiurge, a kind of master soul, which mediates between the material world and the domain of the Forms.[10] Increasingly, post-Platonic philosophy invoked soul or spirit to bring together the domains of being and becoming, of ideality and materiality, of Form and thing, which Platonic ontology distinguished and separated.

Speculatively venturesome yet acutely self-critical, Plato's philosophy is a permanent achievement of realistic thought. It may be an exaggeration to say that Western philosophy consists of a series of footnotes to Plato. Nevertheless, Plato epitomized a perennial temper of mind. This theoretical attitude is humanistically oriented; it is devoted to enlightened discussion as the primary method of attaining truth, and it is inclined to accord reality to whatever is deemed valuable.

ARISTOTLE

In historical contrast with Plato's philosophy is Aristotle's. But the contrast, or contrariety, falls within the same genus. Aristotle, after all, spent twenty years as a disciple in Plato's Academy before setting forth on his own. No less than Plato, Aristotle has contributed one of the lasting formulations of realism as a speculative philosophy. The theoretical attitude which Aristotle expressed is naturalistically oriented. For the method of attaining truth, Aristotle looked to painstaking observation of concrete cases followed by classification and culminating in rigorous systematic organization. He was reluctant to concede reality to anything except what is scientifically warranted.

Specific points of Aristotle's critique of Plato's metaphysics are concentrated in the first book of the *Metaphysics.* The context is characteristically Aristotelian. First philosophy for Aristotle is, among other things, the study of first principles, and in one sense the first principles are the four causes of natural explanation—the formal, the material, the efficient, and the final causes. As Aristotle said:

> Evidently we have to acquire knowledge of the original causes (for we say we know each thing only when we think we recognize its first cause), and causes are spoken of in four senses. In one of these we mean the substance, i.e. the essence [the form] . . . ; in another the matter or substratum, in a third, the source of the change, and in a fourth the cause opposed to this, the purpose and the good (for this is the end of all generation and change).[11]

To support his theory of the four causes, Aristotle performed the role of philosophical scholar, establishing *pari passu* the most influential interpretation of pre-Socratic philosophy. Aristotle regarded the doctrines of his predecessors as preliminary and incomplete statements of the doctrine of causes. He remarked that although "in a sense they [the four causes] have all been described before, in a sense they have not been described at all. For the earliest philosophy is, on all subjects, like one who lisps, since it is young and in its beginnings."[12] Aristotle counted Plato a failure on the same grounds; he alleged that Plato had recognized only the formal and the material causes and had also misconstrued the nature of the formal cause with the doctrine of the Forms.

Aristotle's attack on Plato's doctrine of the Forms is detailed. Two main thrusts are discernible: one against the theory of the Forms similar to Plato's own critique in the *Parmenides,* the other against the mathematical theory of the Forms. As regards the mathematical theory, which Plato's successors in the Academy had advocated, Aristotle dismissed it as unintelligible. Any theory which purports to identify substantial being with numbers and geometrical figures is false, for the latter are abstractions of the mind only. As regards the doctrine of the Forms, Aristotle reiterated points raised in the *Parmenides*—e.g., the third man argument; but he added a new dimension to this critique. He denied that principles separated from the things whose natures they were conceived to explain could explain those things. He doubted that explanation itself could be advanced by the kind of uneconomical duplication of principles which results from the erection of another world of intelligible universals transcending this world of sensible things. He considered the difficulty aggravated when the Forms that are posited to explain things are selected simply because they are universal, in the sense of characterizing many things, and not because they are essential. In brief, Aristotle contended that Forms, if they are to serve as the principles of natural things, cannot be Platonic universals. At the very least they must be essences inherent in the very natures of the things whose formal principles they are. Aristotle's critique of Plato's theory of the Forms pivots on his theory of substance and essence.

In the *Categories,* Aristotle examined the main classes of words, and by tacit assumption, of concepts and of beings. He distinguished ten categories: "substance, quantity, quality, relation, place, time, position, state, action, or affection."[13] For Aristotle, substance is the basic category; the other nine designate kinds of attributes which may be legitimately ascribed to substance. When Aristotle treated the other categories as attributes of substance, he bequeathed serious problems to later philosophers, among which was the problem of ascertaining just what substance is.

In the *Categories,* Aristotle distinguished two senses of the term "substance."

> Substance, in the truest and most definite sense of the word, is that which is neither predicable of a subject nor present in a subject; for instance, the individual man or horse. But in a secondary sense those things are called substances within which, as species, the primary substances are included; also those which, as genera, include the species.[14]

In other passages Aristotle noted still other senses of the term. For instance, he has said: "The word 'substance' is applied, if not in more senses, still at least to four main objects; for both the essence and the universal and the genus are thought to be the substance of each thing, and fourthly the substratum." [15] However, the specification of senses laid down in the *Categories* has governed most discussions of Aristotle's philosophy.

Having stipulated that the concrete individual is the first sense of substance, Aristotle next proceeded to list the marks of substance in this primary sense. First, substance is the ultimate logical subject. Substances are the "entities which underlie everything else, and everything else is either predicated of them or present in them." [16] Second, "all substance appears to signify that which is individual." [17] A substance is denotable by the demonstrative term, "this." A third mark of substance is that "it does not admit of variation of degree." [18] A fourth mark of substance is that it remains the same through change. "The most distinctive mark of substance appears to be that, while remaining numerically one and the same, it is capable of admitting contrary qualities," so that "one and the self-same substance, while retaining its identity, is yet capable of admitting contrary qualities." [19] A fifth mark of substance is independent existence, sometimes called "self-existence." If first substances "did not exist, it would be impossible for anything else to exist." [20]

The fifth mark returns to the first mark. As the first mark suits a logic which rests upon ultimate subjects for predication, the fifth mark fits an ontology which is grounded in self-existent beings. When further explored, the two marks uncover a crucial problem for Aristotle. The first mark displays a distinction between "being present in" and "being predicable of" a substance. Only that which cannot exist except as it is in the subject—e.g., the particular shade of brown of the hair in the head of an individual man—is said to be present in the subject, whereas that which can exist outside the subject also—e.g., the "man" that is predicated of this individual as when it is judged that he is a man—is said to be predicable of the subject. Pressed far enough, it would seem that all genuine essences or natures, all *infimae species* qualify as first substances, at least according to the fifth mark. At this juncture, of course, what is in question is the status of substance in the second sense.

Aristotle's doctrine of substance in the second sense is undeniably obscure. Species and genus are said to be substance in the second sense. But if both are universal—i.e., may be predicated of many—and the genus is explicitly designated an indeterminate universal, neither qualifies as substance. Aristotle is quite clear on the point that the universal is not substance.[21] Substance is an individual—a "this." The universal is a "such" and not a "this." An individual may be characterized by several "suches" and if each "such" is a substance, then each substance is composed of a multiplicity of substances. But this would deprive each substance of its unity, or its independent existence. Further, the numerically distinct individuals which the universal characterizes would, if the universal is a substance, be merged into one individual. Hence the original distinct individuals would not be substances at all, but rather accidents of the universal which had, paradoxically, been predicated of them.

Aristotle and his successors wrestled with the problem of ascertaining the substantiality of first and second substances. Aristotle's own solution, whatever it was in fact, must forever remain a matter of interpretation. But the overwhelming textual evidence seems to favor the view that the *infimae species,* the definitions of which formulated the essences of things, count as substantial individuals. To denote the essence is to denote the substance. As Aristotle said:

"The essence of each thing is what it is said to be *propter se*. . . . What . . . you are by your nature is your essence."[22]

However perplexing his conception of substance may be, Aristotle constructed speculatively a system of beings ranked according to the kinds of substances. In the natural world, a world of change and of changing things, substances are present as composites of form and matter, the form marking the actuality and the matter the potentiality of the thing. The essences of these composite things are hylomorphic, composed of form and matter. Substances are organized in a hierarchy of being.

At the base of the hierarchy lies matter. By analysis and abstraction, it is possible to conceive of matter wholly devoid of any form. This ultimate substrate is called prime matter. It is doubtful that matter without form could be actual; it would be at best sheer potentiality. The matter which we perceive and know is part of a composite of which form is at least equally constituent. The most basic actual material substances are earth, air, fire, and water; they obviously possess forms. All earthly natural substances contain one or more of these four elements. A fifth element is the ether. It is an exceptionally rarified, weightless, and luminous stuff; it is the matter of which the planets and other celestial bodies are made.

Next in the hierarchy of being come the living substances. These especially captivated the mind of Aristotle. Soul is the principle which animates matter; it is the form of the body. Aristotle distinguished three types of soul. The lowest type of soul displays only the functions of nutrition and reproduction; the next type accounts for locomotion and sensation; and the highest type, for rational thought. Among natural substances, plant life manifests merely the lowest type of soul, animal life exhibits the next type as well, and man alone exhibits the highest type.

Beyond the natural substances, there exist eternal separate substances, which he also called pure forms, pure acts, Unmoved Movers, the final causes of the universe, gods. These substances, which Aristotle discussed in Book XII of the *Metaphysics*, unreservedly satisfy the criteria of substantiality. They are the prime instances of what it means to be. By means of arguments based on the physical science of motion as it was known in his day, Aristotle sought to prove the existence of the separate substances. These "proofs," sharpened by later philosophers, will be considered below. Aristotle's own reliance on ancient science was so great that he would not decide whether the Unmoved Movers are 47 or 55 in number. He left that to the astronomers for calculation. The life and thought of the separate substances Aristotle did attempt to describe. Calling each substance "God," he wrote that "God is a living being, eternal, most good, so that life and duration continuous and eternal belong to God."[23] The divine life, moreover, is a life of thought.

> [God] thinks of that which is most divine and precious, and it does not change; for change would be change for the worse, and this would be already a movement. . . . Therefore it must be of itself that the divine thought thinks (since it is the most excellent of things), and its thinking is a thinking on thinking.[24]

MEDIEVAL PHILOSOPHY

Plato and Aristotle bequeathed a host of problems to their successors. The controversies that raged in late ancient and medieval philosophy erupted as a consequence. To these we now turn.

Theory of the Soul—Several intractable issues lurk in Aristotle's theory of the soul. One issue has to do with the immortality of the soul. If the rational soul of a man is also the form of his body, then the soul must perish with the body. Even the mystical doctrine of the resurrection of the body does not resolve the issue, since there is an interval between the natural death of a man and the resurrection of his body on the day of judgment. Suggested solutions have been ingenious, as for instance St. Thomas's thesis that the soul evinces a disposition (*habitus*) for the body in its temporary disembodied state.

Another issue stimulated the so-called plurality of forms controversy. If a type of soul is necessary to explain a given natural life-function, then a living substance is animated by as many souls (forms) as it performs functions. But this would mean that a man, for example, would have three souls at least, one of each major type. Here, too, the doctrines proposed have been ingenious. Noteworthy again is St. Thomas's theory that the higher forms subsume the functions of the lower forms without also containing these lower forms.

Still, a third issue has been raised concerning the rational soul. For Aristotle, the rational soul exercised itself in the intellectual activity of formulating and relating concepts. Referring to this activity in substantive terms, Aristotle spoke of the active intellect. Since the active intellect always reached the same conclusions when it proceeded from the same premises and employed the same rules of inference, it seemed logical to ask whether there is one active intellect for all men. On one side, thinkers as diverse as Plotinus (205–270) and Averroes (1126–1198) implied or taught that there is one active intellect. On the other side, fearing that the extreme doctrine of the unity of the active intellect would destroy the distinction between God and men and would collapse into pantheism, thinkers like St. Thomas Aquinas taught that each man has his own active intellect.

Realism vs. Nominalism—One topic in medieval philosophy aroused more controversy than the plurality of forms—namely, the status of universals. Originating in Plato's dialogues, which first presented and criticized the doctrine of the separate existence of the Forms, the controversy over universals was, in medieval philosophy, cast in the terminology of Aristotle. In an introduction to Aristotle's logic, Porphyry (233–305) had asked whether species and genera (Aristotle's second substances) are genuinely substantial; and in a commentary on Porphyry's introduction, Boethius (480–524) further pondered the question. Through Boethius' *Commentary,* the issue entered medieval philosophy.

At first, the extreme realists, those who agreed with Plato that universals have an existence higher than, and separate from, particular individuals, held the field without battle. St. Augustine (354–430), who lived long before the topic became the basis for dispute, was the leading spokesman for the Platonic point of view. But even

St. Augustine radically revised the doctrine of his master. No longer were universals conceived to exist as separate Forms; henceforth they were considered to be ideas in the mind of God. This *doctrina antiqua,* as it was later dubbed, was so firmly allied to Christianity that an attack on the philosophical theory seemed also to be an attack on the Christian religion. Consider some of the strands of this alliance.

The Roman Catholic Church institutionalized Christianity in the West; and waiving consideration of the split between the Roman Catholic Church in the West and the Greek Orthodox Church in the East, the Church in styling itself Catholic claimed to be universal. To strengthen the Church against lapses in its membership and even in its clergy and its officialdom, theologians esteemed the Church to be a superior reality, a universal sacrosanct from the physical and spiritual vicissitudes of the individuals it embraces. Furthermore, theologians resorted, sometimes unwittingly, to extreme realism to explain the doctrines of original sin and redemption. When Adam fell in the Garden of Eden, not the individual Adam alone but the universal Adam of all mankind fell. Hence each newborn babe bears the taint of Adam's sin. Similarly, Jesus Christ died on the Cross to save not only those who witnessed his life, death, and resurrection, but to redeem all mankind. Moreover, theologians accepted the doctrine of the Forms as prerequisite to proof of the existence of God. St. Augustine himself experienced his "first conversion" by studying the books of the Platonists; he turned away from wholly corporeal conceptions of deity toward a spiritual conception of God.[25] God was for him the Truth; God encompasses all the invisible and immutable Forms from which all visible and mutable things are made.

Despite the reliance of the Church on extreme realism, logicians in the ninth century began to suspect the validity of the doctrine. Poring over the forms of judgment, the categories, and the classifications of subjects and predicates, they detected faults in the thesis that universals are real. Roscellin (1050–1120) brought to a climax stirrings that go back to Eric of Auxerre (841–871). Roscellin held that universals, far from being the ultimate realities, are names only. The things names denote are all individuals, the universals being verbal or linguistic. Since in Latin *nomen* stands for "name," Roscellin's doctrine came to be known as nominalism. The main advantage of nominalism is the economy it offered. Stripping away the separate realm of universals, nominalism reduced the ontological commitments of the philosopher to a belief in the existence of particular individuals. Ever since its institution, nominalism has been a persistent philosophical tendency. Today, as in the ninth century, it flourishes in the field of logic. Willard Van Orman Quine, the American logician, has been the most influential nominalist of recent years; he has contended that a system of logic and mathematics may be constructed without ontological commitment to the separate existence of abstract entities, such as attributes, relations, classes, numbers, functions.[26]

Nominalism has been opposed not only by those philosophers who upheld extreme realism because of the support it renders religion and theology, but also by those who sought to answer the question: How can the same word apply to many different things? In the twelfth century, answers to this question were disputed by two of the most acute minds in the history of thought—William of Champeaux (1070–1120) and his erstwhile student, Abelard (1079–1142).[27]

At first William of Champeaux adhered to extreme realism. Accordingly, the same word may apply to many different things because these things are identical in at least one respect. This identical character, pervading a multiplicity of individuals, is a genuine universal; and the particular individuals, participating in the same universal and being consequently members of the same species, are the same. Although ignorant of the texts, Abelard resurrected the arguments against participation which Plato first broached in the *Parmenides*. If, for example, to judge that Socrates is human is to affirm that he possesses the entire universal of humanity, then he possesses Plato, too; and conversely. If, on the other hand, to judge that Socrates is human is to affirm that he possesses only a part of humanity, then he is less human and/or more human than other men, depending upon the partiality of the part he possesses. Now as long as the universal is considered a separate, self-existent identity in which individuals participate, the dilemma is inescapable.

In dialectical disarray, William of Champeaux retreated to what has been called "the indifference theory." [28] According to the indifference theory, things participating in the same universal are the same thing, not essentially but indifferently. Thus, while individual things belonging to the same species have different essences, these essences are similar. This similarity in the midst of difference allows the word for the species to apply to the individuals. It is not known that Abelard attacked the indifference theory, although the line of attack he could have pursued should be clear. Individual *x* has characters a, b, c, and is said to be similar to individual *y*. But individual *y* also has its own characters; and if *x* is similar to *y*, then *y* must have at least one of the characters *x* has—a or b or c. Let us say both *x* and *y* have character a. It follows that the a of *x* is identical with the a of *y*, and the problem which erupted in respect to the identity in the first place rises again. No wonder William of Champeaux abandoned the defense of realism and yielded the arena to others.

The question remained: How can the same word be applied to many different things? Abelard, unsurpassed in destructive polemic, set out to furnish a constructive answer.[29] The position he attained might well be called "conceptualism." According to conceptualism, universals are concepts the human mind produces; their being therefore is mental. In the natural world apart from the human mind, the really real things are all individuals. By ignoring or confusing the differences of individual things, men form concepts which are universal. Words stand for these concepts; men apply the words to distinct individual things in the light of the mental concepts or abstract images for which the words stand. Needless to say, Abelard's doctrine is defective, too. Either the concepts in the mind are based on the real essences of things, or they are not. If they are based on the real essences of things, then the difficulties to which the positions of William of Champeaux led reassert themselves. If they are not based on the real essences of things, then a veil falls between language and thought on the one side and real things on the other. Not only does metaphysical skepticism ensue, but more pertinently the application of thought and language to reality becomes a mystery.

Among scholastics, St. Thomas Aquinas has traditionally been hailed as the philosopher who solved the problem of universals. Actually, he borrowed his position from Avicenna (980–1037). No doubt, St. Thomas's theory is the most comprehensive.[30] With the Platonists, St. Thomas held that universals exist prior to particular individuals; they exist *ante rem* as ideas in the mind of God. With the Aristotelians, he held that they exist in things; they exist *in re* as the essential natures of things. With the nominalistic conceptualists, he held that they exist after things; they exist *post rem* as concepts in the minds of man reached by processes of abstraction. The Thomistic theory perhaps consoles the major disputants in the controversy over universals by conceding that what each says positively is true. However, the consolation is feeble, since the main objections of each disputant to his adversary's theory stands unaffected by the Thomistic doctrine. The achievement of St. Thomas Aquinas is eclectic synthesis, artificially contrived. Curiously, the angelic doctor who granted universals so much had to rely on matter for his principle of individuation. For if universals exist in things as their essences, things are made individual only by their matter. Nor did he recoil from the striking implication that angels, being immaterial substances, cannot be individuals, but rather must be species.[31]

St. Thomas's realism was exceptionally vulnerable, as the subsequent history of scholastic philosophy reveals. Duns Scotus (1266–1308) demoted universals from their absolute *ante rem* status although he did acknowledge their *in re* and *post rem* status.[32] His reasons are hard to fathom. But it is apparent that he was motivated in large part by an inclination to emphasize the Will of God and, by consequence, to de-intellectualize Him. Hence Duns Scotus subordinated the ideas in the mind of God to the Divine Will. At the same time, Scotus was reluctant to deprive form of its role in individuation. Indeed, he taught that each individual is individuated by a very special form—thisness (*haecceitas*).[33]

William of Ockham (1280–1349) further whittled down the doctrine of universals which St. Thomas had inflated. William of Ockham denied not only their *ante rem* status as ideas in the mind of God, but also their *in re* status as the essential natures of things.[34] He shaved away the universals with his legendary razor, the constant symbol of economy in philosophy. However, he did concede that universals have a *post rem* status as ideas in the minds of men and as words in language.

The controversy over universals has remained alive long after the recession of scholasticism. Mention has been made of the nominalism of Quine, which itself arose in response to the realistic interpretations of modern logic. Extreme realism developed in the direction of Absolute idealism and the theory of the concrete universal, to be discussed in Chapter V. The vagaries of conceptualism, first broached by Abelard, constitute an entire chapter in the history of thought. John Locke presented a theory close to Abelard's when he maintained that words stand for abstract general ideas in the minds of men, that these ideas represent nominal essences only, and that things in nature, whose real essences can never be known, are all particular. George Berkeley demolished the Lockean theory by demonstrating empirically through introspection that no human mind ever entertains an abstract general idea but always a concrete particular one. He exploited an example of which Locke himself had been aware—namely, the idea of a triangle. The idea of the triangle, for which the word "triangle" stands, cannot be abstract or general; it must be the idea of either a scalene triangle or an isosceles triangle, since no mind can form an idea of a triangle which is both or neither. Nevertheless, the word "triangle," standing for a particular idea, may be employed to apply to many particular triangles. David Hume adopted the Berkeleyan position, supporting it by the associationist psychology which claimed to explain how habits are formed in the usage of language. It is doubtful that modern discussions, more sophisticated in respect to psychological inquiry and symbolic representation, have advanced the question much beyond the point at which it rested in the fourteenth century.

Perhaps Ludwig Wittgenstein achieved a breakthrough which

heralds the supercession of the traditional problem of universals.[35] For Wittgenstein taught that the "craving for generality" is a psychological confusion which philosophically inspired the wrong kind of answer to the question: What do words mean? When we answer, words mean abstract entities, we have been plainly led astray. The correct procedure, according to Wittgenstein, is to transform the question into another one: How are words used? In detecting and examining the usages of words in their various contexts, we uncover their meaning, namely, the rules which govern their usage. But for those who believe that Wittgenstein has had the final say on the issue, it must be unnerving to observe that thinkers schooled in linguistic analysis can still be stimulated by the old questions and answers.[36]

The Existence of God—Platonic realism was a central feature in the doctrine of God which the early Christian theologians propounded. St. Augustine christened Platonism. He transformed the Forms from self-subsistent entities into divine ideas.

In St. Augustine's system, God, therefore, performed the role which Plato had assigned to the form of the Good. This conception of God, moreover, became the basis for a unique argument for His existence. As the ground of all the forms God is tantamount to Truth. Every judgment is true so far as it conforms to its idea. In all our intellectual strivings, we test our opinions by the standard of truth, and this Truth is God. Even the skeptic, who ceaselessly suspends judgment because he fears error, unconsciously acknowledges Truth, and hence God. Needless to add, St. Augustine easily connected this doctrine of God as Truth with the religious doctrine of Jesus Christ as the *logos*.[37] In similar fashion, Christian theologians argued for the existence of God on the basis of man's moral strivings. All these moral efforts are directed toward the Good, and this Good is God. Such arguments for the existence of God often seem to confuse what is objectively real with what men desire in their hearts and minds; but presented within the framework of Christian Platonism, they proved to be anticipations of the ontological argument.

St. Anselm (1033–1109) presented the most original and influential statement of the ontological argument. He wrote:

> . . . we believe that thou [God] art a being than which nothing greater can be conceived. Or is there no such nature, since the fool hath said in his heart, there is no God? (Psalms xiv. I). But, at any rate, this very fool, when he hears of this being of which I speak—a being than which nothing greater can be conceived—understands what he hears, and what he understands is in his understanding; although he does not understand it to exist.
>
> For it is one thing for an object to be in the understanding, and another to understand that the object exists. . . .
>
> Hence, even the fool is convinced that something exists in the understanding, at least, than which nothing greater can be conceived. For, when he hears of this, he understands it. And whatever is understood, exists in the understanding. And assuredly that, than which nothing greater can be conceived, cannot exist in the understanding alone. For, suppose it exists in the understanding alone: then it can be conceived to exist in reality; which is greater.
>
> Therefore, if that, than which nothing greater can be conceived, exists in the understanding alone, the very being, than which nothing greater can be conceived, is one, than which a greater can be conceived. But obviously this is impossible. Hence, there is no doubt that there exists a being, than which nothing greater can be conceived, and it exists both in the understanding and in reality.[38]

Since St. Anselm the ontological argument has been reformulated many times by such giants in the history of philosophy as Descartes, Spinoza, Leibniz, Hegel, and, recently in the schema of symbolic logic, by Charles Hartshorne.[39] Common to all versions is the inference from an idea of Him in the mind of the thinker to the existence of God. The ontological argument has also provoked numerous refutations. The first refutation was launched by a contemporary of St. Anselm—the monk Gaunilon.

Gaunilon denied that the inference from idea to existence is legitimate. He charged that it leads to logical absurdity. It would allow one to infer from the idea of a perfect lost island to the existence of the island. To prove the existence of a thing it is not sufficient to show that an idea of the thing exists in the understanding. What is required is to show that the thing which the idea represents exists in reality apart from the understanding.[40] In his own way Gaunilon anticipated the position of Kant.

Kant, too, found the ontological argument invalid. Existence is not a property which thought can deduce from a concept; rather it is a category which is applicable to a thing only when the thing is either encountered in experience or linked by causal laws to a thing or things encountered in experience. Yet Kant conceded a primary place to the ontological argument in natural theology. He held that since all arguments for the existence of God rest on the alleged demonstration of existence from ideas, they all fundamentally presuppose the ontological argument. Since the ontological argument is invalid, according to Kant, all arguments for the existence of God are invalid.

St. Anselm replied to Gaunilon's objection, and by implication to Kant's critique of the ontological argument. St. Anselm rejected Gaunilon's assumption that the idea of God is like any other idea—e.g., the idea of an island. The idea of God is the idea of a being greater than which nothing can be conceived. It is therefore not itself reducible to an object of or within the human understanding. The unsurpassable greatness, the absolute perfection, of the being which it represents, entails the existence of that being. Plainly the idea of God is no subjective state merely; it is an objective idea, or Platonic form.

Nevertheless, St. Thomas Aquinas lent his authority to Gaunilon's view that the difference between the mental existence of an idea and the real existence of the thing represented by the idea is so radical that no inference from the former to the latter is valid for man. St. Thomas also questioned the psychological capacity of the finite human understanding to frame an adequate idea of God. According to St. Thomas, moreover, the ontological argument is tantamount to the thesis that the existence of God is self-evident. Now a proposition is "self-evident" when its predicate is contained in its subject. There are two senses of self-evidence: self-evidence in itself, though not to us; and self-evidence in itself, and to us. St. Thomas wrote:

> . . . this proposition, *God exists,* of itself is self-evident, for the predicate is the same as the subject, because God is His own existence. . . . Now because we do not know the essence of God, the proposition is not self-evident to us, but needs to be demonstrated by things that are more known to us, though less known in their nature—namely, by His effects.[41]

Having ruled out the ontological argument, St. Thomas Aquinas proceeded to contrive proofs of God's existence based on His effects. These proofs are grounded in factual evidence and buttressed by the laws of reasoning. There are five proofs.

The first proof is the proof from motion. From the sensibly evident fact that in the natural world things are in motion, St. Thomas argued that other things must have put these things in motion. If these other things are moving, then they, too, require other things to put them in motion. But, said St. Thomas,

> This cannot go on to infinity, because then there would be no first mover, and, consequently, no other mover, seeing that subsequent movers move only inasmuch as they are moved by the first mover; as the staff moves only because it is moved by the hand. Therefore it is necessary to arrive at a first mover, moved by no other; and this everyone understands to be God.[42]

The second proof is based on the nature of efficient causation. The alleged factual evidence for the proof is that every thing or event in nature is the effect of a prior cause which produced it. Once again an infinite regress—this time, of causes—is ruled out. Therefore, St. Thomas concluded, "it is necessary to admit a first efficient cause to which everyone gives the name of God."[43]

The third proof is based on possibility and necessity. The alleged factual evidence for the proof is that all actual things, including nature itself, are permeated with possibility; otherwise there would be no change, no coming into being and passing away, for possibility is the power to be or not to be. However, for any actual thing infected by possibility, its actualization requires a prior actuality. Since an infinite regress of prior actualities is ruled out, St. Thomas inferred that "there exists some being having of itself its own necessity, and not receiving it from another, but rather causing in others their necessity. This all men speak of as God."[44]

The fourth proof is based on "the gradation to be found in things."[45] The factual evidence for the proof is the alleged observation of a hierarchy of beings ranked according to value and culminating in an uppermost bound of absolute value. Assuming that the existence of degrees of value and reality requires an absolute standard of perfect value for their measurement and their being, St. Thomas inferred that such an ultimate cause of being, goodness, and every other perfection exists; and that this cause is what we call God.

The fifth proof is based on "the governance of the world."[46] From the alleged observation of purposive order even in the case of inanimate things which lack knowledge, St. Thomas inferred the existence of some being endowed with knowledge and intelligence which directs inanimate things to achieve their ends unconsciously but designedly. He concluded that "some intelligent being exists by whom all natural things are directed to their end; and this being we call God."[47]

For many scholastics the five proofs belonged together, mutually strengthening one another. However, it is transparent that they could also be argued separately. The first three proofs do, in one sense, belong together; they are cosmological proofs and rest upon an Aristotelian interpretation of the physical universe. The first proof has, consequently, been rendered obsolete by Newtonian physics; it is no longer thought that the natural state of a body is to remain at rest. The second proof depends upon a principle of causation which is suspect not simply because of Hume's critique, but because contemporary physics, with its focus on microscopic particles and events, has abandoned classical causation for probabilistic concepts. The third proof is wholly bound up with metaphysical distinctions between possibility and necessity, and even if valid, the distinctions are not empirically evident, as the proof assumes. The fourth proof owes as much to Plato as to Aristotle; and the hierarchy of being according to value is no more empirically evident than the metaphysical concepts essential to the third proof.

The fifth proof, often termed "the teleological argument," has had a long and independent life. It has had widespread acceptance in modern times. During the eighteenth century it was employed by the Deists for whom the physical universe was a well-regulated machine. They contended that, just as the watch requires an intelligent craftsman for its maker, so the well-designed physical universe requires an intelligent being, God, for its creator. During the eighteenth century, however, natural theology, and in particular "the teleological argument," received its most shattering criticism from David Hume in his *Dialogues Concerning Natural Religion* (1779). According to Hume, not only is there insufficient evidence for design in the universe, but even if such design exists, it could have been produced by a being imperfect in intelligence and power or by a company of such beings. In the nineteenth century, John Stuart Mill (1806–1873) nevertheless resorted to the teleological argument in his *Three Essays on Religion* (1874), although he maintained that it proved the existence of a limited deity, because a God with infinite power and knowledge would not need means to attain his ends.

The Problem of Analogy—However effective or ineffective the arguments for the existence of God, they betray a tendency common to realists—the tendency to posit a world rich with kinds and levels of beings and climaxing in a supreme being, God. Despite the differences of position on crucial issues among Plato, Aristotle, and sundry medieval and modern realists, they concur in regarding the world as a hierarchy or a great chain of being.[48] The theory that the world is a hierarchy or chain of being is not restricted to realism. Mysticism, which may be interpreted as the antithesis of realism, subscribes to the hierarchy theory. The most consummate of mystics, Plotinus, has stressed the unity that transcends all multiplicity, a One that absorbs all within its majestic nonentity, and yet on the other hand, he distinguished levels of being—in his terminology, hypostases. Topmost stands the One, next the Intellectual-Principle, and third the Soul. The material world of changing particulars is somehow "grounded in" or "stands upon" these hypostases. The insuperable task for the mystic is to explain why and how the simple unity fractures into multiple stories of being.

The task for the realist is to explain how the different levels or kinds of being can be related in a hierarchically ordered cosmos. This task is nothing short of explicating the bond of being.

Plato approached the task in different ways. According to Plato, there are different degrees of being, and the criteria of being are the criteria of intelligibility and value. Hence the more intelligible and the more valuable, the more real. The Platonic system esteems the perfect universal to be the highest degree of being, and derives the being of all particular things from the universals they instantiate. For example, a particular thing is *square* and is said correctly to be *square* when it possesses the quality *squareness,* and this quality is the same as the universal *squareness*. The relation is one the medievals called "analogy of attribution." It is consistent with an emanationist interpretation of reality: being flows downward or outward from a source or center of perfect being to less perfect grades of being. However, Plato also employed the analogy of model to copy in order to elucidate the relation of universal form to particular thing. But then, to mediate the two, he needed a principle which belongs to neither the level of the forms nor that of particulars. Thus he invoked the principle of mind, or rather the principle of soul, in which mind is seated. For the soul not only soars as mind above things to forms, but also as creative agent makes things after the patterns of the forms.

Plato sought also to explain how the forms are related to each other. That they participate in one another is essential but not sufficient to explain how they constitute an order of perfect and intelligible beings. Here the form of the Good enters. Lying beyond being and knowing, the Good is the unknowable transcendent principle which supports the hierarchy.

Christian Platonism equates the Good with the Supreme Soul—namely, God, and treats the problem of the relatedness of beings, after the analogy of model and copy. On the one hand, God is the model which the world imitates or copies. On the other hand, statements about God are attributions based on analogy drawn from created things. The man is father to the boy; God is father to man. Since God lies beyond knowing, He eludes philosophical investigation. Philosophy terminates, and revealed theology commences.

Aristotle, too, approached the problem of integrating the many substances in different ways. According to Aristotle, the hierarchy is a hierarchy of kinds, and each kind is substantial in the sense of its kind. Reality is no continuum exhibiting diversity in degree; rather it is stratified into abrupt qualitative levels. At the lowest level of the hierarchy are the physical substances such as the natural elements, at the highest are the separate substances, and mediate are the biological species. Aristotle's task of relating the various kinds of substances is threefold. In logic it revolved around the endeavor to bring first substance and second substance together. In physics it centered on the attempt to bring the four causes to unity. In metaphysics it focused on the effort to bring the diverse substances together in a single system.

Fundamentally, Aristotle's problem is a problem of relation; and it is aggravated by the consideration that relation is one of the categories of accidents and not itself substantial. Thus, for example, the judgment that "John is taller than Mary" does not represent a relation between two substances; instead, it predicates to John the relational attribute of "being taller than Mary." This conception stunted the growth of logic for centuries, and symbolic or mathematical logic developed only after the rejection of the Aristotelian conception of relation. However, the issue here is not logical, but metaphysical. If, as Aristotle contended, the relation is a property inhering in the substances, how can it extend outside each substance and so connect each to the others? How, moreover, can all the diverse substances be integrated into a systematic whole? The answer Aristotle suggested is the analogy of proportionality. By virtue of the operation of this analogy, a single system comprehends matter, intermediate natural substances, and the separate substances of theology. As potency is to act in the particular substances, so the physical world is to the absolute actuality of the separate substances. Christian Aristotelianism explicitly adopted the analogy of proportionality. The God who satisfied the requirements of Aristotelian philosophy, however, lacked those personal qualities which the God of religion possesses.

DESCARTES AND MODERN REALISMS

The history of thought has not exhausted the tenability of the variant Platonisms and Aristotelianisms. These philosophical types are recurrent versions of realism. In addition, modern realisms have appeared. Although modern realisms are less significant than their ancient forbears, they present arresting, original conceptions.

Modern realism began with Descartes. Cartesian realism affirms a world existing independently of knowledge, and although it is silent on the status of universals, it recognizes, perhaps as a consequence of its theory of knowledge, that there is more than one kind of being in the world. Cartesian realism, moreover, is susceptible to the difficulty that besets philosophical realism in general —the problem of relating the beings acknowledged to exist. The term "dualism" is customarily used to denote this aspect of Cartesian philosophy. Descartes upheld epistemological dualism because of his dichotomy of thought and its objects as well as psychophysical dualism because of his division of substances into mind and matter. The problem for epistemological dualism is how to guarantee the imputed cognitive relation between thought and its objects. Typically it is held that cognition is true when thought corresponds to its object, and just as typically, it is charged that the correspondence, if said to be known, falls on the side of thought and cannot be objective, and, if objective, falls on the side of the object outside of thought and so cannot be known. The problem for psychophysical dualism is how to relate the two substances: body and mind. Typically it is held that mind and body interplay in human experience, and just as typically, it is charged that the interplay as a mode of substance is either material or mental, and that if it is mental, it cannot affect the body, or if material, the mind.

Descartes opened his *Meditations on First Philosophy* (1642) in a skeptical mood. He subjected all his inherited beliefs to doubt by demonstrating that their main source—sense-perception—is unreliable. In addition, he argued that, since human reason may have been created by a malignant demon who deliberately intends to deceive, it too is unreliable. From a state of complete skepticism Descartes, in the second "Meditation," discovered an indubitable truth—namely, his own existence. Granting that there is a powerful and cunning deceiver forever deceiving me so that I doubt the existence of all objects external to me, including my own body, as Descartes reasoned, "without doubt I exist also if he deceives me, and let him deceive me as much as he will, he can never cause me to be nothing so long as I think that I am something."[49] Hence the proposition—*cogito, ergo sum* (I think, therefore I am)—is the first certain principle which enabled Descartes to escape skepticism and upon which he built what he considered to be a certain system of knowledge.

The *cogito* argument did not lead Descartes directly to realism. After all, the only being of which Descartes was certain at this point was merely his own being—a solitary thinking self, and on the basis of the *cogito* argument some philosophers have spun out idealistic systems. Descartes, however, refrained from drawing an idealistic conclusion. Instead, he took stock of the ideas in the mind of his thinking self, and he found one idea which could not have been produced by this self—namely, the idea of God. From this idea he proceeded, in the third "Meditation," to demonstrate the existence of God.

Descartes' formulation of the ontological argument is unique. First, he invoked the scholastic distinction between formal reality and objective reality. Briefly, formal reality marks the status of things in the world, and objective reality belongs to ideas so far as they represent or refer to objects beyond themselves—i.e., are the vehicles of logical meaning. Second, Descartes ranked all beings—suspending momentarily the question of their existence—in a hierarchy according to their formal reality. Third, he held the objective reality of ideas to be proportional to the formal reality of their objects, and he ranked all ideas accordingly. Fourth, Descartes held "by the natural light that there must be as much reality in the efficient and total cause as in its effect."[50] Now in respect to objective reality, the idea of God is the greatest of all ideas, so great that it exceeds the power of the finite mind to produce it, so great that only God Himself could have produced it. Thus Descartes wrote:

> By the name God I understand a substance that is infinite (eternal, immutable), independent, all-knowing, all-powerful, and by which I myself and everything else, if anything else does exist, have been created. Now all these characteristics are such that the more diligently I attend to them, the less do they appear capable of proceeding from me alone; hence, from what has already been said, we must conclude that God necessarily exists.[51]

Descartes advanced two other arguments for the existence of God. In the third "Meditation," he also sought to prove the existence of God from the continued existence of the self in time. Assuming that time is atomic, Descartes reasoned:

> It is as a matter of fact perfectly clear and evident to all those who consider with attention the nature of time, that, in order to be conserved in each moment in which it endures, a substance has need of the same power and action as would be necessary to produce and create it anew, supposing it did not yet exist.[52]

In the fifth "Meditation," Descartes argued from the essence of God to His existence. He wrote:

> Existence can no more be separated from the essence of God than can its three angles equal to two right angles be separated from the essence of a (rectilinear) triangle, or the idea of a mountain from the idea of a valley; and so there is not any less repugnance to our conceiving a God (that is, a Being supremely perfect) to whom existence is lacking (that is to say, to whom a certain perfection is lacking), than to conceive of a mountain which has no valley.[53]

It is unnecessary here to criticize Descartes' proofs of the existence of God. The third proof is vulnerable to St. Thomas's attack on the ontological argument. The second proof depends on a special theory of time and is vulnerable to some of the criticisms of the cosmological arguments. As for Descartes' first proof, its assumptions are so disputable that it deserves admiration solely as a brilliant yet specious expression of inventive speculation. Suffice it to remark that, however invalid these proofs, they furnished Descartes the needed route of escape from subjective idealism. For with God, the self is no longer solitary; there is at least one Other.

Since God is a perfect being, Descartes eliminated the possibility that a deceiving demon has the self in his clutches. Whatever error the self commits is the self's own fault. Within its limits, human reason is infallible. Indeed, reason alone may elaborate an entire system of certain truths in rational theology, mathematics, and physics, at least so long as the last science is restricted to the investigation of the essence of matter and its laws.

Still the task remained to explain how it is possible to know the existence of external physical objects, including the existence of one's own body. In the sixth "Meditation," Descartes presented an extremely complex argument for the existence of an external world, the major promise of which is belief in the existence of the perfect God as our creator. According to the argument, the self becomes aware of its intimate connection with a physical body first through the operation of the imagination, and then through the experience of locomotion. Meanwhile, the self has perceptions, which seem to refer to other existent physical objects. Since the self is the creature of God, and since God is perfect and not a deceiver, it is plausible to suppose that the self has a body, and, further, that there exists an external world of corporeal objects corresponding to the self's perceptions. Belief in the existence of external physical objects does, of course, lack absolute theoretical certainty, but it is so highly probable that it is practically certain.

Having begun as a skeptic, Descartes in his *Meditations* concluded as a commonsense realist. Cartesian epistemological realism displays the gravity of the difficulty stemming from the dichotomy of idea and object; for Descartes, only God could heal the breach.

Equally grave is the difficulty of psychophysical dualism stemming from the division of substance into mind and matter. After proving the existence of the self in the second "Meditation," Descartes inquired into its nature, or essence. He wrote:

> . . . what then am I? A thing which thinks. What is a thing which thinks? It is a thing which doubts, understands, (conceives), affirms, denies, wills, refuses, which also imagines and feels.[54]

Hence he ascertained that the self is a thinking substance, a mental thing. On the other hand, before demonstrating that material substances exist, Descartes in the fifth "Meditation" investigated the essence of matter. He wrote:

> I am able distinctly to imagine that quantity which philosophers commonly call continuous, or the extension in length, breadth, or depth, that is in this quantity, or rather in the object to which it is attributed. Further, I can number in it many different parts, and attribute to each of its parts many sorts of size, figure, situation and local movement, and, finally, I can assign to each of these movements all degrees of duration.[55]

Hence he determined that matter is extended substance. Now the problem of psychophysical dualism is how to relate mind and matter, self and body. As Descartes observed in the sixth "Meditation," "there is a great difference between mind and body."[56]

Descartes proposed a theory of interaction to solve the problem of relating body and mind. According to interaction, physical causes affect mental events—e.g., a pinprick causes pain; and similarly, mental causes affect physical events—e.g., my will causes my arm to rise. Descartes sought to locate the mechanism for interaction in the pineal gland within the brain. Cartesian interaction theory has encountered objections. Once the world is divided into two kinds of substances existing separately of one another and having exclusive properties, that a cause in one kind of substance may have an effect in another kind of substance is metaphysically inexplicable. The transmission of causal efficacy is neither of one substance nor of the other; hence it is nothing. Physics joins metaphysics in rejecting interaction between mind and matter conceived as separate kinds of substances. The physical law of the conservation of energy postulates a constant quantity of energy in the physical world. However, if action passes from matter to mind, the quantity of physical energy would decrease, and if action passes from mind to matter, the quantity of physical energy would increase.

Descartes' successors grappled with the problem of psychophysical dualism in different ways. Spinoza, to consider one post-Cartesian thinker, adopted a monistic view of substance. He defined substance as "that which is in itself and is conceived through itself," [57] and he identified substance with God. He meant by God, "Being absolutely infinite, that is to say, substance consisting of infinite attributes, each one of which expresses eternal and infinite essence." [58] By attribute, Spinoza meant "that which the intellect perceives of substance, as if constituting its essence." [59] Among the attributes of God are thought (mind) and extension (matter). He wrote:

> Thought is an attribute of God, or God is a thinking thing.[60]
>
> Extension is an attribute of God, or God is an extended thing.[61]

Individual minds and bodies are modes. By mode, Spinoza meant "the affections of substance, or that which is in another thing through which also it is conceived." [62] There is for Spinoza no interaction between a mode of thought and a mode of extension. Causation prevails within each attribute but does not operate across attributes. Since the attributes are grounded in the single substance, God, and are infinite, they parallel each other. Thus there is a one-to-one correlation between modes of thought and modes of extension. This theory is known as parallelism. Spinoza's parallelism is found objectionable because it assumes that there exists a mode of thought corresponding to the most remote physical event in the farthest reaches of the universe and that there exists a mode of extension corresponding to the most hidden mental state in the depths of the self.

Having placed a field of ideas between the objects known and the knowing mind, epistemological dualism led inexorably, as the development of philosophy from John Locke through George Berkeley to David Hume shows, to metaphysical skepticism. In reaction the Scottish school of commonsense realism, founded by Thomas Reid (1710–1796), emerged. Reid diagnosed the germ of Humean skepticism to be the doctrine that the mind knows only its ideas, which he eradicated with his theory that the mind knows objects by means of ideas. Scottish realism flourished during the seventeenth and eighteenth centuries, but it receded during the high tide of idealism in the nineteenth century, when it yet remained a strong undercurrent in Anglo-American thought. Although Scottish realism inspired no vast speculative systems, it served as a stabilizing influence on minds lured by the fancies of romanticism and transcendentalism.

CONTEMPORARY REALISM AND SANTAYANA

In the twentieth century, realism, nurtured in part by the tradition of Scottish realism, rose to dominance over idealism in England and the United States. In England, G. E. Moore (1873–1958), Bertrand Russell (1872–1970), and Samuel Alexander (1859–1938) led the realists in their united purpose of demolishing idealism. Excepting Samuel Alexander, whose system of process philosophy will be considered in Chapter VI, the English realists tended to shy away from speculation; they were practitioners of analytic methods which prepared the way for ordinary language analysis. In the United States the realists joined with their English colleagues in their common assault on idealism. American realism has swept by in three waves: new realism, critical realism, and what may be called neo-classical realism.

The new realists, who published their platform in 1910, were Edwin B. Holt (1873–1946), Walter T. Marvin (1872–1944), W. P. Montague (1873–1953), Ralph Barton Perry (1876–1957), Walter B. Pitkin (1878–1953), and E. G. Spaulding. Focusing on the theory of knowledge, the new realists proposed a theory of epistemological monism—at least in regard to perception. Thus the percept in the mind and the object in the physical world are said to be identical ontologically; their distinction is functional only, the percept being in the mental context of cognition and the object in the physical context of causal laws. New realism entailed a singular theory of mind, a theory heavily influenced by William James's 1904 article,

"Does Consciousness Exist?" The new realists taught that mind or consciousness does not exist as a substance; rather it is a function of the physical organism. The theory had affinity with psychological functionalism which was eventually superseded by behaviorism, and has inspired the philosophy of neutral monism, which will be considered in Chapter IV.

Ironically, new realism suffered its undoing in the very arena in which it chose to be engaged—in the theory of knowledge. Because of its doctrine of the identity of percept and object, new realism could never satisfactorily explain the occurrence of errors. Either perception is always true, or perceptual errors are objective, belonging presumably to a realm separate from the physical context. The first alternative is excluded by the obvious existence of perceptual error—e.g., the perception that a stick half in water and half out is bent. The second alternative alone is permissible, but it entails a sort of perverse Platonism, positing a realm of subsistent being which is populated with all possibilities, including errors, dreams, fictions, hallucinations.

The failure of new realism became the opportunity of critical realism. The critical realists were Durant Drake (1878–1933), Arthur O. Lovejoy (1873–1962), James B. Pratt (1875–1944), Arthur K. Rogers (1868–1936), George Santayana (1863–1952), Roy Wood Sellars (1880–   ), and Charles A. Strong (1862–1940). They concurred on one main thesis—that an adequate theory of knowledge capable of explaining error requires an epistemological dualism of idea and object.

Leading realists who did not expressly affiliate themselves with new realism and critical realism were Frederick J. E. Woodbridge (1867–1940), John Elof Boodin (1869–1950), and Morris Cohen (1880–1947). More recently, on the analytic side, thinkers like Herbert Feigl and Wilfrid Sellars have resorted to the principles of realistic philosophy, while on the speculative side, James K. Feibleman in his *Ontology* (1952) has undertaken to build an ambitious system of philosophy along realist lines. Since World War II, a third movement of realism has appeared—a neo-classical realism founded and initially led by John Wild.[63]

Among the realists, George Santayana (1863–1952) merits special consideration. His is the most original and comprehensive system of philosophy to which contemporary realism has led. Santayana presented his theory of knowledge in *Scepticism and Animal Faith* (1923). It is introductory to the system of ontology expounded in his four-volume *Realms of Being* (1927–1940).

Santayana's critical theory of knowledge opens with an examination of belief. Beliefs conflict with one another, inducing skepticism. Like Descartes, Santayana employed the skeptical method, and carried it as far as it would go. The skeptical method in Santayana's application leads, however, not to the *cogito* argument, but to "the solipsism of the present moment." [64] This state is so permeated by doubt that neither a self nor a temporal structure with past and future is credible; the experienced datum now is all there is. It is preliminary to "ultimate skepticism." [65] The ultimate skeptic is one for whom no belief in any existent thing is tenable. Santayana's critical method exposes the principle upon which ultimate skepticism is based: "Nothing given exists." [66]

The denial of existence to what is given logically compels acknowledgment that something is given—namely, the qualities immediately apprehended (or intuited) in experience. Santayana used the term "essence" to denote these nonexistent qualities. (Other critical realists preferred the term "sense-data.") Unlike Descartes, Santayana found no essence which entailed existence. Indeed, the mind, as long as it entertains essence alone, is not inclined to believe in existence. Experience confined to the intuition of essence is primarily contemplative and aesthetic. Plainly, the experience of a living animal, like man, cannot be long confined to the purely contemplative and aesthetic. The animal is entangled in nature; its encounters with its environment and other animals register as shock. To survive, the animal must act; and to act, he must believe in the existence of objects and their causative powers.

Santayana described belief in terms of "compulsion" and "brute necessity"; he qualified it as "instinctive" and "practical." [67] Hence he called belief "animal faith." Belief attributes existence to the essence or to things represented by the essences. Animal faith is made up of beliefs in the existence of the self, the existence of substance (matter), and the existence of Nature. Although these fundamental beliefs cannot be proved, they constitute a sort of naturalistic a priori; they prevail wherever and whenever men live and think. Santayana's critical realist epistemology is superbly summed up in the formula: "Knowledge is faith mediated by symbols."[68] Essences are the symbols; they are interpreted to stand for or represent objects in the external world.

Epistemological dualism, upheld by Descartes, is reaffirmed by Santayana. But the difference in the doctrines of the two thinkers is remarkable. Whereas Descartes established the cognitive relation between idea in the mind of the thinker and physical object in the external world by demonstrating that God, a perfect being, exists, Santayana established the role of essence intuited by the thinking animal as symbolic of existent substances in the material world by invoking the irrational agency of animal faith. Needless to add, animal faith is no more trustworthy than God's existence to guarantee the truth of knowledge.

The ontological categories implicit in Santayana's dualistic epistemology are the subject of his system, *Realms of Being*. Each of the major ontological categories received treatment in a separate volume: *Realm of Essence* (1927), *Realm of Matter* (1930), *Realm of Truth* (1938), and *Realm of Spirit* (1940).

An essence is just the character or quality it is: its principle is identity; and it is "perfectly individual" and also universal.[69] Restricted to no place and no time, essences are reminiscent of Plato's forms. However, "essences do not exist."[70] Further, the realm of essence is "infinitely extended and freed from all confusion with natural forces."[71]

Matter (substance) is not intuited as essence is; it is posited or believed to exist. Matter therefore is believed to have the following indispensable properties: it is external to thought; it consists of parts which are external to one another and so constitutes a physical space; it is in flux and constitutes a physical time; it is unequally distributed in space and time; and it "composes a relative cosmos."[72] In addition to these indispensable properties, matter has the property to assume "sometimes . . . the form of animals in whom there are feelings. These mental facts are immaterial." [73] The animal, a material substance, possesses a psyche. The psyche is "a habit in matter"; it is "the specific form of physical life, present, and potential, asserting itself in any plant or animal." [74]

Truth is correspondence of ideas to objects, of judgments to facts. It is the standard for thought. The realm of truth is the absolute truth: "that segment of the realm of essence which happens to be illustrated in existence." [75]

Spirit is one of the two levels of life, the other of which is psyche. It is only, Santayana said, "that inner light of actuality or attention which floods all life as men actually live it on earth. It is roughly the same thing as feeling or thought; it might be called consciousness." [76]

Santayana's ontology discloses the dualisms to which realism is susceptible. First, there is the dualism of essence and matter (existence). Originating with Plato, this dualism is transmuted into the epistemological dualism of symbolic essence and represented existent. Second, there is the dualism of matter, including psyche, and spirit. This dualism is an eccentric formulation of psychophysical dualism.

Now Santayana was a materialist; he maintained that, among the categories of being, matter alone exists, although he acknowledged the being of the nonmaterial realms of essence and of spirit. The common charge against him is that he failed to relate matter and the nonmaterial realms in a coherent fashion. Essence and spirit testify to a type of philosophy which is emphatically idealistic. Many materialistic naturalists, who followed Santayana when he expounded his doctrines of essence and matter, turned against him when he advanced his theory of spirit. The crux of the issue was the status of spirit. Either spirit is an epiphenomenon of matter, an impotent by-product of physical processes, or it bespeaks a separate realm of being. It could not consistently be both. Yet Santayana seemed to advocate that spirit was both a materialistic epiphenomenon and a separate nonmaterial realm of being.

Santayana's philosophy with its multiple realms and its dualisms may be taken as the paradigm for realism. It displays the richness of realism in recognizing a plurality of levels, degrees, or types of being. It also exhibits the dualistic tensions to which realism is prone. The philosophies to which we now turn—materialism and idealism—are ontologically simpler than realism. They reduce all being ultimately to mind or matter.

IV

MATERIALISM

Materialism, defined generally, is the theory that matter alone is real. Materialism as a speculative philosophy is ontological to its core. It asserts that being is matter; and that nothing is, except matter and its modifications. From the beginning, materialism has been considered a reductionist theory. As reductionists, materialists stand opposed to realist and to process philosophers. Both materialism and idealism are reductionist theories, their disagreement residing in the principles to which everything is reduced.

Materialists disagree as to what matter is. Perhaps the most crucial disagreement has arisen over the question whether matter is discrete or continuous. Discrete matter is atomistic; continuous matter is fluid, and fluidity suggests energy. Atomism lends itself to a substantialistic interpretation of the cosmos. The fluid, energist conception of matter leans toward process philosophy, and it favors a field theory of matter rather than the view that matter consists of simply located particles. These differing conceptions of matter find their way into nonmaterialistic philosophical theories. In materialistic philosophies, however, the conception of matter exerts a controlling influence on the character of all other conceptions.

One form of materialism is known as anthropological materialism; it defines man, including morality and mind, so as to reduce him and all his qualities to matter and material relations. Another form of materialism is cosmological; it presents a total view of the world in the light of the principle that matter is the ultimately real. In its central meaning materialism has proved to be a most durable philosophy at once very ancient and very contemporary.

ANCIENT ATOMISM

Leucippus of Miletus (circa 450 B.C.), the most shadowy figure of early Greek philosophy, originated the atomic theory. Democritus of Abdera (460–370 B.C.), one of the major philosophical authors of antiquity, perpetuated Leucippus' atomism; he wrote on physics, cosmology, and metaphysics and worked out the implications of atomism in epistemology and ethics. Epicurus (341–270 B.C.) revived the atomism of Democritus when he strove to furnish the cosmological context for his ethical theory. Lucretius (95–55 B.C.), who carried on the Epicurean moral tradition in Rome, gave atomism its most complete expression in his famous poem, *De rerum natura.*

Atomism was the first major philosophical materialism viable and comprehensive enough to explain natural processes. It may be spelled out in five categories.

The first category is the atom. Leucippus is credited with having formed the conception of the atom when, in response to Melissus, he described the atom as like Parmenidean being but insisted that there are many atoms. Thus atomism is pluralistic materialism; it holds that atoms are the ultimate real constituents of things. The number of atoms is infinite. Atoms, moreover, have constant and variable properties. Indivisibility is the primary characteristic of the atom. An atom cannot be generated, nor can it perish; it is unchangeable, neither growing nor diminishing in quantity; it is homogeneous, finite, and full. The variable properties of atoms are their size, shape, and weight. That atoms differ from one another is due to these properties. According to Democritus, the shapes of atoms are infinite, and their sizes vary, some atoms being very large. Epicurus, however, disagreed with Democritus; he denied that atoms differed in shape or size on the grounds that, if they did, they would cease to be minute and imperceptible.[1] Epicurus did attribute variable weights to the atoms; he reasoned that weight accounted for their downward fall in the void and their resistance to rising up. It is not the intrinsic properties of the atoms which account for their individuality; rather it is their local positions in the void.

The second category of atomism is the void. Parmenides denied the existence of not-being and accepted the consequence—namely, that motion is unreal. Aristotle apprehended Leucippus' reasons for positing the void when he related that Leucippus had "granted that there could not be movement without the void, that the void was 'not being,' and nothing of what is is not being; for what, strictly speaking, *is,* is completely full. But such being, he claimed, is not a unity. It consists of a plurality of things infinite in number and too small to be seen. They move in the void (for there is void)."[2] The void is absolutely empty space, and while the atomists accepted space in the guise of the void as an important category, they disregarded time. Rather they treated time as a perception of change in the atoms moving in the void, regarding it as a special kind of accident.[3]

The third category of atomism is change. Although known before the atoms and the void, change is posterior in being to the other two categories. It is analyzed as the motion of atoms in the void. Motion is the translation of a body from one position in space to another. The space a moving body vacates is empty until or unless occupied by another body. The space into which a body moves must be emptied in order to be occupied. When atoms move in such a way as to occupy adjacent spaces, they form a compound; the compound in this instance is said to be generated, or to come into being. When, on the other hand, the atoms forming a compound move apart, the compound is dissolved; it is said to pass away. Which atoms fit together to compose compounds is determined in part by the shapes and in part by their jostling about and striking against each other in empty space. The same features operate to produce dissolution. What caused the original motion of the atoms in the void? Being eternal, such motion had and needed no cause. What kind of motion is it? It was probably "a confused and aimless motion in all directions."[4] Certain terms, which have been attributed to Leucippus' lost work, *The Great World-Order,* throw light on the types of motion: rhythm, contact, entanglement, eddy. Although the motions of the atoms in the void received scant comment from Epicurus, they inspired some of Lucretius' most stirring lines.[5] Lucretius pictured the atoms as wandering, each carried by its own weight, or randomly struck by other atoms, their motions varying, some entangling to compose concrete macroscopic objects, others falling disconnected in the void. The downward fall of the atoms in the void is not, however, uniform. At undetermined times and positions the atoms deviate from their downward courses, swerve, and collide with each other. Otherwise they would have fallen straight down in the fathomless void, and none touching any other, Nature would have produced nothing. Lucretius, it seems, imputed a measure of freedom to the falling atoms, and in this respect he adopted a qualified position in regard to the next category of atomism—strict causation.

Strict causation, the fourth category, is announced in the sole complete sentence in the fragments imputed to Leucippus: "Nothing happens at random; everything happens out of reason and by necessity."[6] The atoms bump into each other, and through such direct physical contacts, all changes are explained. The cause-effect relationships holding between atoms are strictly efficient, strictly mechanical; the motion of the atom, called cause, is temporally prior, spatially contiguous, and connected by physical impulse to the motion of the atom called effect. Final causes are ruled out. Although atomists have been accused of having enthroned chance over the cosmos, it should also be clear that by chance they meant simply unknown efficient causes.

The fifth category of atomism is the evacuation of sensible qualities from ultimate reality. Whereas atoms possess the properties of size, shape, weight, motion, and number, they lack the qualities of color, sound, scent, and taste. Democritus said:

> Sweet exists by convention, bitter by convention, colour by convention; atoms and Void (*alone*) exist in reality. We know nothing accurately in reality, but (*only*) as it changes according to the bodily condition, and the constitution of those things that flow upon (the body) and impinge upon it.[7]

Clearly the Greek atomists were forerunners of the modern doctrines of primary and secondary qualities.

The categories of atomism had wide-ranging implications. Although atomism does not logically entail a sensationalistic epistemology or an Epicurean moral philosophy, these doctrines do seem to fit together more tightly than the mere coincidence of their having been advocated by the same thinkers. In fact, F. A. Lange (1828–1875), the leading historian of materialism, has affirmed direct logical connections. He has dubbed the ethics of pleasure "ethical materialism," and he has equated epistemological sensationalism with metaphysical materialism. "What stuff or matter is in the outer world of nature," he wrote, "sensation is in the inner life of man." [8] There is little doubt that Epicurus' conception of the good life as the life of pleasure, along with his definition of pleasure as the absence of pain, makes sense in the cosmic setting of atomism, as does his program for the attainment of the good life, a strategy of withdrawal and escape from troubles. The logical implications of atomism may be easily traced in the fields of cosmology, psychology, and theology.

First, the jostling about of atoms in empty space, colliding with one another according to the principle of efficient causation, projects a stark cosmogony. A collection of atoms isolated in a region of the void somehow begins to form a whirl or vortex. This vortex-action causes atoms of similar character to join each other, and so a world is in the making. No world, however, endures forever, so that any world is just one among many worlds that have been and will be.

Second, the human soul is reduced to a collection of atoms; it, too, is corporeal. Democritus is believed to have thought that, since the most mobile shape is the sphere, fire and soul both consist of spherical atoms. Going beyond Democritus, Epicurus taught that the soul is a body of fine particles, like breath and heat, and that the soul feels because the atoms, distributed throughout the body, are in harmony with one another, at least through the duration of a life. As a collection of indestructible atoms, each soul is nevertheless mortal; it dissolves. Yet instead of destroying hope, the atomists' denial of immortality removed fear—the fear of a shadowy existence such as ghosts were believed to suffer in the afterlife which pagan literature and religion depicted. As Epicurus said: "Death is nothing to us; for that which is dissolved is without sensation; and that which lacks sensation is nothing to us."[9]

Third, the atomists conceived the gods as corporeal. Epicurus defined a god as "a being immortal and blessed, even as the common idea of a god engraved on men's minds. . . . For gods there are, since the knowledge of them is by clear vision."[10] Nevertheless, neither the world nor man's conduct in it is under the governance of gods. As Epicurus said: "The blessed and immortal nature knows no trouble itself nor causes trouble to any other, so that it is never constrained by anger or favour."[11] On these points Lucretius followed his master, having addressed his poetry to the task of liberating men from the superstitions which oppress their happiness—belief in an immortality worse than death and belief that the gods interfere with the world.

GASSENDI'S ATOMISM AND DESCARTES' MATHEMATICAL THEORY OF MATTER

In the seventeenth century, Pierre Gassendi (1592–1655) resurrected atomism.[12] Gassendi presented his atomism mainly as a scientific theory. Gassendi's ultimate atoms had magnitude and figure, as Democritus taught; they have weight, as Epicurus held; but further they have solidity, or impenetrability. Atoms, however, are not eternal; rather they are produced by God, and once produced, they move about in such ways as to make the world. Gassendi, therefore, was not a materialist; he believed in the existence of God and of souls.

Although Gassendi's atomism was eventually absorbed in modern science, it did not in his own time gain the acceptance won by the rival conception of matter held by his more famous contemporary, Descartes. The Cartesian conception of matter was not atomistic, mainly because for Descartes physics is tantamount to geometry. Thus Descartes described matter as "extended in length, breadth, and depth, the various parts of which have various figures and motions, and give rise to the sensations we have of colours, smells, pains, etc." [13] He denied that the perceptions of the senses can teach us what matter really is. Sensible properties, such as weight, hardness, color, and so forth, are variable, differing in different perceptual situations; hence they do not belong to the nature of matter. According to Descartes, matter is solely extension in length, breadth, and depth.

Given this mathematical field theory of matter, Descartes repudiated two of the basic categories of atomism: the conceptions of the atom and of the void. There is no void, empty space or vacuum, Descartes contended, because "the extension of space . . . is not different from that of body." [14] Nor do atoms exist. Recall that atoms were conceived to be indivisible particles of matter. Against this conception Descartes wrote:

> However small the parts [of matter] are supposed to be, yet because they are necessarily extended we are always able in thought to divide any one of them into two or more parts; and thus we know that they are divisible. For there is nothing which we can divide in thought, which we do not thereby recognize to be divisible; and therefore if we judged it to be indivisible, our judgment would be contrary to the knowledge we have of the matter. And even should we suppose that God had reduced some portion of matter to a smallness so extreme that it could not be divided into smaller, it would not for all that be properly termed indivisible. For though God had rendered the particle so small that it was beyond the power of any creature to divide it, He could not deprive Himself of His power of division, because it is absolutely impossible that He should lessen His own omnipotence.[15]

HOBBES

Descartes' conception of matter influenced later materialism, including the philosophy of Thomas Hobbes (1588–1679). Hobbes, like Descartes, rejected the categories of the atom and the void as the key to the nature of matter, but unlike Descartes, he opposed rationalism and dualism. While resident in Paris, Hobbes joined, under the auspices of Père Mersenne, a group of philosophers and theologians, including Gassendi, who raised objections against Descartes' *Meditations* (1641). Hobbes's objections number sixteen, several of which are pertinent to the claims of materialism.

Objection II expresses Hobbes's famous reductionist attack on the *cogito.* According to Hobbes, it is correct to infer from the proposition that "I think" the further proposition that "I exist." The ground of the inference is "that fact alone, that we can conceive no activity whatsoever apart from its subject, e.g., we cannot think of leaping [walking] apart from that which leaps [walks], of knowing apart from a knower, or of thinking without a thinker."[16] But it is illegitimate to infer anything about the nature of the subject from the character of the activity of the subject. If Descartes were right to hold that because I think I am a subject whose essence is thinking, then by equal right one could assert: *sum ambulans, ergo sum ambulatio;* I am walking; hence I am the walking.[17] Against Descartes, Hobbes maintained that the subject underlying these activities—thinking, walking, and so forth—is "something corporeal; for, as it appears, the subjects of all activities can be conceived only after a corporeal fashion, or as in material guise."[18]

Objections VII, IX, and X deal with the idea of God. Hobbes was an empiricist; for him all ideas are based on sense-perception. In Objection IX he maintained that "there is no idea either of God or of soul."[19] In Objection X he challenged one by one the attributes Descartes ascribed to God—infinity, independence, omniscience, omnipotence. He did so in order to disprove the alleged innateness of the idea of God, but in the process he also showed that no finite human thinker could have an idea of a subject with such attributes.

In modern philosophy Hobbes ranks as the first major proponent of a thoroughgoing materialistic metaphysics. He presented his theory in his work, *De Corpore* (1655), which has been translated into English under the title, *Elements of Philosophy.* No survey of materialism would be adequate without due attention to Hobbes's thought, and such attention would place Hobbes's position *vis à vis* atomism within a more general comprehension of his thought. First

Hobbes's uniquely materialistic conception of the logic of philosophy should be considered. Then the basic categories of his materialism and the grounds of his repudiation of atomism should be examined. Finally Hobbes's startling application of materialism to moral and political topics should be noted. Indeed, it is as a moral and political philosopher, as the author of the singular classic, *Leviathan* (1651), that Hobbes has earned his place in the history of philosophy.

Hobbes defined philosophy as "such knowledge of effects or appearances as we acquire by true ratiocination from the knowledge we have first of their causes or generation: And again, of such causes or generations as may be from knowing first their effects."[20] Amplifying this definition, Hobbes examined philosophy in its formal, final, efficient, and material aspects. Formally, philosophy is ratiocination, which Hobbes identified with computation. Centuries before the advent of cybernetics, Hobbes contended that rational thinking is computing, and that computation consists of addition (composition) and subtraction (division). Thus he said, "we add and subtract in our silent thoughts, without the use of words."[21] Subscribing to the Baconian principle that "the end of knowledge is power,"[22] Hobbes maintained that philosophy has a practical end. Philosophy is useful in two ways: it furnishes us with commodities which are products of our control over nature, and it enables us to avoid calamities. Philosophy performs its purpose, its end, or final cause, supported by its efficient or methodological features. Philosophical method, Hobbes said, "is the shortest way of finding out effects by their known causes, or of causes by their known effects."[23] This method goes backward and forward—from effects to causes and from causes to effects. Further, it may start with a whole, whether cause or effect, and resolve it into its parts, seeking through the parts the causes thereof. Or it may be compositive, adding part to part until a whole is attained, or until a part, either cause or effect, is known. Though an empiricist, Hobbes took the formal method of Euclid to be the model for philosophical method; he insisted that the procedure in philosophy is properly deductive.

Hobbes's materialism comes forward when he treats the subject-matter of philosophy. "The *subject* of Philosophy," he asserted, "is every body of which we can conceive any generation, and which we may, by any consideration thereof, compare with other bodies, or which is capable of composition and resolution; that is to say, every body of whose generation or properties we can have any knowledge."[24] Hobbes deliberately excluded from the compass of philosophy fields which were traditionally included: theology, angelology, and so forth. He defined Theology as "the doctrine of God, eternal, ingenerable, incomprehensible, and in whom there is nothing neither to divide nor compound, nor any generation to be conceived;" and he excluded it and angelology on the grounds that there is "in them [noncorporeal beings] no place neither for composition nor division, nor any capacity of more and less, that is to say, no place for ratiocination."[25] Philosophy, he continued, has two principal parts: natural and civil. "For two chief kinds of bodies, and very different from one another, offer themselves to such as search after their generation and properties; one whereof being the work of nature, is called a *natural body,* the other is called a *commonwealth,* and is made by the wills and agreement of men."[26]

Hobbes's materialism is based on a dynamic conception of matter. Scientific knowledge extended indefinitely seeks the causes of universal things—i.e., "such accidents as are common to all bodies, that is to all matter."[27] Consequently, scientific knowledge is knowledge of motion, since there is

> one universal cause, which is motion. For the variety of all figures arises out of the variety of those motions by which they are made; and motion cannot be understood to have any other cause besides motion; nor has the variety of those things we perceive by sense, as of *colours, sounds, savours,* and other causes than motion, residing partly in the objects that work upon our senses, and partly in ourselves, in such manner, as that it is manifestly some kind of motion, though we cannot, without ratiocination, come to know what kind.[28]

Hobbes distinguished the various branches of science and philosophy by reference to the universal cause—motion. Geometry studies the motions productive of single parts of bodies and of single bodies, inasmuch as, to illustrate Hobbes's conception of geometrical entities, "a line is made by the motion of a point, superficies by the motion of a line, and one motion by another motion, etc."[29] Physics studies "what effects one body moved worketh upon another."[30] It may do so without consideration of their sensible qualities. One branch of physics inquires into "such effects as are made by the motion of the parts of any body, as, how it comes to pass, that things when they are the same, yet seem not to be the same, but changed."[31] It deals with the sensible qualities of light, color, transparency, opacity, sound, odor, savor, heat, cold, and the like. Another branch of physics investigates the causes of seeing, hearing, smelling, tasting, and touching. Next comes moral philosophy; it considers "the motions of the mind, namely, appetite, aversion, love, benevolence, hope, fear, anger, emulation, envy, etc.; what causes they have, and of what they be causes."[32] Last is civil philosophy; its principles, Hobbes maintained, may be known introspectively and without ratiocination, since "the causes of the motions of the mind are known . . . by the experience of every man that takes the pains to observe those motions within himself."[33]

The basic categories of Hobbes's materialism—what he called "the first grounds of philosophy"—are Space, Time, Motion, Causation, and Body, which merit attention here, in addition to Quantity, Power and Act, Identity and Difference. Each of these categories is defined by reference to phantasms (images or representations) in the mind.

> Space is the phantasm of a thing existing without the mind simply; that is to say, that phantasm, in which we consider no other accident, but only that it appears without us.[34]
>
> Time is the phantasm of before and after in motion.[35]
>
> Motion is a continual relinquishing of one place, and acquiring of another.[36]
>
> [A cause is] the aggregate of all the accidents both of the agents how many soever they be, and of the patient, put together; which when they are all supposed to be present, it cannot be understood but that the effect is produced at the same instant; and if any one of them be wanting, it cannot be understood but that the effect is not produced.[37]

Hobbes's conception of body involves the Aristotelian distinction between substance and accident. Body is "that, which having no dependence upon our thought, is coincident or coextended with some part of space."[38] Certain accidents "can never perish except the body perish also;"[39] these are extension and figure, without which no body can be conceived to be.[40] All other accidents, such as the states of rest and motion, color, hardness, "do perish continually, and are succeeded by others; yet so, as that the body never perisheth."[41] Thus Hobbes distinguished variable from invariable accidents. This distinction should not be equated with the distinction between secondary and primary qualities, although Hobbes adopted the latter distinction, too. All bodies possess magnitude and motion, which, though variable, are classified as primary qualities. Hobbes's conception of secondary qualities emerges in his discussion of sense and of the objects of sense.

> The object is the thing received; and it is more accurately said, that we see the sun, than that we see the light. For light and colour, and heat and sound, and other qualities which are commonly called sensible, are not objects, but phantasms in the sentients.[42]

Hobbes's materialism contradicts atomism. Hobbes rejected the category of the void (or vacuum) on experimental and logical grounds. Experimentally, he pointed to the fact that, though full of water, a gardener's watering vessel, with holes in the bottom, will not sprinkle water as long as the hole at the top is stopped. He took this "for a sign that all space is full; for without this, the natural motion of the water, which is a heavy, downwards, would not be hindered."[43] Logically, he attacked the arguments of Lucretius and others. If empty space exists between bodies, then, since a body can be put in motion only by a contiguous moving body, bodies at rest can never be put in motion.

Further, Hobbes denied that matter consists universally and ultimately of atoms. Instead, he recognized three types of body: 1) consistent and visible bodies, such as the earth and the stars; 2) invisible bodies, such "as the small atoms which are disseminated through the whole of space between the earth and the stars;"

and 3) "that most fluid ether, which so fills all the rest of the universe, as that it leaves in it no empty space at all."[44] While Hobbes allowed atoms a place in his theory of matter, he regarded the indivisibility of atoms to be relative, not absolute. And he posited the existence of a nonatomic, fluid ether. He devoted the concluding chapter of the *Elements of Philosophy* to explain gravity, a physical fact which raised difficulties for the atomists who, with their doctrine of the void, had to suppose the doctrine of action at a distance—namely, that bodies act on each other at a distance from one another without a connecting medium. Hobbes, in his own way, was groping for concepts which Newton later furnished.

Hobbes's materialism found application in his theories of man, morality, and politics. In this respect Hobbes must be counted as one of the leading anthropological materialists in the history of philosophy. Sketched in the first part of the *Leviathan,* his theory pictures man as a complex body with motions of its own and with sense to register the effects of the motions of external bodies. From sense are derived the cognitive faculties of man: memory, imagination, understanding, and reason. The motions of the human body are of two sorts: 1) vital motions which begin at birth, which need no assistance from the imagination, and which concern the functions of the various organs—e.g., breathing, blood circulation, and so forth, and 2) voluntary motions, such as walking, speaking, and so forth, which the imagination initiates. Moral philosophy treats of the voluntary motions. Hobbes employed the term "endeavour" (*conatus*) to designate the "small beginnings of motion, within the body of man, before they appear in walking, speaking, striking, and other visible actions."[45] He distinguished two sorts of endeavor: 1) appetite, or desire, and 2) aversion. Appetite is motion toward an object, aversion motion away from it. Hobbes defined good as "the object of any man's appetite or desire," and evil as "the object of his hate and aversion."[46]

It should be noted, moreover, that when Hobbes qualified the motions studied by moral philosophy as "voluntary," he did not mean to suggest that they are free in any metaphysical sense. On the contrary, Hobbes was a thoroughgoing determinist. Deliberation, which is the mental process that precedes the doing or the not doing of a deed, consists, he taught, of appetites and aversions, hopes and fears arising alternately in the mind and accompanied by thoughts concerning the good or evil consequences of the action. He added: "In deliberation, the last appetite, or aversion, immediately adhering to the action, or to the omission thereof, is what we call the WILL; the act, not the faculty, of *willing*."[47]

Hobbes's materialism is not only deterministic; it is emphatically mechanical. Perhaps no passage in the literature of philosophy surpasses the first paragraph of the Introduction to the *Leviathan* as an expression of mechanism. It is worthy of quotation.

> Nature, the art whereby God hath made and governs the world, is by the *art* of man, as in many other things, so in this also imitated, that it can make an artificial animal. For seeing life is but a motion of limbs, the beginning whereof is in some principal part within; why may we not say, that all *automata* (engines that move themselves by springs and wheels as doth a watch) have an artificial life? For what is the *heart,* but a *spring;* and the nerves, but so many *strings;* and the *joints,* but so many *wheels,* giving motion to the whole body, such as was intended by the artificer? *Art* goes yet further, imitating that rational and most excellent work of nature, *man.* For by art is created that great LEVIATHAN called a COMMONWEALTH, or STATE, in Latin CIVITAS, which is but an artificial man; though of greater stature and strength than the natural, for whose protection and defence it was intended; and in which the *sovereignty* is an artificial *soul,* as giving life and motion to the whole body; the *magistrates,* and other *officers* of judicature and execution, artificial *joints; reward* and *punishment,* by which fastened to the seat of the sovereignty every joint and member is moved to perform his duty, are the *nerves,* that do the same in the body natural; the *wealth* and *riches* of all the particular members, are the *strength; salus populi,* the *people's safety,* its *business; counsellors,* by whom all things needful for it to know are suggested unto it, are the *memory; equity* and *laws,* an artificial *reason* and *will; concord, health; sedition, sickness;* and *civil war, death.* Lastly, the *pacts* and *covenants,* by which the parts of this body politic were at first made, set together,

> and united, resemble that *fiat,* or the *let us make man,* pronounced by God in the creation.[48]

Only less striking than the extended mechanical analogy in the above passage is Hobbes's twice mentioning God. Was the mechanistic, deterministic materialist merely playing lip service to orthodoxy in religious matters? The evidence seems to tell otherwise. Hobbes was a theist, and paradoxically, his conception of the world as a causally determined materialistic mechanism was one of his strongest reasons for belief in God. As he said, "Curiosity, or love of the knowledge of causes, draws a man from the consideration of the effect, to seek the cause; and again, the cause of that cause; till of necessity he must come to this thought at last, that there is some cause, whereof there is no former cause, but is eternal; which is it men call God."[49] Hobbes, as revealed in the first sentence of the above quoted paragraph, prepared the way for the position adopted by the eighteenth-century Deists, and superbly elucidated by C. D. Broad[50]—namely, that the conception of the world as a machine entails the conception of a cosmic mechanic, God. Not only did Hobbes accept this theological conclusion on a rational basis, he also adhered to the Anglican religion, from the conviction that the religion established by the law of the kingdom could admit of no dispute without the risk of civil war.

FRENCH MATERIALISM

Materialism as a comprehensive philosophy flourished in France in the eighteenth century. Julien Offray de la Mettrie (1709–1751), Denis Diderot (1713–1784), Jean le Rond d'Alembert (1717–1783), Claude-Adrien Helvetius (1715–1771), Paul-Henry Thiry, Baron d'Holbach (1723–1789), and Pierre Jean George Cabanis (1751–1808) are historically the most important representatives of French materialism. Here it is useful to cite the works only of La Mettrie and of Holbach to convey a sense of the import of French materialism, an import which is operative even in contemporary thought.

La Mettrie—A physician turned philosopher, La Mettrie illustrates in exemplary fashion anthropological materialism. His philosophy actually climaxes a long chain of thought that originated with Descartes.[51] Descartes cited the revolutionary theory of the circulation of the blood advanced by William Harvey (1578–1675), who pictured the human heart as a pump. Generalizing from it, Descartes proposed a thoroughly mechanistic interpretation of the living body. He wrote:

> . . . this will not seem strange to those, who, knowing how many different *automata* or moving machines can be made by the industry of man, without employing in so doing more than a very few parts in comparison with the great multitude of bones, muscles, nerves, arteries, veins, or other parts that are found in the body of each animal. From this aspect the body is regarded as a machine which, having been made by the hands of God, is incomparably better arranged, and possesses in itself movements which are much more admirable, than any of those which can be invented by man. . . . If there had been such machines, possessing the organs and outward form of a monkey or some other animal without reason, we should not have had any means of ascertaining that they were not of the same nature as those animals. . . . It is nature which acts in them [the brute animals] according to the disposition of their organs, just as a clock, which is only composed of wheels and weights, is able to tell the hours and measure the time more correctly than we can do with all our wisdom.[52]

Descartes, in effect, proposed the doctrine of the beast-machine. Meanwhile, he denied that man is a machine. No matter how much the human body resembles a machine, there were, according to Descartes, two tests which would distinguish the man from the machine: 1) the use of language or of other signs by man; and 2) the flexibility and diversity of man's responses to various contingencies. These tests, Descartes concluded, show that men have reason, or rather that their bodies are inhabited by rational souls. Descartes' point of view was dualistic; Gilbert Ryle has caricatured it as "the dogma of the Ghost in the Machine."[53]

La Mettrie extended Descartes' machine analogy to man. Descartes had supposed that in nature there exists a radical separation of men from brute animals. La Mettrie at first returned to the widely accepted tradition of Aristotelian naturalism to undermine Descartes' position. In his *Histoire naturelle de l'âme* (1745) La Mettrie applied the method of medical science to the soul to show that the soul is dependent on the specific constitution of the physical organism, that, indeed, the soul with all its faculties is nothing but the unity of forms enveloped in and emerging out of matter. In *L'homme machine* (1747), La Mettrie went a step further. For, as the title of his book makes plain, La Mettrie taught that man himself is a machine. Affecting a popular style and flippantly disregarding the orthodoxies of the age, he won instant notoriety.

The theory of the man-machine was a scientific hypothesis based on experiment and observation. Ruling out as vain the a priori speculations of the philosophers, La Mettrie held that "it is only a posteriori, while seeking to unravel the soul as throughout the organs of the body, that one can, I do not say, discover with certainty the very nature of man, but attain the greatest degree of probability possible on the subject."[54]

La Mettrie maintained that "the human body is a machine which itself winds up its springs; a living image of perpetual movement."[55] He elaborated his thesis by reference to these biological facts: that food fuels the body, that different substances affect states of consciousness and health differently, that the brain is the organ of thinking, and so forth. He mixed these facts with conjectures of dubious truth-value: that brain size determines mental capacity, that the large apes can be taught to speak, and so forth. The ascription of linguistic capacity to the apes was itself bound up with the more credible hypotheses that the transition in nature from the animals to man is not violent and that thought itself consists wholly in using symbols. La Mettrie's comparison of the brain to a musical instrument beautifully illustrates his mechanical conception of particular organs. He wrote: "As a violin string or a key of the clavichord vibrates and renders a sound, so the brain's cords struck by sound waves are stimulated to render or to repeat the words which touch it."[56] Particular organs do not by themselves account for the mechanical nature of the human body. "Organization," declared La Mettrie, "is the first merit of man."[57] And organization in the human organism is simply a self-adapting mechanical system which fulfills its own ends.

Hence human values are naturalized, man is assigned a place in nature alongside the other animals, and the status of God is esteemed to be problematic. Although La Mettrie declined to choose between theism and atheism on the grounds that neither side had sufficient evidence in its support, he quoted approvingly a statement which he attributed to a friend—namely, that "the universe will not be happy unless it is Atheistic," for only then will it be rid of religions with their wars.[58] La Mettrie's materialism was, then, implicitly linked to cosmological materialism; but it was explicitly anthropological.

Having shown that the body is a machine, he proceeded to eliminate the spiritualistic conception of the soul. "The soul is a vain term of which one has no idea, and which a person of intelligence ought to use only in order to name the part which thinks in us."[59] He based his view on the behavior of the body as a whole or of its parts after death, arguing that life and action may be explained without supposing that the soul is a separate substance. He defined the soul as "only a principle of movement, or a sensible material part of the brain, which one can, without fearing error, regard as a principal spring of the entire Machine."[60] Imagine the body to be a clock; then the soul is its pendulum. In effect, La Mettrie offered an almost contemporary materialistic conception of mind; he identified the soul (or mind) with an actual physical part of the organism and with the actions and states of that organism.

Holbach—In his *System of Nature* (1770), Holbach furnished the most comprehensive statement of French materialism. He absorbed anthropological materialism within the sweeping context of cosmological materialism, and he made the latter explicit.

The basic categories of Holbach's system are 1) matter, 2) motion, and 3) causation. "The universe, that vast assemblage of every thing that exists," he wrote, "presents only matter and motion."[61] Matter is no inert substrate. "Every thing in the universe is in motion; the essence of matter is to act; if we consider its parts attentively, we shall discover, there is not a particle that enjoys absolute repose."[62] To account for the incessant motions of matter, Holbach revived the Greek doctrine of the four elements.

> Elementary fire appears to be in nature the principle of activity. . . . Earth appears to be the principle of the solidity in bodies, from its impenetrability, and by the firm coherence of its parts. Water is a medium, to facilitate the combination of bodies, into which it enters itself as a constituent part. Air is a fluid, whose business it seems to be to furnish the other elements with the space requisite to expand, to exercise their motion.[63]

The whole universe, moreover, "offers to our contemplation nothing but an immense, an uninterrupted succession of causes and effects."[64] Determinism prevails throughout the system.

> *Order* is never more than the necessary, the uniform connection of causes with their effects, or that series of action which flows from the peculiar properties of beings. . . . In the universe all is necessarily in order, because every thing acts and moves according to the properties of the beings it contains. . . .There is neither *chance* nor any thing fortuitous in this nature, where no effect is produced without a sufficient, without a substantial cause.[65]

Holbach employed the term "Nature" in two senses. In the broad sense, Nature is the great whole that results from matter in motion. In the narrow sense, Nature is the whole that results from the essences.

> An immense variety of matter, combined under an infinity of forms, incessantly communicates, unceasingly receives a diversity of impulses. The different properties of this matter, its innumerable combinations, its various methods of action, which are the necessary consequence of these combinations, constitute for man, what he calls the *essence* of beings.[66]

At this juncture Holbach's materialism displays a fourth category: essence. According to Holbach, essence is a specific combination of matter with determinate properties and lawful propensities—i.e., "that which constitutes a being such as it is; the whole of the properties or qualities by which it acts as it does." [67] Because the term "essence" is loaded with connotations derived from its long usage since ancient times, it might be better to substitute the term "organization."

The category of essence (or organization) is well illustrated in Holbach's theory of man.

> MAN is as a whole, or in his nature, the result of a certain combination of matter, endowed with particular properties, competent to give, capable of receiving, certain impulses, the arrangement of which is called *organization,* of which the essence is to feel, to think, to act, to move, after a manner distinguished from other beings with which he can be compared. Man, therefore, ranks in an order, in a system, in a class by himself, which differs from that of other animals, in whom we do not perceive those properties of which he is possessed.[68]

Man, then, is "a material being organized after a peculiar manner," and "like all other beings, man is a production of nature, who resembles them in some respects, and finds himself submitted to the same laws; who differs from them in other respects, and follows particular laws, determined by the diversity of his conformation." [69] Holbach even entertained as plausible the hypothesis that man is a natural product formed in the course of time and in consequence of environmental conditions. He expressly excluded the Cartesian dualistic thesis that man has an incorporeal soul. "The doctrine of spirituality," he emphasized, "offers nothing but vague ideas; or rather is the absence of all ideas." [70] And he repudiated the Cartesian thesis that matter cannot think. He wrote: "Those who have distinguished the soul from the body, appear only to have distinguished their brain from themselves." [71] Holbach asserted, therefore, a theory of identity materialism with respect to the mind-body problem. The mind (or soul) is the brain, for

> the brain is the common centre where all the nerves, distributed through every part of the body, meet and blend themselves: it is by the aid of this interior organ, that all those operations are performed which are attributed to the soul: it is the impulse, the motion, communicated to the nerve, which modifies the brain: in consequence,

it re-acts, gives play to the bodily organs, or rather it acts upon itself, and becomes capable of producing within itself a great variety of motion, which has been designated intellectual faculties.[72]

As the subtitle of his masterpiece reveals—"The Laws of the Moral and Physical World," Holbach was particularly concerned to demonstrate the dependence of human morality on physical reality. "The distinction which has been so often made between the *physical* and the *moral* man is," he explained, "evidently an abuse of terms. Man is a being purely physical: the moral man is nothing more than this physical being considered under a certain point of view, that is to say, with relation to some of his modes of action, arising out of his particular organization."[73] In moral philosophy Holbach adopted happiness as the supreme good for man. He located the achievement of happiness in a social context where the virtues of goodness, truth, and reason are crucial. Now it is not germane in this sketch of Holbach's materialism as a speculative philosophy to discuss at length his moral philosophy, but it is germane to note that Holbach excluded human freedom and God from his system.

Holbach, as noted above, was a thoroughgoing determinist. "Man's life," he said, "is a line that nature commands him to describe upon the surface of the earth, without his ever being able to swerve from it, even for an instant."[74] Holbach's determinism, moreover, was explicitly fatalistic. "FATALITY is the eternal, the immutable, the necessary order established in nature, or the indispensable connection of causes that act with the effects they operate. . . . In man, free agency is nothing more than necessity contained within himself."[75]

Finally, Holbach audaciously proclaimed a doctrine tacitly held by many *philosophes*—atheism. The entire second part of his *System of Nature* is devoted to the case for atheism. The argument is, of course, multifaceted. By "atheism" Holbach meant the denial of all theories, arguments, beliefs, and superstitions supporting allegedly supernatural agency or agencies. Much of Holbach's argument is a detailed examination of the proofs philosophers and theologians have offered to elucidate the nature of God and to prove His existence. Holbach contended, in brief, that the very conception of an incorporeal being is meaningless. At the same time he sought to show that, since the alternatives to atheism involve falsehood and are backed by priests, only atheism is genuinely compatible with human morality.

SCIENTIFIC CONTRIBUTIONS TO MATERIALISM

Materialism has owed much to scientific conceptions.

Anthropological materialism received extraordinary impetus from the work of Charles Darwin (1809–1882). In *The Origin of the Species* (1859), Darwin showed that all forms of living things (species) descend by means of gradual changes from a few simple life-forms, perhaps even a single life-form. According to Darwin, accidental variations, produced by antecedent physical causes, modified individual organisms, and natural selection, determining the adaptability of the organism to its environment, explained which variations survived. Darwin implied that man is an animal wholly natural in origin, and that mind is seen either as an appendage to the physical organism or, like man's other organs, as an instrument employed in his struggle for survival. Inspiring process philosophy as well as anthropological materialism, Darwin's theory of evolution furnished the life sciences with an original unifying principle supported by a convincing array of empirical evidence.

Thomas Henry Huxley (1825–1895), Darwin's leading disciple, maintained, in his celebrated essay, *Man's Place in Nature* (1864), that man is descended from the apes; he advocated this thesis, which shocked the nineteenth-century mind, as a hypothesis confirmed by an array of evidence found in anatomy, embryology, and paleontology. In the *Descent of Man* (1871), Darwin lent clinching support to Huxley's thesis. The theory of the natural origin of man gave the anthropological materialists a scientific weapon with which to combat the theologians and the religious thinkers who adhered to the dogma of man's supernatural origin and destiny.

Furthermore, changing scientific theories of matter influenced the shape and sweep of cosmological materialism. At the beginning of the modern scientific era, several theories of matter competed for acceptance: the atomic theory of Gassendi, the field theory of Descartes, and mixed theories held by such thinkers as Hobbes. The latter eventually crystallized as the corpuscular theory. Thus Robert Boyle (1627–1691) was too much of a chemist to be satisfied with atoms. Having only the quantitative properties of indivisibility, extension, figure, weight, and motion, atoms seemed incapable by themselves of explaining the variety of qualities. Hence Boyle settled upon corpuscles as the ultimate entities. In effect, he moved in the direction of a theory of chemical elements.

However, it remained for Antoine Lavoisier (1743–1794) to establish a quantitative rule for chemical analysis. Instead of Boyle's theory of corpuscles, i.e., concretions with divers qualities, Lavoisier supposed a constancy of weight for each fundamental type of chemical element.

In 1808 John Dalton (1766–1844) revived atomic theory to explain chemical changes. Walton wrote:

> From the relative weights in the mass, the relative weights of the ultimate particles or atoms of the bodies might have been inferred, from which their number and weight in various other compounds would appear, in order to assist and to guide future investigations, and to correct their results. Now it is one great object of this work, to show the importance and advantage of ascertaining the relative weights of the ultimate particles, both of simple and compound bodies, the number of simple elementary particles which constitute one compound particle, and the number of less compound particles which enter into the formation of one more compound particle.[76]

Dalton established the atom as a scientific principle.

After Dalton, the theory of the atom underwent rapid scientific elaboration. Prior to Dalton, Rudjer Boscovich (1711–1787) had advanced the conception of the atom as a center of force. In 1844 Michael Faraday (1791–1867) revived this conception. Proposing a theory of matter consistent with electrical conduction, Faraday conceived the atom as a simple center of force, its form elastic and its shape constituted by the disposition and the intensity of its force. He pictured the atom as a mathematical point in a dynamic field, as inseparable from its field, which nevertheless is so related to the fields of other atoms that each atom, in a sense, pervades the entire universe.[77] Paradoxically, each atom has a zero radius with infinite repulsive force. Not only has the development of atomic theory conduced to a field theory which equates matter with force or energy, it has also led to the abandonment of the ancient attribute of the indivisibility of the atom.

By the end of the nineteenth century the atom was understood to have a structure and to consist of small negatively charged electrons and larger positively charged ions. Twentieth-century physicists have proposed models to represent pictorially mathematical theories of atomic structure. Bohr's model pictured the atom's nucleus as consisting of ions, around which revolve the electrons in fixed orbits, electrons capable of jumping from one orbit to another in the emission or absorption of radiation. This model was widely accepted. Advances in theory and experiment, especially developments in quantum mechanics, however, have made it exceedingly difficult to imagine the structure of the atom. Even the number of subatomic particles has increased: neutrons, protons, electrons, neutrinos, and so forth. Nevertheless, mathematical sophistication has enabled theoretical physicists to represent atomic structure, at least to other expert physicists, if not to humanists.

It is of course plausible to adhere to the scientific conception of matter without being a materialist. A materialist asserts more than simply that matter exists, whatever it is conceived to be; he further asserts that ultimately nothing but matter exists. It is not plausible, however, to found a materialistic philosophy on an outmoded conception of matter. Ancient atomism, for example, can hardly appeal to the contemporary student as scientifically credible.

GERMAN MATERIALISM

It may be taken as a principle that no materialism is admissible unless its conception of matter is scientifically credible. Indeed, German materialism in the nineteenth century exemplified conformance to this principle; at the same time it illustrated the absolute limitation of the principle. For scientific conceptions of matter change, and a materialism compatible with the science of its day, as perforce it must be, is often outmoded the day after. Here two nineteenth-century German philosopher-scientists are worthy of brief study: Ludwig Büchner (1824–1899) and Ernest Haeckel (1834–1919).

Haeckel, the biologist-philosopher, provides the preface to the discussion of German materialism. In the first chapter of his widely read book, *The Riddle of the Universe* (1899), Haeckel formulated the basic tenets of the cosmology which nineteenth-century science warranted. These tenets, which he called "cosmological theorems," are

(1) The universe is eternal, infinite, and without limits.
(2) Its substance fills infinite space and is in perpetual motion.
(3) The motion continues through endless time as a continuous development, with periodic cycles from life to death.
(4) The bodies throughout infinite space obey the same laws of nature, although in some regions of space they are evolving into new forms of life and development, and in other regions they are devolving toward disintegration and destruction.
(5) Our sun and our earth are themselves among the innumerable perishable bodies in the universe.
(6) Our earth has emerged from a fiery mass and has undergone a long process of cooling.
(7) Life-forms have evolved on the surface of the earth during a course of time spanning many millions of years.
(8) In evolution the kind of animals with vertebrates has outstripped all other kinds.
(9) Mammals, the most highly developed branch of the vertebrates, arose much later in the evolutionary process.
(10) The primates are the most highly developed branch of mammals and began to evolve about 3 million years ago.
(11) Man, the youngest and most perfect twig of the branch of primates, sprang from a series of manlike apes.
(12) The period of human history, stretching over the few thousand years during which civilization has existed, is "merely a small portion of the history of our planetary system; and as our mother

> earth is a mere speck in the sunbeam in the illimitable universe, so man himself is but a tiny grain of protoplasm in the perishable framework of organic nature."[78]

Haeckel's twelve cosmological theorems are a mixture of scientific commonplaces and valuations. With minor revisions, they could stand today as an acceptable summary of what a tough-minded scientific position, naturalistic and materialistic, would teach about the ultimate nature of the world and of man's place in it.

Haeckel, whose masterpiece was published the same year during which Büchner died, reflected in his work the impact of the theory of evolution upon materialism. Büchner, whose major work, *Force and Matter* (1855), went through twenty editions before the end of the nineteenth century, relied heavily on the facts and hypotheses of scientific investigations in physics, optics, biology, physiology, genetics, chemistry, geology, physical anthropology, and so forth.

Büchner—The basic principle of Büchner's thought, summed up in the title of his book, is "No force without matter—no matter without force!"[79] Matter is uncreatable and indestructible. Despite its various transformations, it remains the same. It is infinite in time, i.e., immortal, and infinite in space, i.e., without beginning or end. Büchner considered the ultimate constitution of matter to be beyond understanding, although he found the concept of the atom to be helpful. As he said,

> the word *atom* is merely an expression for a necessary conception, required for certain purposes. We have no real notion of the thing we call *atom;* we know nothing of its size, form, composition, etc. No one has seen it.[80]

Büchner's materialism, therefore, is monistic. There is for him but one material substance, of which atoms are merely useful conceptions.

Another noteworthy feature of Büchner's materialism is his emphasis on force as an inseparable (an essential) property of matter. Force is "that system of mutual attraction and repulsion which holds them [the minute particles of which a body consists] together, and gives form and shape to the body."[81] Büchner contributed his part to the rise of the electromagnetic theory of matter, but he had no inkling of the requisite higher mathematics. He wrote: "Nothing but the changes which we perceive in matter by means of our senses could ever give us any notion as to the existence of power which we qualify by the name *force*. Any knowledge of them by other means is impossible."[82]

In the nineteenth century and afterward anthropological materialism advanced by focusing on the mind-body problem and by propounding materialistic theories of mind. The psychophysical relation was made subject to quantitative empirical investigations, and a causal connection between the brain and the mind (consciousness) came to be accepted as scientifically verified, although scientists disagreed about the philosophical significance of that relation. Cabanis and Karl Vogt (1817–1895) had maintained that thought stands to the brain as bile to the liver and as urine to the kidneys. Büchner explicitly rejected their viewpoint. Nevertheless, he held that "thought, spirit, soul, are not material, not a substance, but the effect of the conjoined action of many materials endowed with force or qualities."[83] He illustrated the connection of body and mind by means of an analogy.

> The steam-engine is in a certain sense endowed with life, and produces as the result of a peculiar combination of force-endowed materials, a united effect, which we use for our purposes, without, however, being able to see, smell, or touch the effect itself. The steam expelled by the engine is a secondary thing, it has nothing to do with the object of the machine, and may be seen and felt as matter. Now, in the same manner as the steam-engine produces motion, so does the organic complication of force-endowed materials produce in the animal body a sum of effects, so interwoven as to become a unit, and is then by us called spirit, soul, thought. The sum of these effects is nothing material: it can be perceived by our senses as little as any other simple force, such as magnetism, electricity, etc.—merely by its manifestations. We have defined force as a property of matter, inseparable from it, yet, with regard to our *conception,* they are widely

distinct, and in a certain sense opposed to each other. At last, we know not how to define force or spirit otherwise than by something immaterial or opposed to matter.[84]

Büchner's doctrine is obviously ambiguous; it makes two points: 1) that thought is force, a complex property working in and inseparable from the body; and 2) that thought is also the ineffectual by-product of the bodily activity which, like the steam expelled by the engine, is irrelevant to the activity. The first point would qualify Büchner as an identity materialist. Assume the convertibility of force and matter and mind is reducible to matter. Mind would be synonymous with the chemical or electrical processes occurring in the brain. The second point, however, recognizes that thought has a conscious aspect which is distinct from the physical processes; and, furthermore, it dismisses this conscious aspect as a secondary effect which is impotent to affect subsequent causal processes. The second point constitutes a theory which is termed epiphenomenalism. He wrote: "The brain is, then, only the carrier and the source, or rather the *sole cause* of the spirit, or thought; but not the organ which secretes it. It produces something which is not materially permanent, but which consumes itself in the moment of its production." [85]

Büchner might, it would seem, avoid the charge of inconsistency by rejecting the assumption upon which his theory is construed to entail identity materialism—namely, the convertibility of force and matter. But the escape route is one which leads first to a new dualism: force (inclusive of mind) and matter, and, secondly, to contradiction, since part of mind (hence of force) is forceless (a secondary impotent by-product).

Haeckel—In contrast to Büchner's philosophy, Haeckel's is unequivocally monistic. For Haeckel the great "riddle of the universe" is the problem of substance: how to reconcile matter with spirit (force or energy) in a coherent theory. The so-called law of substance was his solution to the riddle. The law of the conservation of matter, discovered by Lavoisier in 1789, established that the sum of matter, which fills infinite space, is constant; and the law of the conservation of energy, discovered by Robert Mayer in 1843, established that the sum of energy (force), which is at work in infinite space and is the cause of all phenomena, is constant. Haeckel embraced both laws under his law of substance, which he called "the supreme and all-pervading law of nature, the true and only cosmological law."[86] Just as Spinoza, whom Haeckel acknowledged as his predecessor in monism, had maintained that extension and thought are two infinite attributes of one substance, so Haeckel held that "matter (space-filling substance) and energy (moving force) are but two inseparable attributes of the one underlying substance."[87]

Haeckel's theory of the mind (or soul) was materialistic. All mental activity is based in a substratum called "psychoplasm," which, he believed, chemical analysis has shown to consist of albuminoid carbon-combinations. In the higher animals the "psychoplasm" yields to "neuroplasm," upon which the nervous systems depend. Minds, or souls, have a natural development as well as a material basis, so that Haeckel devoted one chapter to "the embryology" and another to "the phylogeny" of the soul. Free will and immortality were ruled out. Scientific knowledge disallows, according to Haeckel, the action of the will without causation; it supports instead the explanation of all human actions in terms of hereditary and environmental causes. "We now know," wrote Haeckel, "that each act of the will is fatally determined by the organization of the individual and as dependent on the momentary condition of his environment as every other psychic activity."[88] Furthermore, Haeckel, who used the term "soul" to denote the "sum of cerebral functions," rejected outright the doctrine of immortality; he was rather a professed "thanatist"—that is, one who holds that "at a man's death not only all the other physiological functions are arrested, but his 'soul' also disappears."[89] Science, he maintained, furnishes solid empirical evidence demonstrating that cerebral functions depend on the physical condition of the brain, and therefore supports thanatism. On the question of belief in God, Haeckel adopted the position of pantheism.

> Pantheism teaches that God and the world are one. The idea of God is identical with that of nature or substance. . . . Pantheism is *the world-system of the modern scientist.*[90]

At the same time Haeckel admitted that his pantheism was tantamount to atheism. "Atheism," he said, "affirms that there are no gods or goddesses, assuming that god means a personal, extramundane entity. This 'godless world-system' substantially agrees with the monism or pantheism of the modern scientist; it is only another expression for it, emphasizing its negative aspect, the non-existence of any supernatural deity."[91] Indeed, he even quoted approvingly Schopenhauer's remark: "Pantheism is only a polite form of atheism."[92]

Caution should be exercised when labelling Haeckel's philosophy "materialistic." Perhaps the terms "monistic" or "naturalistic" would serve better. For Haeckel's philosophy presents three categories: (1) substance, (2) matter, and (3) force, or energy, with substance posited as the primary category and matter as a secondary one. Haeckel, in one sense, proposed a monism which is neutral, its ultimate substance being neither material nor mental. However, Haeckel did stress the materialistic character of this ultimate substance.

NEUTRAL MONISM

Several recent philosophers, including William James and Bertrand Russell, have proposed neutral monism. In his 1904 essay, "Does Consciousness Exist?" James answered the question posed by the title negatively so far as the term "consciousness" may be taken to stand for an entity. Nevertheless, he did insist

> . . . most emphatically that it does stand for a function. There is, I mean, no aboriginal stuff or quality of being, contrasted with that of which material objects are made, out of which our thoughts of them are made; but there is a function in experience which thoughts perform, and for the performance of which this quality of being is invoked. That function is knowing. . . . My thesis is that if we start with the supposition that there is only one primal stuff or

> material in the world, a stuff of which every thing is composed, and if we call that stuff "pure experience," then knowing can easily be explained as a particular sort of relation towards one another into which portions of pure experience may enter. The relation itself is a part of pure experience; one of its "terms" becomes the subject or bearer of the knowledge, the knower, the other becomes the object known.[93]

For James, then, there was but one stuff; he termed it "pure experience." Parts of the stuff enter into cognitive relations and are then called mental; they equally enter into physico-causal relations and are then called material.

Russell—In *The Analysis of Mind* (1921), Bertrand Russell criticized James's usage of the phrase "pure experience." It exhibited, he said,

> a lingering influence of idealism. "Experience," like consciousness, must be a product, not part of the primary stuff of the world. It must be possible, if James is right in his main contentions, that roughly the same stuff, differently arranged would not give rise to anything that could be called "experience." [94]

Russell expressly committed himself to the position of neutral monism, declaring that "the 'stuff' of the world is neither mental nor material, but a 'neutral stuff,' out of which both are constructed." [95]

In *The Analysis of Matter* (1927), Russell expanded his argument for neutral monism. He attacked and demolished the concept of substance. "The physical object is a group of events arranged about a 'center,' and there is no reason to suppose there is a substance in the center, since the group of events will produce exactly the same events with or without the supposition. Similarly, matter in physics is but a string of events with its intrinsic physical laws; and motion, too, is a string of events connected with each other according to the laws of motion." [96] Thus Russell's neutral monism is tantamount to phenomenalism. A physical object, whether a chair or an electron, is simply a logical construction from sense-data, or perception. "The matter that we construct is impenetrable as a result of definition: the matter in a place is all the events that are there, and consequently no other event or piece of matter can be there."[97] It might appear at first that Russell is no less guilty than James of bearing "a lingering influence of idealism," since experience, sense-data, and percepts all belong to the same family. For Russell, however, percepts are emphatically not mental; they are "really part of the matter of the percipient's brain."[98]

Hence it would appear that, in escaping idealism, Russell's monism has succumbed to materialism. Russell of course saw it otherwise. He embraced what has been called the "double aspect" theory. In the percept physical and mental events are compresent.

> The relation of compresence is between a percept and a physical *event,* and physical events are not to be confounded with pieces of matter. A piece of matter is a logical structure composed of events; the causal laws of the events concerned, and the abstract logical properties of their spatio-temporal relations, are more or less known, but their intrinsic character is not known. Percepts fit into the same causal scheme as physical events, and are not known to have any intrinsic character which physical events cannot have, since we do not know of any intrinsic character which could be incompatible with the logical properties that physics assigns to physical events. There is therefore no ground for the view that percepts cannot be physical events, or for supposing that they are never compresent with other physical events.[99]

As for mental events, Russell continued: "What are called 'mental' events, if we have been right, are part of the material of the physical world, and what is in our heads is the mind (with additions) rather than what the physiologist sees through his microscope."[100] The materialistic cast of Russell's theory, however, is evident in the primacy he accorded physics among the sciences. "Inference from one event to another, where possible, seems only to acquire exactness when it can be stated in terms of the laws of physics."[101]

Physicalistic Theories of Mind—Russell's neutral monism was less than neutral in its bias for a materialistic—or at least a physicalistic—theory of mind. And most scientific theories of mind in the twentieth century have leaned toward materialism. Unable to rely upon the reports of introspection, psychologists have turned to the objective and experimentally testable observation of behavior. Since 1919, when John Watson (1878–1958) published his programmatic text book, *Psychology from the Standpoint of a Behaviorist,* academic psychology in the United States has been dominated by behaviorism. Either for methodological or for substantial reasons, psychologists have reduced mind and its processes to physical patterns of behavior. On the grounds of linguistic analysis, Gilbert Ryle in his *Concept of Mind* has also lent support to the behaviorists. While Ryle and his followers might perhaps, for fear of metaphysics, shy away from identity materialism—i.e., the doctrine that mental event and cerebral event are one and the same, other thinkers are far less restrained.

Cybernetics, the relatively new science of machines, has presumed that the close analogy between computers and human thought is strong enough to justify calling the computers "thinking machines." To construct such a machine is, for some, literally to design a brain, thought being equated indifferently with the mechanical functions of the computer as well as the organic events occurring in a brain. Closely linked with these developments in cybernetics and psychology is the rise of a theory of mind known as "central state physicalism." Briefly, this theory equates mental states with states of the central nervous system which present themselves in a disguised form. Paul K. Feyerabend, J. J. C. Smart, and Herbert Feigl have been proponents of this theory with differing degrees of certitude.[102]

DIALECTICAL MATERIALISM

The recent exponents of materialism in the Anglo-American world, with rare exceptions,[103] have lacked the desire to furnish their anthropological materialism the context of a synoptic materialistic metaphysics. Yet it would be wrong to conclude that cosmological materialism no longer exists. On the contrary, cosmological materialism, in the guise of dialectical materialism, is the official philosophy of hundreds of millions of people.

Marx—The founding father of dialectical materialism was Karl Marx (1818–1883). Although he is best remembered as a social revolutionary whose theories, after much interpretation and revision, have come to constitute the official ideology of the Soviet Union, he deserves an impartial place in the history of social science, particularly in the fields of economics, sociology, and political science. In *The Critique of Political Economy* (1859), Marx showed that the material conditions of life determine the social, political, and intellectual life-process of men in general. Marx's discovery is summed up in the formula: "It is not the consciousness of men that determines their existence; but, on the contrary, their social existence determines their consciousness."[104] Marx, whose theory was primarily economic and sociological, meant by "social existence" the material conditions of life—in particular, the mode of production. Further, he distinguished two aspects of the mode of production: 1) the forces of production, and 2) production relations, or property relations. In the course of history, contradictions between the forces of production and property relations erupt, leading to revolutionary changes in social structures. Marx presented his theories as scientific. Empirical evidence tends to confirm the hypotheses that economic conditions affect human society and culture and that contradictions within the mode of production cause social revolutions, although it does not allow the deduction of economic determinism from the first hypothesis and the claim of universality for the second. Nevertheless, Marx had opened the way for a new phase in the history of materialism, and Frederick Engels (1820–1895), Marx's leading disciple, recognized and appreciated Marx's originality. He heralded his master's works as expressions of "the materialist conception of history," or simply "historical materialism."[105]

Cosmological materialism had interested the young Marx, as his doctoral dissertation, *The Distinction Between the Democritean and Epicurean Philosophies of Nature* (1841), reveals. Marx, then a young Hegelian, considered Epicurus' philosophy to be a dialectical advance on Democritus' philosophy. Epicurus, he contended, solved the basic problem of Greek atomism—namely, the problem of knowledge when he attended to the activity of consciousness.

The mature Marx was a dialectical materialist. The transition from one philosophical position to its near opposite is often imputed to the influence of Ludwig Andreas Feuerbach (1804–1872) on Marx.

Feuerbach was a mechanical materialist, or at least he espoused a type of materialistic philosophy which has lent itself to this interpretation. In *The Essence of Christianity* (1841), Feuerbach presented four tenets: 1) that the objects of knowledge have an existence independent of the knower, 2) that all knowledge originates in the senses, 3) that no spiritual or immaterial beings exist, and 4) that ideas or ideals exist for man and have a determining role in human history. These tenets represent a realistic point of view in opposition to epistemological idealism and at the same time imply a materialistic theory of reality.

Marx's own materialism arose in part in reaction to Feuerbach's materialism, as his famous "Theses on Feuerbach," jotted down in Brussels in 1845, makes plain. But, as these theses also make plain, Marx rejected Feuerbach's materialism because it was intrinsically speculative. Thus he wrote:

> I. The chief defect of all hitherto existing materialism—that of Feuerbach included—is that the object, reality, sensuousness, is conceived only in the form of the *object* of *contemplation,* but not as *human sensuous activity, practice,* not subjectively. . . .
> II. The question whether objective truths can be attributed to human thinking is not a question of theory but is a practical question. . . .
> XI. The philosophers have only *interpreted* the world in various ways; the point however is to *change* it.[106]

Marx, who condemned Feuerbach for excessive theorizing, naturally found Hegel the dialectical idealist too much in the clouds to be relevant to the social requirements of human history. Hegel was standing on his head, and had to be put rightside up. The correction, however, was not a mere metaphysical readjustment; it demanded nothing less than a thoroughgoing scientific understanding of society and its material foundations. Marx, who set out to banish the abstract categories of speculative metaphysics, regarded economics—

not the Absolute Spirit—to be the causative force in history. Mind and matter disappear from Marx's philosophical vocabulary; economic relations—viz., production, property, value—come to the fore. Categories themselves are translated into social classes, the dialectic of the categories becoming the warfare of the classes.

Stalin—The expansion of Marx's practical historical materialism into the full-scale metaphysics of dialectical materialism is due to Engels.[107] Vladimir Ilyich Ulyanov, alias Lenin (1870–1924),[108] and Joseph Vissarionovich Dzhugashvili, alias Stalin (1879–1953),[109] finished the job of making dialectical materialism a full-fledged philosophy. In perhaps its clearest definition, Stalin wrote:

> Dialectical materialism is the world outlook of the Marxist-Leninist party. It is called dialectical materialism because its approach to the phenomena of nature, its method of studying and apprehending them, is *dialectical,* while its interpretation of the phenomena of nature, its conception of these phenomena, its theory, is *materialistic.*[110]

Although Stalin's conception of dialectical materialism differs from Engels', and although it has been superseded, even ignored, by more recent Soviet philosophical discussions, it is noteworthy for two reasons: it is exceptionally lucid, and it typifies the main features of dialectical materialism as metaphysical speculation. For despite the dialectical materialists' insistence that their doctrines are scientific and not metaphysical, it soon becomes apparent to all but the adherents that those doctrines go far beyond what science proves. As Stalin's definition of dialectical materialism asserts, there are two aspects to the position: one, the method, which is dialectical; two, the content, which is materialistic. Each should be considered in its turn.

Stalin regarded dialectics to be the direct opposite of metaphysics. He distinguished four principal features of the dialectical method. First, rather than view nature "as an accidental agglomeration of things, of phenomena, unconnected with, isolated from, and independent of each other," the dialectical method accepts nature "as a connected and integral whole, in which things, phenomena are organically connected with, dependent on, and determined by each other," and in which, "any phenomenon can be understood and explained if considered in its inseparable connections with surrounding phenomena, as one conditioned by surrounding phenomena."[111] Second, "dialectics holds that nature is not a state of rest and immobility, stagnation and immutability, but a state of continuous renewal and development, where something is always arising and developing, and something always disintegrating and dying away," so that to understand phenomena requires that they be considered "from the standpoint of their movement, their change, their development, their coming into being and going out of being."[112] Third, dialectics holds that the process of development "passes from insignificant and imperceptible quantitative changes to open fundamental changes, to qualitative changes."[113] Moreover, the qualitative changes occur rapidly and abruptly and "as the natural result of an accumulation of imperceptible and gradual quantitative changes."[114] Consequently, the process of development "should be understood not as a movement in a circle, not as a simple repetition of what has already occurred, but as an onward and upward movement, as a transition from an old quantitative state to a new qualitative state, as a development from the simple to the complex, from the lower to the higher."[115] Fourth, "dialectics holds that internal contradictions are inherent in all things and phenomena of nature, for they all have their negative and positive sides, a past and a future, something dying away and something developing."[116] Thus, according to the dialectical method, "the process of development from the lower to the higher takes place not as a harmonious unfolding of phenomena, but as a disclosure of the contradictions inherent in things and phenomena, as a 'struggle' of opposite tendencies which operate on the basis of these contradictions."[117]

Turning next to the materialism, Stalin stressed three principal features:

> (1) . . . the world is by its very nature *material,* that the multifold phenomena of the world constitute different forms of matter in motion, that interconnections and interdependence of phenomena, as

established by the dialectical method, are a law of the development of moving matter, and that the world develops in accordance with the laws of movement of matter and stands in no need of a "universal spirit."[118]

(2) . . . matter, nature, being, is an objective reality existing outside and independent of our mind; that matter is primary, since it is the source of sensations, ideas, mind, and that mind is secondary, derivative, since it is a reflection of matter, a reflection of being; that thought is a product of matter which in its development has reached a high degree of perfection, namely, of the brain, and the brain is the organ of thought; and that therefore one cannot separate thought from matter without committing a grave error.[119]

(3) . . . the world and its laws are fully knowable, that our knowledge of the laws of nature, tested by experiment and practice, is authentic knowledge having the validity of objective truth, and that there are no things in the world which are unknowable, but only things which are still not known, but will be disclosed and made known by the efforts of science and practice.[120]

Later dialectical materialists have revised some of Stalin's points. They have, for example, contended, in opposition to Stalin's position, that nature "is in a state of eternal, uninterrupted and regular (lawlike) movement, change, and development,"[121] that, in effect, the dialectical process is devoid of abrupt change. Other recent materialists have rejected outright the dialectical method, preferring instead the experimental methods of science.[122] But the fact remains that among materialisms dialectical materialism stands today as a comprehensive system of thought embraced by hundreds of millions of adherents. No other philosophy enjoys equivalent status.

CONCLUDING REMARKS

Materialism poses a number of paradoxes. It is at once the oldest and the most contemporary of philosophies. It has been subjected to more contempt in the history of thought than any rival philosophy; yet its adherents now outnumber those of any other philosophy and it is the only official philosophy of a major State. Materialists, more than other thinkers, have allied themselves with the natural sciences from which their speculative theories have derived exceptional credibility; yet their close association with the sciences has also rendered them extraordinarily vulnerable. When natural science has been stagnant and unattended, materialism has faded from sight. When, on the other hand, natural science has been vital and productive, materialists have been hard-pressed to cope with the new discoveries, for each scientific advance threatens to undermine the foundations of the materialist system which has been erected too soon and too absolutely on the passing phases of progressing scientific knowledge. Despite these paradoxes, and regardless of its type, materialism is unequivocal in its acceptance of matter however conceived, and of space (void), motion (dialectics), force (energy), as its fundamental categories. In the future, as in the past, it may be expected, systems of speculative philosophy will continue to be erected upon these categories.

V
IDEALISM

Ralph Barton Perry (1876–1957) has said that "the cardinal principle of idealism" is the assertion of "the priority of the cognitive consciousness, the assertion that being is dependent on the knowing of it. . . ."[1] But Perry may have overemphasized the epistemological argument for idealism.

Idealism is derived from the term "idea." This term refers to two sets of characteristics: those characteristics pertaining to ultimacy or absoluteness in reality and value (as in Plato's system) and those pertaining to mind, consciousness, and subjectivity (as in Descartes' system). The idealist as speculative philosopher is one who synthesizes both sets of characteristics into a single systematic theory of all that is. When he focuses on the first set of characteristics, he moves toward cosmology and axiology (value theory); when on the second set, he stresses epistemology. Despite these variant emphases, however, idealism as speculative philosophy is unified in its core ontology—that mind, or spirit, is ultimate. Corollary to this conviction is the belief that the world exhibits teleology or design, that mind, in other words, guides the processes in the world toward the attainment of ends. Of course, these ends may be subject to pessimistic interpretations which afford little satisfaction to those who seek security for human values. At any rate, the idealists maintain that from mind all else is derived; within mind all else dwells.

Idealists disagree about the interpretations and implications of the core ontology. Epistemological idealists, who are preoccupied with the problem of knowledge, differ from cosmological idealists, who are concerned mainly with the place of ideal values in the world. Subjective idealists, whose criterion of mind and hence of reality is the solitary self, conflict with objective (or Absolute) idealists, whose criterion is the cosmos as a whole. Pluralistic idealists, who claim that there are many minds, contradict and are contradicted by monistic idealists, who claim that there is but one true Individual. Hence idealism assumes many forms, and to these we shall now attend.

LEIBNIZ

Leibniz upheld a pluralistic idealism called monadism. The ultimately real things are psychical entities, and there are multitudes of these psychical entities. The justification of this extraordinary doctrine is complex. The subject-predicate logic which Leibniz inherited from Aristotle has been a determining factor. Since Aristotle analyzed the structure of judgment to consist of subject and predicate, with the subject denoting a substance, the predicate an attribute, and the copula the inherence of an attribute in a substance, Leibniz simply followed the Greek logician when he concluded that there must be substances corresponding to the subjects of judgments; he was logically more rigorous than Aristotle when he added that all attributes (essential and accidental) belong equally to the individual substance. Considerations of physics induced Leibniz to deny that these ultimate substances are material atoms; the essence of body, he held, is not static extension but dynamic force. Meanwhile, the invention and use of the microscope in the emerging life sciences made him aware that there are forms of life invisible to the naked eye. Finally, as an inventor of the infinitesimal calculus, Leibniz could readily accept the conception of the continuity of infinitely small entities. Furthermore, the method which Leibniz inherited from Descartes required that there be basic simple entities as the termini of analysis. And the traditional conceptions of final causation and teleology in nature which Leibniz revived lent credence to the view that mind is ubiquitous.

The consequence of this confluence of reasons was, for Leibniz, the proposal of monadic idealism. The basic categories of Leibniz's monadic idealism, or monadism, are 1) monad, 2) compound substance, 3) hierarchy, 4) continuity, 5) plurality and fullness of being, 6) final causation, and 7) preestablished harmony.

Monadic idealism is the opposite to atomistic materialism. The key concept of monadism is the concept of the monad. Leibniz defined substance as being capable of action; and he distinguished two kinds of substances: simple and compound. Compound substances—e.g., a tree, an animal, a chair—are collections of simple substances. Leibniz defined monad as a simple substance; he called monads "the true atoms of nature."[2] Each monad is a unity, whereas each compound is a multitude. Monads have no parts; they have neither figure nor extension; they have no shape; otherwise they would be divisible and so lack unity. But monads do have some qualities; otherwise they "would be indistinguishable from one another . . . seeing . . . that they do not differ in quantity."[3] Observation of change in nature, which is composed of compound substances, depends upon an observation of differences which can be supplied only by the qualities in the monads. Change prevails throughout the created universe, and applies to created monads as well as to compound substances. But the changes in monads must proceed from internal principles. No monad can begin or perish naturally, and so each lasts as long as the universe. Even created monads are absolutely independent of one another; none can be altered or changed in its inner being by any other created monad. Leibniz expressed the point quaintly when he wrote: "The monads have no windows through which anything can enter or depart."[4] Examples Leibniz gave of monads are lives, souls, spirits, and since nature consists ultimately of monads, he asserted that "all nature is full of life."[5] Monadism is, therefore, a form of panpsychism.

Leibniz's panpsychism is paramount in his treatment of the internal principle of change in each monad. This principle is twofold: it involves perception and appetition. Perceptions are "representations of the compound, or of what is external, in the simple;" and appetitions (desires) are "its tendencies to pass from one perception to another."[6] Leibniz's objection against the Cartesians is worthy of note; he criticized them for "having taken no account of the perceptions of which we are not conscious" and for having consequently believed that "spirits only are monads and that there are no souls of brutes or of other entelechies." [7] All monads have quality; but quality, dependent on the internal principle of change, is ultimately psychical, in that it derives from perception and appetition. Hence all monads are psychical.

Leibniz ranked monads in a hierarchy of continuous gradation according to their psychical qualities. At the base of the hierarchy are monads which have only perception. Leibniz called them "entelechies." Entelechies "have within themselves a certain perfection . . . ; there is a certain sufficiency which makes them the sources of their internal activities, and so to speak, incorporeal automata." [8] These simplest monads have perceptions similar to our experiences when "we remember nothing and have no distinguishable perception, as when we fall into a swoon or when we are overpowered by a profound and dreamless sleep." [9] Leibniz called these perceptions "minute perceptions." [10] No matter how muffled and indistinct, the perception of the monad is its inner state representing external things. Hence Leibniz asserted that "each monad is a living mirror, or endowed with internal activity, representative according to its point of view of the universe, and as regulated as the universe itself." [11]

It is by degrees, by the continuous gradation of qualities, that the hierarchy is completed; and the hierarchy is full, having no gaps. Although all monads could be designated "souls" in the most general sense, Leibniz preferred to apply this term strictly to only those monads "whose perception is more distinct [than minute perception] and is accompanied by memory." [12] Memory furnishes souls with a sort of consecutiveness among their internal states. Recalling past states, it enables the monad to respond appropriately to its present states and to anticipate future states. Leibniz defined "feeling" as "perception accompanied by memory," [13] and he called monads that have feeling "animals."

Apperception enters at this point in the continuous hierarchy of monads. Leibniz defined apperception as *"consciousness,* or the reflective knowledge" of perception.[14] Animals in small degree approach apperception. When apperception operates clearly, the apperceiving monad is properly called a rational soul, or spirit. Such a monad reasons; it attains "knowledge of necessary and eternal truths."[15]

A man is a compound substance; his self, however, is a monad. A man exhibits the characteristic qualities of the various levels of monads. In swooning and dreamless sleep, he experiences the minute perceptions of the entelechies. In irrational appetition, he acts like a brute animal. A man, however, is essentially rational. As Leibniz said, "by knowledge of necessary truths, and by their abstractions, . . . we rise to *acts of reflection,* which make us think of that which calls itself I, and to observe that this or that is within *us.*"[16] The ego is the supreme monad in the aggregate or colony of monads that make up a man.

There are monads higher than the human ego. In at least one passage Leibniz avowed that there are genii.[17] Be that as it may, it was certainly orthodox for him to affirm the existence of supernatural spirits such as angels and God. God is axiomatically the supreme monad, and by reflection man knows that and what God is.

God is "the supreme substance, . . . unique, universal and necessary, having nothing outside of itself which is independent of it, and being a pure consequence of possible being."[18] He is an absolutely perfect being, and his creation is also perfect. Leibniz is emphatic that God is the final and sufficient reason of all that is. But there are serious problems, to be noted below, in relating God to his creation.

Leibniz's monadism is bizarre; certainly it is contrary to commonsense beliefs about the nature of the physical world. Monadism imposed a radical reinterpretation of the conceptions of matter, time, space, and causation. Time and space are not to be taken for real things which somehow envelope or enclose monads; they are rather appearances of relations within the monads. Time is the succession of states within the monads; space is the representation of the coexistence of monads. Similarly motion is not real; change is real, but change is qualitative differentiation within monads.

Leibniz's most penetrating analysis was reserved for the concept of matter. In the seventeenth century, matter was considered to be atomic, and the essence of the atoms was held to be extension. Such material atoms, Leibniz insisted, "are contrary to reason."[19] An extended body is divisible, but by definition an atom is indivisible; hence the prevalent conception of matter is self-contradictory. Leibniz substituted monads for material atoms: monads are metaphysical and substantial points; they are sources of actions, are exact and real. Matter is then appearance, but it is well-founded appearance—*phenomena bene fundata*. As Leibniz strikingly put the issue: "Matter can only be considered like an army or herd, or like a pond full of fish, or like a watch made up of springs and wheels."[20]

Causation, too, is reinterpreted. It cannot be viewed as inherently efficient causation; such causation is apparent only. For the monads cannot act on one another. Genuine causation is final; it testifies to the purposiveness of Mind.

That the monads act together, in a manner which appears to indicate interaction, is simply due to preestablished harmony. Leibniz expounded his doctrine of preestablished harmony in the context of the mind-body problem bequeathed by Descartes. Leibniz called upon the reader to imagine two clocks in perfect agreement, one standing for the soul, the other for the body. He cited three ways of accounting for this agreement. The first way is the way of mutual influence, favored by Descartes and popular philosophy. Leibniz ruled out this way because "we cannot conceive of material particles which can pass from one of these substances to another."[21] The second way is "to have a skillful worker continually adjust them and keep them in agreement;" it involves, in other words, "the continual assistance of the Creator."[22] This way is the one favored by the occasionalists, Nicholas Malebranche (1638–1715) and Arnold Geulincx (1624–1669). Leibniz rejected it because it "introduces *Deus ex Machina* in a natural and ordinary occurrence where, according to reason, it ought not to intervene except as it operates in all other natural things."[23] The third way is Leibniz's own hypothesis, the way of Harmony. As Leibniz wrote: "From the beginning God has made each of these two Substances of such a nature that each by following its own laws, given to it with its being, still agrees with the other, just as though there were a mutual influence or as though God always took a hand in it beyond his general supervision of things."[24] Increase the number of clocks in the illustration to infinity, and substitute monads of all degrees of life and mind, and the reader will have a good picture of Leibniz's cosmos of monads operating in preestablished harmony.

A serious problem in monadism breaks out at this point. The autonomy of the monads has been undermined by the special position of God, the supreme monad. God created the world, for Leibniz, in the sense that He envisioned all possible worlds of monads and elected to actualize the best one. Constrained by the rule of the best, God is not a free creator. The category of final causation guarantees that the best that may be, must be. But then the monads that are have come into existence as logical deductions of the Divine Nature. As Leibniz said in one passage: "God alone is the primitive unity or the original simple substance; of which all created or derived monads are the products, and are generated, so to speak, by continual fulgurations of the Divinity, from moment to moment, limited by the receptivity of the creature, to whom limitation is essential."[25] Fulgurations from the Divinity recall the emanations from the One, and monadism veers dangerously close to collapsing into monism.

BERKELEY

Whereas the idealism of Leibniz is primarily ontological, that of Berkeley is primarily epistemological. Of course Berkeley had metaphysical intentions which reach beyond the theory of knowledge to apply to the theory of being; the gravamen against matter is launched to eradicate skepticism and, lest we forget, atheism. Nevertheless, Berkeley's philosophy arose in the context of British empirical epistemology, and was especially dependent on the doctrines of Locke.

In the *Essay Concerning Human Understanding* (1690), John Locke had sought to show that all knowledge consists of relations between ideas, and that all ideas originate in the immediate data of experience. Simple ideas are of two sorts: ideas of sensation such as white, soft, square, heavy, and so on; and ideas of reflection such as perceiving, willing, and so on. From these simple ideas the mind by means of various operations constructs ideas of relations, complex ideas, and abstract ideas. But every idea, in principle, is either a simple idea or reducible to simple ideas. Only the idea of substance, a complex one, escaped Locke's conception of the absolute derivation of complex ideas from simple ones. As Locke said:

> The mind being, as I have declared, furnished with a great number of the simple ideas conveyed by the senses, as they are found in exterior things, or by reflection on its own operations, takes notice also, that a certain number of these simple ideas go constantly together; which being presumed to belong to one thing, and words being suited to common apprehensions, and made use of for quick dispatch, are called, so united in one subject, by one name; which, by inadvertency, we are apt afterward to talk of and to consider as one simple idea, which indeed is a complication of many ideas together: because, as I have said, not imagining how these simple ideas can subsist by themselves, we accustom ourselves to suppose some *substratum* wherein they do subsist, and from which they do result which therefore we call *substance*.[26]

Hence three factors enter into the idea of substance: 1) a name, 2) a collection of properties that go constantly together, and 3) a substratum. With regard to the conception of substance as a collection of properties, Locke's distinction between primary qualities and secondary qualities is pertinent. For physical substances as they exist in nature possess hardness, extension, figure, bulk, texture, motion, number; but they are not colored, scented, hot or cold, sweet or bitter or sour or salt, silent or noisy. Physical substances contain powers to produce such sensations in the human understanding; but they contain no resembling properties. With regard to the conception of substance as substrate, it turns out to be no idea supplied by sensation or reflection. As Locke said: "The idea, then, we have, to which we give the general name substance, being nothing but the supposed, but unknown, support of these qualities we find existing, which we imagine cannot subsist *sine re substante,* without something to support them, we call that support *substantia;* which, according to the true import of the word, is, in plain English, standing under, or upholding."[27] To accommodate the idea of substance in general to Locke's classification of ideas is to treat it as an abstract idea, but it is a peculiar one in that it would be an abstraction from which all quality is eliminated. Nevertheless, Locke retained the idea of substance in general for three types of being: matter, mind, and God.

Berkeley pressed the empirical epistemology further than Locke had done. With the intention of refuting the theory of matter, Berkeley attacked the conception of the abstract idea. In consequence he produced an original type of empirical idealism. Berkeley's system contains two major categories: 1) Ideas, and 2) Minds; and he distinguished two kinds of minds: 2a) finite and 2b) infinite. The first seven sections of *The Principles of Human Knowledge* state and elucidate Berkeley's two major categories and the arguments which he employed to justify them. Almost as an afterthought and in the second edition of his *Principles,* Berkeley added to these major categories a third category: the notion. Furthermore, in presenting and defending his categories, and in demolishing the theory of matter, Berkeley advanced arguments which have become part of the permanent heritage of idealism.

The category of idea is presented in Section 1 of *The Principles of Human Knowledge*. An idea, according to Berkeley, is the object of knowledge, or of consciousness. Ideas divide into three classes: 1) sense-data, such as sensations of light and color furnished by the sense of sight, sensations of hardness and softness, of heat and cold, of motion and resistance, gained through touch, odors furnished by smell, tastes by the palate, and sounds by hearing; 2) perceptions arising from our attention to the passions and operations of the mind; and 3) ideas which the memory and the imagination construct by compounding, dividing, or representing ideas in the first two classes. Berkeley next defined the physical thing which is the object of knowledge, or of consciousness, as a collection of ideas. "For example, a certain colour, taste, smell, figure and consistence having been observed to go together, are accounted one distinct thing, signified by the name *apple*." [28]

The category of mind is presented in Section 2. According to Berkeley's definition, mind, or the knowing subject, is "something which knows or perceives them [ideas]; and exercises divers operations, as willing, imagining, remembering about them. This perceiving active being," wrote Berkeley, "is what I call MIND, SPIRIT, SOUL, or MYSELF." [29] Mind, moreover, is distinct from ideas; it is that "wherein they [ideas] exist, or, which is the same thing whereby they are perceived—for the existence of an idea consists in being perceived." [30]

In Sections 3 through 5 Berkeley presented his definition of existence for things—i.e., the objects of knowledge treated in Section 1 as collections of ideas. The things in question are of course sensible things; they consist of sense-data ideas. Berkeley's definition is summed up in his famous formula that for sensible things: "their *esse* is *percipi*."

Berkeley considered this formula to be intuitively certain. He wrote:

> I think an intuitive knowledge may be obtained of this by anyone that shall attend to *what is meant by the term exist when applied to sensible things*. The table I write on I say exists, that is, I see and feel it; and if I were out of my study I should say it existed—meaning thereby that if I was in my study I might perceive it, or that some other spirit actually does perceive it. There was an odour, that is, it was smelt; there was a sound, that is, it was heard; a colour or figure, and it was perceived by sight or touch. This is all that I can understand by these and like expressions.[31]

Berkeley also considered the formula certain because of the impossibility, as he declared, "for me to conceive in my thoughts any sensible thing or object distinct from the sensation or perception of it." [32] Berkeley, who somehow fused both logic and psychology, was referring to psychological impossibility only in part, while in the main he intended to indicate a logical impossibility. This method of justifying his basic formula he employed in a later passage. He wrote: "When we do our utmost to conceive the existence of external bodies, we are all the while only contemplating our own ideas. But the mind, *taking no notice of itself,* is deluded to think it can and does conceive bodies unthought of or without the mind, though at the same time they are apprehended by or exist in itself."[33]

Berkeley's formula for existence in *The Principles,* audacious as it is, is restricted in its application to things. Things have their existence by virtue of being perceived, but not minds. In his *Commonplace Book,* Berkeley had recorded a more precise formula for existence: "existence is *percipi* or *percipere,* or *vellem* i.e. *agere."*[34] Hence for Berkeley the formula for existence is double-pronged: For objective things, to be is to be perceived; for subjective minds, to be is to perceive, or to act.

A brief account of the being of minds is presented in Sections 6 and 7, thereby completing the basic structure of Berkeley's system. Berkeley, in effect, offers an argument for the existence of minds. Things existing in being perceived are ideas; therefore, there must be minds to perceive them. Berkeley assumed the conception of substance advanced by Locke, but he limited it to mind. Ideas must inhere in a substance, in this case the being that perceives them. But since "an idea to exist in an unperceiving thing is a manifest contradiction; for to have an idea is all one as to perceive," Berkeley concluded: "it is evident that there is not any other Substance than *Spirit,* or *that* which perceives."[35]

A serious danger that threatens Berkeleyan idealism is extreme subjectivism, or solipsism. Solipsism is the philosophy according to which there exists nothing except the solitary knowing subject and his ideas; or in mitigated form it may hold that something else besides the subject may exist but that it cannot be known. Solipsism may very well be irrefutable; nevertheless, it can never be affirmed or defended, since these procedures assume the possibility of communicating with really existing others. Now in the *Three Dialogues between Hylas and Philonous,* Berkeley's spokesman Philonous, the lover (φίλος) of mind (νοῦς), is so concerned to demonstrate to Hylas, the matterist,* that the object of knowledge

* The name "Hylas" is derived from the Greek word ὕλη, meaning matter. A materialist is one who believes that matter and its patterns are the only real existences;

depends on the knowing subject that he seems to slip into an inescapable subjectivism. However, in Section 6 of the *Principles,* in advance of the demolition of matter, Berkeley safeguarded himself against this pitfall. He wrote:

> All the choir of heaven and furniture of the earth, in a word those bodies which compose the mighty frame of the world, have not any subsistence without a mind—that their *being* is *to be perceived or known;* that consequently so long as they are not actually perceived by me, or do not exist in my mind or that of any other created spirit, they must either have no existence at all, or else subsist in the mind of some Eternal Spirit.[36]

The existence of the world throughout interperceptual intervals testified to its being perceived by an Eternal Spirit other than the finite subject. This same Spirit also guarantees that the world, though dependent on being perceived, is not a private world known only to a solitary finite mind, but rather a genuinely public world.

Berkeley's idealism never impugned the existence of the world outside his own finite mind or other finite minds. On the contrary, Berkeley agreed with the plain men that *"those things they immediately perceive are the real things,"* while he concurred with the philosophers that *"the things immediately perceived are ideas which exist only in the mind."* [37] His philosophy has a realist as well as an idealist cast, although the idealism is paramount. Berkeley's type of idealism would be called phenomenalism, were it not for the fact that he affirmed the existence of finite minds and of God. Phenomenalism is the theory that physical objects are simply collections of ideas, or logical constructions of actual and possible sense-data.* [38] Berkeley's position on the nature of the physical world is phenomenalism. Not only did he construe physical objects as

a matterist is one who believes matter exists. See A. A. Luce, *Berkeley's Immaterialism* (London: Thomas Nelson and Sons, Ltd., 1945), p. 25.

* Linguistic phenomenalism is a recent and sophisticated formulation of the position. It has been designed to meet the objections that collections of sense-data lack the unity and substantiality of material objects and that possible sense-data are too shadowy to enter into the constitution of physical things. Advocated by Alfred Jules Ayer, linguistic phenomenalism maintains that "the propositions which are ordinarily expressed by sentences which refer to material things could also be expressed by sentences which referred exculsively to sense-data. . . ." [39]

collections of ideas, but also he reinterpreted the basic categories of natural philosophy along phenomenalist lines. Causation, as regards nature but not mind, is "consistent uniform working."[40] Time is "the succession of ideas in our minds."[41] Space has no existence distinct "from that which is perceived by sense and related to bodies."[42] Motion is relative to bodies. Berkeley, however, held back from phenomenalism when he acknowledged the existence of finite minds and of God.

What Berkeley sought, above all, to disprove is the existence of matter. As Cartesians and Lockeans were wont to do, Berkeley defined matter as "an inert, senseless substance, in which extension, figure and motion do actually exist."[43] The idea of matter, he claimed, is an example of an abstract idea, and the theory of abstract ideas, he argued in the Introduction to his *Principles,* is false. According to Locke, who authored the theory, an abstract idea is the idea men entertain when they use words understandingly; it is the common meaning a word has for different minds; and it is attained by representing the common characteristics of a class of particular ideas and omitting the particular characteristics of these ideas. Berkeley attacked this theory on logical, psychological, and linguistic grounds. Logically, some abstract ideas would perforce be self-contradictory—e.g., the idea of a triangle having both unequal and equal sides. Psychologically, men think only particular ideas, as introspection reveals. Linguistically, men are not restricted to using words to refer to meanings. Men learn to use words and ideas, both particulars, in a way which makes them general—that is, applicable to many things.

The idea of matter is the first casualty of Berkeley's emphasis on concrete thinking. The idea of matter is doubly abstract. First, philosophers had abstracted the primary qualities of extension, figure, motion, number, and solidity from the secondary qualities of color, sound, taste, odor, felt temperature, and had considered that the primary qualities belong to corporeal objects whereas the secondary qualities do not. Secondly, philosophers following Locke had abstracted substance in general from the sensible qualities and had conceived the former to be the substrate in which the latter inhere.

Against the doctrine of primary and secondary qualities Berkeley launched an attack, which he sustained by detailed considerations in the first of the *Three Dialogues between Hylas and Philonous.* What Berkeley, in sum, demonstrated is that all concrete thought and experience show the togetherness, rather than the separation, of these qualities, and further that the same arguments which are employed to maintain the subjectivity of secondary qualities may equally well be employed to maintain the subjectivity of primary qualities. For these arguments hinge on the relativity of the quality to the perceiver, so that if the fact that variability in taste of an object from perceiver to perceiver is evidence for the subjectivity of qualities of taste, then by parity of reasoning variability in extension as seen by different perceivers is evidence for the subjectivity of extension.

Against the doctrine of matter as a substrate devoid of all qualities, except that of being a mere support, Berkeley also argued at length. As the most vacuous of abstract ideas, it contains no content and so is meaningless. It is, moreover, useless; it can explain nothing at all. To suppose, for example, that it is the cause of our ideas is to muddle disputatious points. Not only is it difficult to establish a causal connection between matter and mind, between like and unlike; but also it is difficult to impute any activity to so vacuous and inert an entity as matter is. Finally, matter as that which exists independently of mind is inconceivable, since to conceive anything is to relate it to mind. In effect, Berkeley had, besides demolishing Locke's conception of matter as substrate, anticipated and rejected the celebrated definition of John Stuart Mill: matter as "a Permanent Possibility of Sensation."[44]

Curiously, Berkeley's objection to matter as pure substrate could have also been brought to bear on his conception of mind as substance. If man's only cognitive avenue to mind is through ideas, then it would seem that mind, no less than sensible objects, would depend on being perceived, and then regress of minds within minds, without end, would be the logical consequence. In addition, just as sensible things reduce to collections of ideas, minds, too, would be nothing more than collections of ideas. David Hume had followed the argument to its logical conclusion when he wrote: "what we call a *mind,* is nothing but a heap or collection of different perceptions, united together by certain relations, and suppos'd, tho' falsely, to be endowed with a perfect simplicity and identity."[45] Berkeley, however, did not foresee Hume's conclusion, although he did apprehend that knowledge of mind as active substance could not be attained by means of ideas.

Hence Berkeley introduced, almost as an afterthought and in the second edition of his *Principles,* a third category—the category of notion. And so he could say: "We may not, I think, strictly be said to have an *idea* of an active being, or of an action, although we may be said to have a *notion* of them."[46] In the case of one's self, each has a notion which is tantamount to intuitive knowledge. In the case of other finite minds, our knowledge is based on inference from analogy. Because of the observed analogy between the behavior of one's own body, which is explicable by reference to one's own intuitively known mind, and the behavior of another's body, it is legitimate to infer the existence of a mind to explain that body's behavior.

Berkeley's category of notion enabled him to claim knowledge of mind as active substance. It also provoked the charge of inconsistency. However fertile the notion would be in later Hegelian idealism, it did seem anomalous in a system as emphatically empirical as Berkeley affirmed his own to be.

The allegation of incoherence in fundamental concepts is simply one objection among many hurled against Berkeley. Indeed, Berkeley has perhaps provoked more refutations than any philosopher in history. One of the earliest occurred in his own time. Samuel Johnson thought he had devastated Berkeley's idealism when he kicked a stone; as another philosopher remarked, Johnson's action showed that he could hit a stone but miss a point.

Immanuel Kant, who proposed a system of transcendental idealism, undertook to dispose of Berkeley's so-called "dogmatic material idealism." According to Kant, Berkeley had maintained that "space, with all the things of which it is the inseparable condition, is something which is in itself impossible," and that therefore "the things in space . . . are merely imaginary entities."[47] Against Berkeley, Kant offered his own conception of space as an a priori form, to be considered below; and he contended that subjective states of consciousness enjoy no superiority in ontological status or epistemological certainty over physical objects existing in space. For Kant, subject and object are equally indispensable for experience and knowledge, and they are on a par.

Realist Criticisms—Philosophical realists in the twentieth century have continued the onslaught against Berkeley's idealism. In a famous article, entitled "The Refutation of Idealism,"[48] G. E. Moore scrutinized the principle: *esse* is *percipi*. The crux of this principle, according to Moore's analysis, resides in the proposition that whatever is *must necessarily* be perceived. The idealist holds this proposition to be a synthetic necessary truth, synthetic because otherwise the proposition would be trivially tautologous, necessary because otherwise there would be *esse* without *percipi* in contradiction with the principle. Now, according to Moore, the idealist is refuted once the distinction is recognized between consciousness, on the one side, and the object or content of consciousness, on the other side. For it is then discerned that there is no proof of a necessary (internal) relation between consciousness and content for consciousness.

A related line of attack was offered by Ralph Barton Perry.[49] Perry contended that idealism rested on "the fallacy of the argument of the egocentric predicament." The egocentric predicament consists in the fact that no matter how much we seek in thought to find an item unrelated to our thinking about it, it must nevertheless be so related. To conceive an object independent of thinking is still to conceive it and hence to find it related to thought. The fallacy occurs when the idealist, like Berkeley, infers from this predicament. For the conclusion of this inference, when logically analyzed, reduces either to the redundancy that all objects of consciousness are objects of consciousness or to the unproven and indemonstrable proposition that all things are objects of consciousness.

Stace's Defense—The argument against idealism and for realism is by no means terminated. In full awareness of the realist writings, Walter T. Stace (1886–1967) has proceeded, in his important paper, "The Refutation of Realism,"[50] in a manner which Berkeley would have applauded. Stace has argued that we do *not* know that any single entity exists unexperienced, and that, even if such entities do exist, we cannot possibly know that they do. Finally, he held, since we do not know and cannot know that unexperienced entities exist, we have *no reason* to believe that such entities do exist.

Stace's metaphysics is interesting in its own right; it is offered as a phenomenalist metaphysics, in which elements of the philosophies of Berkeley and of Leibniz are blended. Thus Stace wrote:

> The universe is fundamentally a colony of multitudes of minds. I hold back from saying that the ultimate stuff or reality of the universe is mind. . . . Moreover, in addition to minds there are givens, floating colours and sounds, relations between these, mental states as themselves intuited and given. Each monadic mind possesses and dwells in its own self-enclosed world of givens.[51]

Stace refused to assert that mind is more fundamental than what is given; to have done so would have required him to desert his empirical standpoint and to make claims not warranted by the evidence. Reaffirming his position in a later work, Stace presented his metaphysics as "the hypothesis that the universe is a plurality of cells, all cells being of the same fundamental structure, though apart from structure they vary indefinitely."[52] He continued: "The structure of every cell in the universe is correctly described if we say that it consists of two essential abstract elements, namely consciousness and datum."[53] Stace dissociated his position from Berkeley's on three points: 1) he declined to consider the objects of consciousness (data, givens) to be mental, 2) he did not suppose these objects to have been created by mind, and 3) he did not agree that there is a gap in the metaphysical system—the interperceptual levels—which necessitates the concept of God. For Stace, it is not necessary for objects to exist when they are not perceived, and so God is "not a necessary concept of metaphysics," although He is "a legitimate contingent concept."[54]

KANT

The epistemological argument for idealism advanced to a new stage with the advent of the transcendental idealism of Immanuel Kant. In *The Critique of Pure Reason* (1781), Kant wrote: "By *transcendental idealism,* I mean the doctrine that appearances are to be regarded as being, one and all, representations only, not things in themselves, and that time and space are therefore only forms of our intuition, not determinations given as existing by themselves, nor conditions of objects viewed as things in themselves."[55] Kant's definition not only stands in need of further elucidation of such terms as "appearance" and "thing in itself"; it also presents transcendental idealism as a quite special doctrine concerning the status of space and time. However, the doctrine in question illustrates Kant's method, the method of critique, so well that the term "transcendental idealism" has come to signify Kant's entire philosophy. This critical philosophy, as has been noted in Chapter I, has explicitly eschewed speculative metaphysics; yet it has unleashed a novel and overwhelming impulse to speculation.

Kant, like Berkeley, was troubled by the problem of knowledge, but unlike Berkeley, he did not approach the problem from the restricted standpoint of empiricism. In particular Kant was disturbed by the impasse in metaphysics between dogmatism and skepticism, and with the palpable implication that reason, despite its pretensions, could supply no knowledge in metaphysics. The task set for reason, therefore, was to explicate the conditions of knowledge, the kinds of knowledge, the faculties involved, and finally the limits, if any, to knowledge. Kant concentrated on the kind of knowledge he called "synthetic a priori." He found such knowledge in mathematics, physics, and the claims of such knowledge in metaphysics. Kant never once doubted the existence of synthetic a priori knowledge in the mathematical and natural sciences. His question was not, How do we know? It was rather, How do we explain the knowledge we have? To be more precise, Kant's problem was, How is synthetic a priori knowledge possible?

Let us clarify Kant's problem by summarizing his elucidations of the kinds of knowledge in the Preamble to *The Prolegomena to Any Future Metaphysics*. It should, of course, be kept in mind that Kant accepted unquestioningly the Aristotelian analysis of the structure of judgment into subject and predicate. A judgment in which the predicate concept is contained in the meaning of the subject concept he called *analytic*. For example: "Matter is extended." A judgment in which the predicate concept introduces a meaning not contained in the subject concept, he called *synthetic*. For example: "The typewriter weighs eight pounds." A judgment which is universal and necessary and which, therefore, is independent of experience for its truth, he called "a priori." For example: any analytic judgment. A judgment which is particular and contingent and which, therefore, is dependent upon experience for its truth, he called "a posteriori." For example: the synthetic judgment cited above as an example. All analytic judgments are a priori; their truth is warranted by appeal to the law of contradiction, in that their denial is tantamount to self-contradiction. All a posteriori judgments are synthetic; their truth is warranted by the appeal to experience. Synthetic a priori judgments, existing in mathematics and physics, constitute a special problem, for they are warranted neither by the law of contradiction nor by appeal to experience. Hume had apprehended this difficulty when he saw that the proposition, "Every event must have a cause," although it is employed in all knowledge about experience, expresses neither a relation between ideas known intuitively or demonstratively nor a matter of fact known perceptually. Hume concluded that the proposition is not a rational truth but rather a natural belief, and he explained it psychologically. Kant generalized Hume's problem, uncovering thereby a whole set of basic principles, in arithmetic, geometry, and physics, of which the principle of causation is one; but he sought to explain these principles not as natural beliefs induced by the association of ideas and mental habits, but rather by reference to the nature of the mind itself.

The solution Kant offered for the problem of knowledge involves his conception of the nature of mind, of the faculties and principles which mind itself brings to the knowledge situation. It involves, in other words, Kant's transcendental psychology. In a recent work sure to exert considerable influence on Kant studies, Peter Strawson has credited Kant with having made the most "strenuous attempt" in history to formulate the limits to what we can conceive "as a possible general structure of experience . . . the set of ideas which forms the limiting framework of all our thought about the world and experience of the world."[56] At the same time, Strawson has charged that Kant was misled by the analogy between this investigation and psychology. "Wherever he [Kant] found limiting or necessary general features of experience, he declared their source to lie in our own cognitive constitution; and this doctrine he considered indispensable as an explanation of the possibility of knowledge of the necessary structure of experience."[57] Further, Strawson criticizes Kant for resorting not to empirical psychology, which is a science, but "to the imaginary subject of transcendental psychology."[58] The thrust of Strawson's critique of Kant is to disentangle the transcendental psychology, which he condemns for masking the real character of Kant's inquiry, from "the analytical argument which is in fact independent of it."[59] In fairness to Kant, however, it should be recognized that Kant meant his philosophy to be more than laborious but confused analysis. By means of transcendental psychology Kant sought to establish the centrality of mind in knowledge. And no other means would do for Kant, since empirical psychology presents a passive mind acted upon by influences from the outside. Furthermore, since "knowledge," "experience," and "nature" have ways of becoming synonymous in Kant's writings, the Kantian proposition that mind is central in shaping knowledge is tantamount to the assertion that it is central in shaping experience and nature.

Kant has esteemed his transcendental idealism as the second

Copernican revolution. Just as Copernicus (1473–1543) succeeded in explaining the motions of the planets by shifting their center from the earth to the sun, so Kant sought to explain the nature of knowledge by shifting from the objects to the subject. Thus Kant's transcendental idealism is the forerunner of romantic idealism. It regards the subject as the primary agency in the construction of the world. Or, as Kant more circumspectly put it: "the understanding does not draw its laws (*a priori*) from nature, but prescribes them to nature."[60] The subject is at least the lawgiver, if not the creator.

To explain a priori knowledge, Kant made use of the distinction between form and content. He maintained that while at any phase in the cognitional process—sensation, perception, understanding, reason—content is given to the subject, form is contributed by the subject as forms of intuition (sensibility), categories of understanding, or ideas of reason. The contribution of these formal elements and principles by the subject requires the operation of special transcendental psychological faculties.

Thus Kant explained the possibility of synthetic a priori propositions in mathematics by resort to the a priori forms of intuition. Whereas the subject receives a posteriori the whole complex of qualities found in sensory experience, it imposes upon this complex the a priori forms of space and time which reside in the faculty of intuition itself. Mathematical judgments are universal and necessary and independent of experience because they simply state the structure of these forms which prevail everywhere in experience.

In similar fashion Kant explained the possibility of synthetic a priori propositions in physics by resort to the a priori categories of the understanding. Whereas the subject receives as content the whole manifold of spatio-temporal sensory qualities and relations, it imposes upon this manifold twelve categories: 1) unity, 2) plurality, 3) totality, 4) reality, 5) negation, 6) limitation, 7) inherence and subsistence, 8) causality and dependence, 9) community, 10) possibility/impossibility, 11) existence/nonexistence, and 12) necessity/contingency.

Since the forms and categories upon which knowledge (and experience) depend are contributed by the subject, Kant refrained from ascribing them to things as those things might exist apart from the subject. Consequently, he drew, in addition to the form/content distinction within knowledge and experience, a second distinction between objects as they are present in experience, which he called "appearances," "representations," and "phenomena," on the one hand, and objects as they exist in their own right apart from experience, "things in themselves" or "noumena" as he called them. Kant's rejection of traditional idealism, such as the empirical idealism of Berkeley, emerges in sharp focus. Transcendental idealism, he declared, "did not concern the existence of things (to doubt which properly constitutes idealism in its accepted meaning), for *it has never entered my mind to doubt this.*"[61] Kant's transcendental idealism is phenomenalistic in the sense that it regards all objects of knowledge and of experience as constructs within experience; it is realistic in the sense that it posits the existence of things in themselves outside experience; and it is skeptical in that it shuts off the possibility of knowing these things in themselves.

Kant's metaphysical skepticism, already mentioned in Chapter I, is elaborated at length in the part of *The Critique of Pure Reason* called "the transcendental dialectic." Kant examined the pretensions of speculative metaphysics which, allegedly by means of unassailable arguments, asserted in rational psychology the immortality of the human self, contended in rational cosmology for antithetical propositions, and claimed in rational theology to prove that God exists. He found that these pretensions were illusory yet inevitable. Reason, no less than the faculties of intuition and of understanding, contains a priori formal principles: the Ideas of the Soul, the Cosmos, and God. They urge reason to synthesize conditioned experience and its unconditioned ground, progressing toward the absolute synthesis, that whole of wholes—God. Unfortunately, according to Kant, the results are disastrous in regard to knowledge. Instead of furnishing new knowledge, reason is impugned by fallacy.

The most dramatic frustration of reason in its quest for transcendent knowledge—knowledge of the things in themselves which lie beyond experience—occurs in rational cosmology. Reason is entangled in a series of contradictions, termed by Kant "antinomies." By "antinomy" Kant meant the opposition of two propositions on a given issue, the occurrence, in other words, of a thesis and an antithesis such that the mode of argument utilized in proving the one begins by assuming the other and ends by reducing this assumption to the absurdity of becoming its opposite. The third antinomy is the most significant one; it has as its thesis the doctrine of universal causation throughout nature and as its antithesis the doctrine of human freedom. It involves nothing less than the confrontation of natural science and human morality. Kant's resolution of the antinomy is remarkable. He removed the conflict by applying the thesis to the phenomena and the antithesis to things in themselves. Clearly, from his own analysis, which had restricted knowledge to appearances, Kant could not consistently do this. Kant's direction of our attention to the antinomies as markers of the boundaries of reason paradoxically insinuated that somehow reason could manage a vision of what lies on the other side of its boundaries.

Kant's metaphysical skepticism is mitigated by an additional consideration. Although he explicitly eschewed speculative metaphysics, he nevertheless offered another sort of metaphysics—to use the phrase of H. J. Paton, "a metaphysics of experience." Kant's complete system comprises two forms of intuition, twelve categories of the understanding, and three ideas of reason. Whereas few neo-Kantians would today subscribe to Kant's total list or even his reasons for it, most do support Kant's essential thesis that experience presupposes a priori formal principles which structure and limit it. And no matter how far neo-Kantians, in sketching their own interpretations of the metaphysics of experience may deviate from Kant's list, they almost universally agree that Space, Time, Quality, Relation, and Cause are indispensable forms or categories.

Kant was convinced that once and for all he had formulated and justified the list of categories operative in knowledge and experience. Believing that he was following Aristotle, Kant defined categories as "pure concepts of the understanding which apply a priori to objects of intuition [sensibility] in general."[62] Categories "are concepts of an object in general, by means of which the intuition [sense perception] of an object is regarded as determined in respect of one of the logical forms of judgment."[63] They are "the functions of judgment, in so far as they are employed in determination of the manifold of a given intuition."[64] Kant refrained from endeavoring to define each category. To consider categories in liberation from empirical employment was to make them seem applicable beyond experience, and to grasp their meaning was to descend unstintingly to the conditions of sensible experience to which their employment is restricted. Kant was convinced that in one major respect he had surpassed Aristotle with regard to a theory of categories. Confident that he had successfully performed the task of deducing the categories, he pronounced the superiority of his philosophy over Aristotle's in that "not until now does he [the philosopher] have a *System*."[65]

Kant's deduction of the categories, comprising a large and obscure portion of the *Critique of Pure Reason*, is multifaceted.[66] One segment is termed "the metaphysical deduction"; it is based on Kant's claim that the categories are functions of the understanding, and hence, since the understanding is the faculty of judging, they are forms of judging. Kant's next step was simply to look at how the logicians, who study the forms of judgment, have classified judgments, and from their table of judgments Kant derived his own list of categories.

The second segment of Kant's deduction of the categories, far more complex, obscure, and influential than the metaphysical deduction, is called "the transcendental deduction." Kant radically altered the transcendental deduction in the second edition of *The Critique of Pure Reason;* a procedure which heightened the difficulties in understanding Kant's intentions and arguments. At least three strands may be discerned in the transcendental deduction of the categories. One strand has to do with psychological faculties and processes of perception, imagination, and apperception. Another strand seeks to explain the unity of experience, made possible by the categories, in terms of the psychological faculties which are all subsumed under "the transcendental unity of apperception."

Still a third strand proliferates into a number of detailed accounts of the way each category is implicated in experience.

It is in that part of the transcendental deduction of the categories —the most crucial part—where Kant invoked the doctrine of the transcendental unity of apperception that he overstepped the metaphysics of experience and ventured beyond into a new kind of speculative metaphysics. Kant's argument has at its premise the proposition that experience is a unity. It has as its conclusion the proposition that the transcendental unity of apperception is the reason for this unity of experience.

Strawson, whose lucidity is always desirable, may be helpful here. Calling Kant's premise "the thesis of the necessary unity of consciousness," Strawson presents the following formula as an elucidation of the thesis: "that experience must include awareness of objects which are distinguishable from experience of them in the sense that judgements about these objects are judgements about what is the case irrespective of the actual occurrence of particular subjective experiences of them." [67] Strawson comments that Kant saw this thesis "as inseparably linked with the requirement of the conceptualizability of experience, with the requirement that *particular* contents of experience should be recognized as having some *general* character; and, so linked, may reasonably be seen as a standard-setting definition of what is to count as 'experience,'" and he even doubts "if any philosopher, even the most economical of empiricists, has ever in practice worked, or tried to work, with a more limited conception" [68] But Strawson slips when he identifies the premise with "the transcendental unity of apperception," and his initial error is aggravated when he denies that Kant could legitimately mean more than empirical consciousness. According to Strawson, all Kant is concerned with are "the general conditions of the employment of concepts, of the recognition of the particular contents of experience as having some general character, and he [Kant] regards these conditions as being at the same time the fundamental conditions of the possibility of ordinary or empirical self-consciousness." [69] Strawson's error, in brief, is to collapse the entire argument into the premise. Kant, however, premised the unity of experience, and inferred the transcendental unity of apperception as the guarantor of that unity.

Despite Kant's sober aims the doctrine of the transcendental unity of apperception inspired speculative metaphysics with renewed fervor. What one perceives (introspects) as one's self within the field of experience is always an empirical self, an appearance beyond which lurks the elusive but ever operative transcendental unity of apperception. By "apperception" Kant meant simply the process or faculty of perceiving perception—i.e., consciousness of consciousness, or self-consciousness. By "unity" he meant that the kind of consciousness which has itself truly as its object must be "one"—i.e., the subject being conscious is the object of which it is conscious. Otherwise there would be an infinite regress; subject-consciousness forever receding beyond each emerging object-consciousness. By denominating this unity of apperception "transcendental" Kant meant that it could not be found in any experience, nor be transfixed to any moment of time or position in space; but rather accompanies all self-consciousness as an identity of thinking by means of the necessary categories. Kant resurrected Descartes when he designated the transcendental unity of apperception as the *cogito*—the "I think."[70] Kant also used the terms "transcendental ego" or "transcendental self" to designate the transcendental unity of apperception. In the light of Kant's critique of rational psychology, it is doubtful that he ever intended to ontologize the transcendental ego, to make of it either an Absolute mind or an individual soul. Yet unwittingly he had released a new principle—a universalized, disembodied Cartesian ego—to titillate the metaphysical imaginations of his successors.

In the Preface to the second edition of the *Critique of Pure Reason,* Kant confessed: "I have therefore found it necessary to deny *knowledge,* in order to make room for *faith.*"[71] His thought had obviously outstripped the system of forms and categories which he had found sufficient to sustain a scientific understanding of nature. Moral experience, Kant recognized, required additional principles, the so-called postulates of practical reason: God, freedom, and immortality. A man is free; otherwise he could not be obligated to perform his moral duties, nor be held responsible for his actions. A man is immortal; otherwise he would not have the infinite span of time in which to perfect his moral will as demanded by the moral law. God exists; otherwise there would be no guarantee that virtue is proportionally awarded happiness. Aesthetic experience, too, requires additional categories: Beauty and Sublimity. And even the life sciences cannot be straitjacketed into the forms of judgment adequate for the mathematical and physical sciences, so that Kant acknowledged that there is a special type of judgment which he called "teleological." In these judgments final causes, ends, the purposes of the organisms take precedence in explanation over mechanical and efficient causes, although teleology originates in our reflective understanding of nature, while nature itself is properly mechanical. In sum, Kant's thought, too restless to remain within the confines of his critical system, seemed to contradict itself.

Although Kant felt the lure of speculative metaphysics, he did not succumb to it. His philosophy, in the last analysis, is founded on three basal divisions of being, or *ur*-categories: 1) unknowable things in themselves, 2) experience or nature, and 3) the transcendental ego. Since knowledge is restricted to experience or nature, speculative metaphysics is foreclosed. Kant's successors in German idealism accepted the restriction of knowledge to experience but assimilating things in themselves and the transcendental ego to experience or nature, they reopened the highway to philosophical speculation.

SCHOPENHAUER

Arthur Schopenhauer (1788–1860), who adopted the Kantian dichotomy of appearance and reality, nevertheless maintained that knowledge of reality is possible. Whereas objective knowledge, starting from the idea (representation in consciousness, appearance, phenomenon), can never get beyond the idea, a direct route to knowledge of reality is available. Schopenhauer wrote: "we are not merely the *knowing subject,* but, in another aspect, we ourselves also belong to the inner nature that is to be known, *we ourselves are the thing in itself*; . . . therefore a *way from within* stands open for us to that inner nature belonging to things in themselves, to which we cannot penetrate *from without*." The way from within is "a subterranean passage, a secret alliance, which as if by treachery, places us at once within the fortress which it was impossible to take by assault from without." Thus the thing in itself is not excluded from consciousness; it "can, as such, only come into consciousness quite directly, in this way, that *it is itself conscious of itself*." [72] For Schopenhauer, knowledge as clarified by Kant does not afford the thing in itself entry into consciousness since formal knowledge is empty and empirical knowledge is confined to phenomena; rather the knowledge which each of us has of his own willing is the sole route. Schopenhauer continued: "In fact, our *willing* is the one opportunity which we have of understanding from within any event which exhibits itself, consequently the one thing which is known to us *immediately*, and not, like all the rest, merely given in the idea. Here, then, lies the datum which alone is able to become the key to everything else, or . . . the single narrow door to the truth." [73]

Upon this special knowledge, Schopenhauer erected his metaphysical system of voluntarism. "I teach," he asserted, "that the inner nature of everything is *will*, and I call the will the thing in itself." [74] Schopenhauer also taught that the will which we know intimately to be the thing in itself is a universal will objectified in nature through all the stages of its evolution and manifest in all the multiplicity of individual life-forms. As Schopenhauer declared: "Will is the thing-in-itself, the inner content, the essence of the world. Life, the visible world, the phenomenon, is only the mirror of the will." [75] The will, moreover, displays itself in strife. "Thus everywhere in nature we see strife, conflict, and alternation of victory and defeat, and in it we shall come to recognize more distinctly that variance with itself which is essential to the will. Every grade of the objectification of will fights for the matter, the space, and the time of the others." [76]

Schopenhauer's metaphysical voluntarism is anti-intellectual and pessimistic. The anti-intellectualism is twofold: 1) the will is prior to the intellect, which becomes merely the will's instrument; and

2) the intellect furnishes only false knowledge, or illusion. To relate itself to externals, the will outfitted itself with the intellect, which operates by means of ideas. When the intellect functions, even in knowing the self, it separates the real subject from the subject cognized, the latter being but another object; thus it applies the form of phenomena—time. When the intellect seeks knowledge of objects other than the self, it brings into play such categories of phenomena as space and causality. If the nature of the intellect vitiates the possibility of genuine knowledge, the nature of the will, according to Schopenhauer, entails pessimism. As Schopenhauer said, "the basis of all willing is need, deficiency, and . . . pain."[77] The will "always strives, for striving is its sole nature, which no attained goal can put an end to. Therefore it is not susceptible of any final satisfaction, but can only be restrained by hindrances, while in itself it goes on forever."[78] Should the will attain an intermediate aim, the result is not simply satisfaction but rather ennui, and ennui "is by no means an evil to be lightly esteemed; in the end it depicts on the countenance real despair."[79] Thus the life of the will "swings like a pendulum backwards and forwards between pain and ennui."[80]

FICHTE

Johann Gottlieb Fichte (1762–1814), Kant's leading disciple, also advocated voluntarism, but without pessimism and anti-intellectualism. Although Fichte's main contributions to idealism were made to the practical branches of philosophy—to ethics, politics, and religion, in his *Wissenschaftslehre* (science of knowledge) he did add to the development of speculative idealism. He divided the field of philosophy into two main positions: dogmatism and idealism. Dogmatism, which Fichte further subdivided into materialism, spiritualism, and Spinozism, seeks to deduce the idea from the object; idealism the object from the idea. In practice the philosopher chooses dogmatism or idealism according to his temperament. If he is a passive creature, he adopts dogmatism; if an active one, idealism. At the level of theory, however, the case is closed against dogmatism. Dogmatism can never explain how the idea, the consciousness of the thing, may be derived wholly from the object. Idealism is more successful in explaining how the object is derived from the idea. Fichte grappled with the task of deducing the object from the idea, of deriving first the experience of the thing and then the thing-in-itself from the ego. He left no less than eleven expositions of, and six introductions to, the *Wissenschaftslehre*.[81]

"The absolute, first, and unconditioned fundamental principle of human knowledge," according to Fichte, is "the *deed-act* (*that-handlung*) which . . . is . . . the basis of all consciousness, and first and alone makes consciousness possible."[82] This deed-act is grasped by all and without hesitation, by means of reflection and abstraction, to be the first law of thought—the Principle of Identity: A is A. In psychology this principle is the principle of the Ego—namely, the proposition "I am." Thus Fichte arrived at the first unconditioned principle of his system: "The Ego Posits Originally Its Own Being."[83]

Whereas the first principle of Fichte's system is absolutely unconditioned, the two other major principles, though like the first needing no proof, are conditioned. Logically, the second principle is simply the obverse of the first. Conditioned as regards content, the second principle is simply the logical tautology: Not-A is Not-A. Psychologically it is grounded in those acts of the Ego which are negative positing (oppositing or opposing). The opposite of the Ego is, by definition, the non-Ego; hence "a non-Ego is absolutely opposited to the Ego."[84] Thus Fichte arrived at the second principle of knowledge: "Whatsoever appertains to the Ego, of that the opposite must appertain to the non-Ego."[85]

The first and second principles of knowledge stand apart as antinomies. A third principle is necessary to bring the first two together. This principle is conditioned as regards its form. It incorporates the other two principles, but in a one-sided way—the Ego absorbing into itself the non-Ego. In the process the Ego sets up with itself an Ego counterpart to the non-Ego. For example, the unity the Ego established by the first principle, entails, on the basis of the second principle, the divisibility of the non-Ego. Hence Fichte formulated the third principle of knowledge as follows: "The Ego opposits in the Ego a divisible Non-Ego to an indivisible Ego."[86]

The Ego displays itself in its essential activity of unifying and opposing, so that from the third principle of knowledge Fichte proceeded to deduce all the other necessary categories: time, space, causality. Furthermore, Fichte proceeded from the theoretical part of his system to deduce the fundamental principle of practical knowledge. This principle, correlative to the third principle of the theoretical part of the system, is "The Ego posits itself as determining the non-Ego."[87]

It is noteworthy that Fichte's system of knowledge is not an absolute idealism. The juxtaposition of the Ego and the non-Ego, the former never able wholly to assimilate the latter, reveals that the Ego is finite. Psychologically Fichte seemed to be asserting that consciousness is necessarily finite, since it involves awareness of an other standing over against it. An infinite Ego, such as God is supposed to be, could not then be consciousness or have knowledge. Fichte put the issue as follows: "For a Godhead, that is, for a consciousness (to us unthinkable) for which the self-positing of the Ego is the positing of all, our science of knowledge would have no content; for its consciousness would embrace no other positing than the self-positing of the Ego; but the form of our system would be valid even for God, since it is the form of pure reason itself."[88] At one point in the elaboration of the *Wissenschaftslehre,* Fichte had been charged with atheism, since the denial that God is conscious is tantamount to the denial that God, in the traditional sense of that term, exists. Fichte sought to escape the charge by restricting knowledge to the finite Ego, and by stressing his voluntarism. For him the practical and not the theoretical, the will and not the intellect, activity and not consciousness, was the key to the inmost nature of the world.

SCHELLING

Fichte greeted the early work, *The Ego as the Principle of Philosophy* (1795), by Friedrich Wilhelm Joseph Schelling (1775–1854) as a commentary on his own *Wissenschaftslehre.*[89] Schelling followed Fichte in maintaining that the Ego is the supreme or unconditioned element in human knowledge; but he went beyond Fichte in holding that the Ego as absolute self-consciousness, while somehow residing in the finite consciousness, cannot be merely the finite Ego in contrast with the non-Ego. Schelling suggested that this Ego is an Absolute in which the distinction between finite subject and object is drawn. In his *System of Transcendental Idealism* (1800), Schelling continued to elaborate his original point of view.

Although Fichte's idealism pivots on two major categories: Ego and non-Ego, and remains within the confines of a subjective idealism of the finite consciousness, Schelling introduced the totally new category of the Absolute Ego. The problem of integrating subject and object, which Schelling had declared in the Introduction to his *System of Transcendental Idealism* to be the central problem of knowledge, was solved by him in a manner quite different from Fichte's way. After failing to find the integration in the thesis-antithesis progression of the understanding, Fichte had appealed to the primacy of the will, which as thesis determines its object as antithesis within the field of moral struggle. By contrast, Schelling, who condemned the idealism of both Kant and Fichte as a mere philosophy of reflection (understanding) which was unable to penetrate the essence of the object, appealed to the special faculty of intellectual intuition.

According to Schelling, the faculty of intellectual intuition is revealed at its highest peak in the achievements of the great geniuses in the history of art. It grasps the object as it is in itself. Furthermore, it grasps that the object is not an alien being opposed to the subject but is rather itself an expression of the subject. Here is the crux of Schelling's celebrated philosophy of nature. Nature, at first regarded as the Other opposed to Mind or Spirit, is intuited to be the embodiment of Mind or Spirit. And the antinomies of reflection that mark the philosophies of Kant and Fichte become polarities which are contained within the Absolute unity of subject and object.

Schelling's transcendental idealism invites the application of sundry labels. It is absolutism, indeed the originator of the doctrine of the Absolute. It is identity-philosophy, in that it asserts the ultimate unity (and hence the identity) of subject and object. It is pantheism, in that it contends that Nature is in essence Spirit. Above all, it is romanticism. It elevated the artists to the highest place in the development of mind and the attainment of truth. It put Nature on an equal footing with Mind and in the process idealized Nature. It promoted intuition above understanding. Indeed, Schelling himself personified the romantic as philosopher. Too often he impulsively announced a philosophical program only to abandon it before completion in order to engage in another. Schelling's writings are distinguished by remarkable insights and brilliantly original conceptions, but they are also marred by lack of discipline and method.

HEGEL

Hegel was an early collaborator with Schelling in the fight against the philosophy of reflection advocated by Kant and Fichte. He condemned Kant's philosophy as a mere subjective idealism. Kant's transcendental unity, he remarked, is transcendental and not transcendent, for Kant "meant thereby that the unity was only in our minds and did not attach to the objects apart from our knowledge of them." [90] Kant therefore restricted the categories "to the subject-mind, and his philosophy may be styled subjective idealism; for he holds that both the form and the matter of knowledge are supplied by the Ego—or knowing subject—the form by our intellectual, the matter by our sentient ego." [91] Hegel's objection to Kant, however, is not due to the fact that Kant's subjective idealism denied reality to the objects of knowledge. As Hegel said: "The main point is not, that they [objects] are, but what they are, and whether or not their content is true. . . . Laying aside therefore this distinction between subjective and objective, we are chiefly interested in knowing what a thing is: i.e., its content, which is no more objective than it is subjective." [92] For Kant, "the things that we know about are *to us* appearances only, and we can never know their essential nature, which belongs to another world we cannot approach," all facts of consciousness being "reduced to a purely personal world, created by ourselves alone."[93] For Hegel, on the other hand, the true doctrine is that "the things of which we have direct consciousness are mere phenomena, not for us only, but in their own nature; and the true and proper case of these things, finite as they are, is to have their existence founded not in themselves but in the universal divine Idea."[94] Thus the Kantian philosophy of reflection, with its dichotomy between phenomena and things in themselves, is superseded in the Hegelian philosophy of dialectical reason. The Hegelian philosophy is, as Hegel stressed, "as idealist as Kant's; [it] should be termed absolute idealism."[95]

Hegel broke with Schelling, despite their common alliance against the philosophy of reflection. Hegel was offended by the identity-philosophy, which reduced all differences to identity. Schelling's Absolute, he observed, is "the night in which . . . all cows are black."[96] But Hegel's main objection to Schelling was based on the fact that Schelling had no philosophical method, whereas Hegel placed his own confidence in the dialectical method. This method, in brief, prescribed that the logical implications of concepts be explicated to the point of exhibiting a continuity of thought from an idea, called the thesis, to an opposite idea, called an antithesis, through a struggle between these two culminating in a third idea, called a synthesis, which reconciles and embraces the two earlier ideas. The dialectical method is illustrated in the opening pages of the *Science of Logic* (1812–1816), where Hegel presents the concept of Being, so pure that it has no content whatever, shows then that a concept without any content is the concept of Nothing, dilates on the contradiction between the concept of Being and the concept of Nothing, and finally demonstrates that the contradiction is resolved in the concept of Becoming, which combines Being and Nothing.

The Absolute is the fundamental category of absolute idealism. Few categories in the history of philosophy have been as intractable to conceptual specification as the category of the Absolute. Introduced by Schelling and utilized by Fichte, the category of the Absolute pervades the philosophy of Hegel. As Hegel declared: "Being itself and the special sub-categories of it which follow, as well as those of logic in general, may be looked upon as definitions of the Absolute, or metaphysical definitions of God." [97] In this guise, the Absolute is "the indeterminate subject of predicates yet to come." [98] The remainder of the logic is a dialectical unfolding of these predicates—subcategories—which belong to and are included within the culminating idea of the Absolute.

Were Hegel's metaphysics a mere panlogism, the Absolute would have been simply the logical product of all concepts. But Hegel's metaphysics drew as much from a phenomenology of mind in both its theoretical and practical manifestations and from the history of philosophy as it did from logic. In the Preface to the *Phenomenology of Mind* (1808), Hegel asserted that ". . . everything depends on grasping and expressing the ultimate truth not as Substance but as Subject as well." [99] In effect, Hegel apprehended the category of the Absolute as two-dimensional at least: as Substance and as Subject. What did he mean?

Hegel's meaning is perhaps best clarified by reference to his understanding of the philosophy of Spinoza and his own supersession of that philosophy. As Hegel said: "The simple thought of Spinoza's idealism is this: 'The true is simply and solely one substance, whose attributes are thought and extension or nature; and only this absolute unity is reality, it alone is God.'" [100] Hegel, moreover, conceded that "to be a follower of Spinoza is the essential commencement of all Philosophy. . . . When men begin to philosophize," he continued, "the soul must commence by bathing in the ether of the One Substance, in which all that man has held as true has disappeared; this negation of all that is particular, to which every philosopher must have come, is the liberation of the mind and its absolute foundation." [101] However, Hegel also insisted that although "absolute substance is the truth, . . . it is not the whole truth; in order to be this it must also be thought of as in itself active and living, and by that very means it must determine itself as mind." [102] Spinoza had erected his philosophy on the great proposition that all determination implies negation, and since everything, even thought in contrast to extension, is determined, it is negated.[103] Therefore, "there is . . . in his [Spinoza's] system, an utter blotting out of the principle of subjectivity, individuality, personality, the moment of self-consciousness in Being."[104] Thus Hegel objected to Spinoza's philosophy for being "a rigid and unyielding substance, and not yet spirit; in it we are not at home with ourselves."[105]

Hegel's Absolute is Spinoza's Substance plus. The additional characteristics of the Absolute may be gleaned from a consideration of the terms of Hegel's indictment of Spinoza: spirituality, activity, individuality. These are missing from Spinoza's Substance, but according to Hegel, they belong to ultimate reality once it is understood to be Subject. Whereas Spinoza regarded all determination as negation, Hegel, for whom dialectic is the sole valid method of philosophy, maintained that all negation is determination. The triadic structure of dialectic—thesis, antithesis, synthesis—is repeated in the triadic structure of Hegel's system of philosophy—Logic, Nature, and Spirit. The Absolute exists in itself—Logic; the Absolute exists from itself, standing over against itself as an Other—Nature; and the Absolute exists for itself, reconciling the in-itself and the for-another—Spirit. Hegel's system, then, contained not only a philosophy of logic, but a philosophy of nature and a philosophy of spirit. In particular, Hegel's philosophy of spirit maps the structure of history, a dynamic field in which the universal is actively individualized, and it examines the manifestations of the universal spirit in morality, politics, art, religion, and philosophy.

Hegel had never doubted that his speculative philosophy would succeed. He had subscribed to the principle that the real is the rational and the rational is the real. Little had he anticipated that this principle would soon divide his philosophical following into two opposing groups: those conservatives who held that, since the real is rational, it should be preserved, and those revolutionaries who held that, since the rational is real, it should be instituted despite the cost to existing institutions. Nor had Hegel foreseen how his conception of the Absolute, combining the notions of universality and individuality, of activity and spirituality, would repel as much as entice those idealists who had been touched by the critical temper of Kant. For the latter, the doctrine of the Absolute was an enigma in need of solution.

T. H. GREEN

Thomas Hill Green (1836–1882) had returned to Kant to formulate "the spiritual principle in knowledge and nature," but he did not stay with Kant. Green's variation of Absolute idealism was epistemological in emphasis. Like Kant, he held that the understanding makes nature, that only through the understanding is there an objective world, a world structured by forms and categories. "The terms 'real' and 'objective,'" asserted Green, "have no meaning except for a consciousness which presents its experiences to itself as determined by relations, and at the same time conceives a single and unalterable order of relations determining them, with which its temporary presentation, as each experience occurs, of the relations determining it may be contrasted."[106] Knowledge, in other words, depends upon relations, and relations can exist only for a mind. So far Green's argument iterates in a general formula Kant's transcendental deduction of the categories. But in his next step Green exceeded Kant's critical boundaries. Not only does knowledge require that experiences within the subject be related; but it also requires a single and unalterable order of relations beyond the subject. Nature is a process of change; nevertheless, it is itself just such an order of relations. Hence the being of each objective thing is dependent upon relations. "It is not the case," Green argued, "that it [a thing] first exists in its unity, and then is brought into various relations. Without relations it would not exist at all."[107] Relations, however, are furnished by mind alone. Hence Green concluded that, just as our minds are necessary to provide the relations in experience which make knowledge possible, so "some unifying principle analogous to that of our understanding" is necessary for the existence of the relations that make nature possible.[108]

F. H. BRADLEY

Francis Herbert Bradley (1846–1924) elevated the case for Absolute Idealism to new heights. His *Principles of Logic* (1883) presented a logical argument for absolute idealism which, in simplicity and cogency, is on a par with Leibniz's logical argument for monadic idealism. His *Appearance and Reality* (1893) broadened the epistemological argument for absolute idealism into the argument *a contingentia mundi*.[109] Knowledge, Bradley showed, is only a special case of the relativity of all thought to the Absolute. These works, especially the latter, galvanized idealist speculation in the English-speaking world.

Bradley's logical argument for absolute idealism pressed the implications of Aristotelian logic in a direction the very opposite to Leibniz's. Bradley adhered to the view that logic is the study of judgment and that every judgment consists of a subject and a predicate. He wrote:

> In every judgment there is a subject of which the ideal content [predicate] is asserted. But this subject of course can not belong to the content or fall within it, for, in that case, it would be the idea attributed of itself . . . the subject is, in the end, no idea but always reality.[110]

The predicate, then, is the total ideal content expressed by a statement, including the grammatical subject of that statement; it is "not a fact but a wandering [or *loosened*] adjective."[111] "Judgment proper," he said, "is the act which refers an ideal content (recognized as such) to a reality beyond the act."[112] "The act [of judgment] attaches the floating adjective to the nature of the world, and, at the same time, tells me it was there already."[113] The subject of judgment then is reality, and, as Bradley said, "reality is not a connection of adjectives, nor can it so be represented. Its essence is too substantial and individual."[114] The true subject of every judgment is implicit in, rather than articulated by, the statement (or proposition) which expresses that judgment. For example, the statement (or proposition) "Mary is baking pies" articulates the ideal content of the judgment; this content is the complex fact of Mary-baking-pies; it is the predicate of the judgment. The subject of the judgment is reality; the judgment ascribes the quality of Mary-baking-pies to reality. In Bradley's logic there is one reality, one subject, for all judgments. This reality, this logical subject, is the Absolute. It is the equivalent of Spinoza's Substance. All particular things and qualities, comprehensible as ideal contents and expressible as predicates, are modes of the Absolute.

Bradley's argument *a contingentia mundi* opens yet another route to the Absolute. He argued that, since all the categories of the natural world are self-contradictory and since noncontradiction is the criterion of reality, all the categories of the natural world are unreal—i.e., appearances. He inferred that only the Absolute is self-consistent.

While elaborating the argument *a contingentia mundi,* Bradley attacked what had been central to the idealism which he had inherited—namely, the reality of relations. His treatment of relations illustrates his negative dialectic at its best. Bradley showed that "qualities are nothing without relations." [115] In order for thought about qualities to be possible, qualities must be plural, each identical with itself and some at least different from the others. Plurality, identity, and differences, however, are relations. Hence "qualities, taken without relations, have no intelligible meaning." [116] On the other hand, Bradley continued: "Unfortunately, taken together with them [relations], they [qualities] are equally unintelligible." [117] Qualities, though they require relations, cannot be reduced to relations, since "relations must depend upon terms, just as much as terms upon relations." [118] Hence relations without qualities are unintelligible. In sum, Bradley has demonstrated that relations and qualities mutually implicate each other.

By means of dialectic, Bradley relentlessly pursued the implications of the theory of relations. He had shown that "qualities must be, and must *also* be related." [119] Thus a quality has a double character: it is a term in its own right supporting a relation; and it is a term affected by the relation. A quality has, in other words, an intrinsic character and a relational character. According to Bradley, the relational character is a new quality, which in turn stands in need of a relation to relate it to the intrinsic character, i.e., the original quality. Once begun, this process continues ad infinitum, each new relation producing a new relational quality which in turn needs a new relation. As Bradley said, "We, in brief, are led by a principle of fission which conducts us to no end, . . . [and so] qualities in a relation have turned out as unintelligible as were qualities without one."[120] Furthermore, the same dilemma crops up from the side of relations, which, Bradley argued, "are nothing intelligible, either with or without their qualities."[121] Without their qualities, relations are mere verbiage, false abstractions—in a word, nothing. But then even with their qualities relations prove to be unintelligible. If a relation is nothing in itself and is merely an adjective of its terms, then it cannot relate the terms; it has no being to stand between the terms, external one to the other. And if a relation has such independent being, then it requires a relation to relate it to its term, and this process continues ad infinitum.

Having demolished relations, Bradley applied his negative dialectic to the other categories of thought which depend upon relations: space, time, motion, causation, and so on. He showed that these categories of thought and the aspects of experience they cover are unintelligible and inconsistent, and so he concluded that they are appearance. He did not mean that they are nothing, but rather that, having the being of appearance, they must be grounded in reality, where alone their contradictions are overcome.

Bradley's appeal to the distinction between appearance and reality rests on a special conception of the criterion of reality. Since self-contradiction is the mark of appearance, the real must be devoid of contradiction.

> Ultimate reality is such that it does not contradict itself; here is an absolute criterion.[122]
>
> Reality is one in the sense that it has a positive nature exclusive of discord. . . . Its diversity can be diverse only so far as not to clash. . . . Appearance must belong to reality, and it must therefore be concordant and other than it seems. The bewildering mass of phenomenal diversity must hence somehow be a unity and self-consistent; for it cannot be elsewhere than in reality, and reality excludes discord. Or again we may put it so: the real is the individual. It is one in the sense that its positive character embraces all differences in an inclusive harmony.[123]

Furthermore, the unity of absolute reality is not for Bradley the unity of a unit reality set in a plurality of unit realities; for then the dialectic of relations would recur to vitiate this plurality as itself an appearance. "Relations," said Bradley, "are unmeaning except within and on the basis of a substantial whole, and related terms, if made absolute, are forthwith destroyed. Plurality and relatedness are but features and aspects of a unity."[124] Hence there is one reality, the universe, "one whole, beyond which there is nothing,"[125] —in Bradley's word, the Absolute.

What is the Absolute? It is so far seen to be "an individual and a system."[126] But it is more than that. Pursuing a line of argument inherited from Berkeley, Bradley identified ultimate reality with experience. Unable to find or to conceive any existent apart from experience, Bradley concluded that "experience is the same as reality" and that the supposition of an existent apart from experience is "a mere word and a failure, . . . an attempt at self-contradiction . . . a vicious abstraction whose existence is meaningless nonsense, and is therefore not possible."[127] Thus, "the Absolute is one system, and . . . its contents are nothing but sentient experience. It will hence be a single and all-inclusive experience, which embraces every partial diversity in concord."[128] The Absolute, moreover, is valuational. As Bradley said:

> Our main wants—for truth and life, and for beauty and goodness—must all find satisfaction. And . . . this consummation must somehow be experience, and be individual. Every element of the universe, sensation, feeling, thought, and will must be included within one comprehensive sentience.[129]

Paradoxically, however, Bradley's Absolute undermines the values for which it stands. It is a whole in which all parts are internally related, a concrete universal embracing all its elements in the grip of necessity. It is the goal of speculation. But thought is discursive and relational, whereas the Absolute, as Bradley once said, is "a positive non-distinguished non-relational whole."[130] Thought therefore must in a sense commit suicide in attaining its goal, and consequently, it is doubtful that the Absolute as Bradley conceived it can be the goal of thought, or even that it is intelligible.[131] A related problem in Bradley's conception of the Absolute is derived from his philosophical logic. The Absolute as logical subject is the only individual, all finite individuals being mere attributes of its ultimate reality. In this respect, Bradley reverted to the abstract monism of Spinoza which Hegel sought to surpass; it was a reversion which did not attract Bradley's fellow idealists: Bernard Bosanquet (1848–1923), Josiah Royce (1855–1916), and John McTaggart Ellis McTaggart (1866–1925).

BOSANQUET

Bosanquet took individuality "to be the principle which must ultimately determine the nature of the real and its constituents."[132] By "reality" Bosanquet meant "that which must stand; that which has nothing without to set against it, and which is pure self-maintenance within;" he regarded individuality to be "the criterion of the ultimately real."[133] He added, "there can only be one individual, and that, *the* individual, the Absolute."[134] The Absolute, also termed by Bosanquet the world or cosmos, is the concrete universal, which he defined as "a system of members, such that every member being *ex hypothesi* distinct, nevertheless contributes to the unity of the whole in virtue of the peculiarities which constitute its distinctness."[135] It is a unity within diversity, "a macrocosm constituted by microcosms."[136] The Absolute, moreover, is mind. By "mind" Bosanquet meant "a 'whole' of a special kind, with a structure and concreteness of its own,"[137] adding that "the best general description of mind is to call it a world."[138] Although Bosanquet subscribed to the doctrine of the Absolute, he disavowed interest in carrying the doctrine further. "My purpose," he declared, "is rather, accepting ultimate Individuality as the character which our fullest experience tends to approach, to draw conclusions as to the nature and position of the human beings to whom in a secondary sense we apply the term Individuals."[139] Thus Bosanquet set out to establish the degree of individuality (reality) appropriate to the finite individual.

> The essence of individuality is to be a world in oneself. And this holds good in its degree for the most finite "individual." In him, however incompletely, we see what it is to have experience, or, in the most general sense of the term, to be conscious.[140]

Bosanquet added "that every possible gradation of reality must be occupied; and the Absolute is enriched by experience of all conceivable grades and varieties of content."[141] Despite this concession to monadism, however, Bosanquet recognized the Absolute, as the principle of individuality and value, to be paramount in his system. Within the Absolute, which at one point he described as "the high water mark of fluctuations in experience, of which, in general, we are daily and normally aware,"[142] all finite individuals live, and move, and have their being.

ROYCE

Royce focused on the problem of relating the Absolute to the finite individuals, the Absolute being One and the finite individuals being Many. From the beginning to the end of his philosophical career Royce adhered to the Hegelian doctrine of the concrete universal, but he did so in his own singular way, and not without radical changes in the mode of argumentation.[143] In *The Religious Aspect of Philosophy* (1885), Royce argued from the finitude of human experience to the existence of the Absolute. In moral experience the awareness of one's own particular aim, in conflict with the aims of others, leads to the moral insight which seeks an aim which reconciles all aims. As Royce said: "In the midst of the warfare of individual wills, we have caught sight of an Universal Will."[144] Discernible in the strugglings of the finite wills, the Universal Will is the Absolute in a moral guise; it later became the basis of Royce's morality of loyalty. In *The Religious Aspect of Philosophy,* however, the moral argument for the Absolute joined with an epistemological argument. He wrote: "All the many Beyonds, which single significant judgments seem vaguely and separately to postulate, are present as fully realized intended objects to the unity of an all-inclusive, absolutely clear, universal, and conscious thought, of which all judgments, true or false, are but fragments, the whole being at once Absolute Truth and Absolute Knowledge."[145] As the moral argument proceeded from conflicting individual wills, the epistemological argument proceeded from finite and even erroneous thoughts. The Absolute as Truth, like the Absolute as Universal Will, overcomes by embracing the finite consciousness. There is no nihilation of finitude, but a completion and preservation.[146]

In *The World and the Individual* (1899), Royce tightened up his treatment of the relation between the individual and the Absolute, mainly by a greater mastery of the technicalities of epistemology and ontology. To this he added, particularly in his supplementary essays, the tools of mathematical logic. Each finite individual is himself not merely a part of a greater system but a representation of the Absolute. Thus Royce viewed the world as a distinctive sort of system of beings, as an Absolute Self-Representative System whose acts of iteration, each with its own uniqueness and representational capacity, are infinite.[147]

Royce's final masterpiece, *The Problem of Christianity* (1913), contains a theory of interpretation which reveals another dimension of the Absolute. The simple activity of interpreting a textual meaning discloses a will to interpret which treats not texts alone but even individual selves, and this will to interpret has as its goal an all-embracing community in which every individual knows every other and all are bound together by the love or loyalty that accompanies self-knowledge in the knowledge of others. Thus the will to interpret in the individual selves reveals the Absolute in the form of the Will-to-Interpret—God in the person of the Holy Ghost, pervading the world, and guiding it to its goal, the Beloved Community.[148] While Royce may seem to reduce the Absolute to total immanence in historical communities, he actually teaches that a community permeated by the will to interpret genuinely represents or expresses the Absolute. In order to guarantee communication of meaning, community in the true sense of the word, the process of interpretation presupposes a transcendent interpreter—the Absolute as God.

MCTAGGART

McTaggart, better than any of his predecessors, stressed a pluralistic and personalistic interpretation of Hegelian Absolute Idealism. In his *Studies in Hegelian Cosmology* (1901; 2nd ed., 1918), he contended "that the element of differentiation and multiplicity occupies a much stronger place in Hegel's system than is generally believed," and on the basis of this principle, he sought to show that "all finite selves are eternal, and that the Absolute is not a self."[149] Rejecting the view that ". . . a self is merely a bundle of attributes, whose substance is the Absolute," he took instead "a view which puts the self higher, and makes each self, not an attribute of one sole self-subsistent substance, but itself a self-subsistent substance, though not an isolated one."[150] In maintaining that each self is an eternal substance, McTaggart supported by logical arguments the thesis that the self is a substantial identity which endures throughout a multiplicity of lives. He held that the self is immortal in the peculiar sense involved in the doctrine of the transmigration of souls entertained in Greek and Indian mythology, according to which the self not only survives but preexists this life.

McTaggart was no less paradoxical in his theory of the Absolute. "The nature of reality," he wrote, "is the manifestation of the Absolute in individuals, or the unity of individuals in the Absolute—in other words, the relation of self to self."[151] In *Studies in Hegelian Cosmology,* McTaggart equated God with the Absolute, and consequently passed over the question whether God exists, since if the Absolute (Reality) does not exist, nothing exists. He focused instead on the question as to the nature of God, or the Absolute. This question took the form: Is the Absolute a Person? The characteristic which determines personality is, McTaggart held, "generally placed in the 'I'—the synthetic unity of apperception."[152] A personal being is one that can distinguish itself from its content, or rather detect in that content an element which is never absent, is always the same, and, though present always in relation to a content, determines that this content is always a content of its own being.

McTaggart illustrated his point: "I know that I can say 'I am.' I know that a College cannot say 'I am.' "[153] Keeping in mind this criterion of personality, McTaggart concluded that the Absolute is not a person. Consciousness of self, a necessary condition for the existence of personality, cannot be possessed by the Absolute, since "there is nothing outside it, from which it can distinguish itself."[154] Although McTaggart held that "the unity of the Absolute is as real as its differentiations, and as real as the unity of a perfect finite self—while it is much more real than the unity of a finite self as it manifests itself imperfectly in this imperfect world," he admitted that "the Absolute is a unity of system, and not a unity of centre, and the element of unity in it cannot be a simple and indivisible point, like that of the finite self."[155] Lacking this indivisible unity, the Absolute, therefore, "cannot have the personality we have."[156] Nor can it have any other kind of personality. On this point McTaggart was emphatic:

> The sense of self *is* the indivisible unity in consciousness. The Absolute has not the indivisible unity, and therefore it has no sense of self. Therefore it is not a person. There is no room left for any further possibilities.[157]

In his two-volume work *The Nature of Existence* (1921, 1927), McTaggart further elaborated his paradoxical idealism.[158] Using the term "Universe" instead of the term "Absolute," McTaggart never wavered in his conviction that the Universe exists. He wrote: "There is therefore a substance which contains all content, and of which every other substance is a part. This substance is to be called the Universe."[159] He refused, however, to apply the term "God" to it. Rather, he took "the word God to mean a being who is personal, supreme, and good,"[160] and he argued carefully that such a being does not exist. To identify God with the Universe—all that exists —is to deny that He is a person; and to treat the Universe as a person would be to deny the reality of finite persons, since no person can be part of another person.[161] To suppose that God is but part of the Universe is to undermine both his alleged primacy of being and his privileged role as creator or governor of the Universe. In regard to ultimate existence, God cannot be more primary than the finite selves. This consideration affects the conception of God as creator. As McTaggart declared, ". . . the natures of primary parts are ultimate facts. It would not, I think, be possible to combine this co-equal primacy of the selves with such predominance of one self as would be involved in creation."[162] To conceive God as Designer or as Controlling Agent in the Universe, just as to conceive Him as Creator requires the concept of causation, and causation, which brings an effect into existence, involves time. But time is unreal. Therefore, God can neither create nor govern the Universe.[163]

The doctrine of the unreality of time, favored among absolute idealists, has received its most trenchant formulation in the philosophy of McTaggart.[164] It is useful here to consider McTaggart's theory. Time, he pointed out, has three determinations: Past, Present, and Future; but these determinations are incompatible. "Every event must be one or the other, but no event can be more than one."[165] This exclusiveness is essential to change and to time, "for the only change we can get is from future to present, and from present to past."[166] Despite the incompatibility of these determinations, however, "every event has them all."[167] McTaggart entertained the strategy of employing the tenses of verbs to remove the contradiction of ascribing simultaneously the three temporal determinations to an event. Accordingly, it is said that an event *is* present, *will be* past, and *has been* future, or it *is* past and *has been* future and present, or again it *is* future and *will be* present and past. But this strategy, according to McTaggart, will not do. An event, he held, is a particular X with a character Y. To say that X has been Y is to assert X to be Y at a moment of past time; to say that X will be Y is to assert X to be Y at a moment of future time; and to say that X is Y is to assert X to be Y at a moment of present time. "But every moment, like every event, is both past, present, and future. And so a similiar difficulty arises."[168] If an event is present, "there is no moment of past time at which it is past. But the moments of future time, in which it is past, are equally moments of past time, in which it cannot be past."[169] And so on. Hence time and temporal determinations are self-contradictory. What is self-contradictory is unreal. Therefore, McTaggart concluded, time is unreal.[170]

To return now to McTaggart's position on the existence of God, it should be clear that he adopted atheism. "There can be no being," he insisted, "who is a God, or who is anything resembling a God that the name would not be very deceptive."[171] Despite his atheism, however, McTaggart upheld the immortality of the finite self. He wrote: "To regard ourselves as substances which are, but which cease to be, is erroneous. To regard ourselves as substances which are, and which do not cease to be, is correct."[172] Absolute idealism took, in McTaggart's philosophy, an emphatically personalistic turn. For him, eternal selves journey through a multiplicity of lives, lives caught up in error and the illusions of temporality, but destined ultimately to attain the fullness of eternal being. And the nature of this fullness of eternal being in which eternal life resides is, he believed, love—"passionate, all-absorbing, all-consuming love."[173]

RECENT DEVELOPMENTS

Absolute idealism, which may well claim to be the highest expression of idealism as a speculative philosophy, has moved, as if compelled by an internal dialectic, from early monistic emphases to pluralistic interpretations verging on monadism. In its heyday the Absolute was esteemed not only as a logical and cosmic whole but as a value whole as well. As idealism entered the twentieth century, however, the two sides of the Absolute began to tear apart. William Ernest Hocking (1873–1966) carried on in the tradition of Josiah Royce, but he had been affected by William James, too. Adopting the pragmatic demand that concepts yield their meaning in the concrete terms of human experience, Hocking sought to work out the meaning of the Absolute as God in human experience. His case for Absolute idealism rested ultimately on the values of religious experience. Wilbur Marshall Urban (1873–1952) was still more explicit on the connection between Absolute idealism and values. After Urban, the case for Absolute idealism has been so altered that the very term "Absolute" disappears and the term "idealism" is replaced by the phrase "philosophia perennis." In stressing the valuational aspect of Absolute idealism, thinkers like Hocking and Urban reveal greater sensitivity to religious and moral values than to the requirements of speculative metaphysics in the intellectual atmosphere of the twentieth century. Advances in the natural sciences and realism and analysis in contemporary philosophy have constituted new challenges for Absolute idealists, most of whom have abandoned the label. John Elof Boodin (1869–1950) proposed a cosmic idealism within its framework; he sought to assimilate the teachings of the sciences. Boodin's kind of philosophical cosmology, in turn, has been absorbed and perfected in the process philosophy of A. N. Whitehead. In more disciplined fashion Errol Harris has restated fundamental theses of Absolute idealism when he revived the case for holistic concepts in natural science by summing up and interpreting a vast array of recently acquired evidence. Brand Blanshard, who prefers to call his philosophy "rationalism" instead of "idealism," has met the challenge of analysis. He has propounded a philosophy of mind in consonance with the thinking of the British Hegelians, Bradley and Bosanquet, and in the context of contemporary empirical psychology. He has also presented the world as a concrete universal, an intelligible whole of internally related parts, which reason strives to grasp in a coherent system of necessary judgments. But Blanshard has so far made it plain that, although he considers the world to be a logical whole, he does not regard it to be a moral (or valuational) whole.[174]

The dissolution of the Absolute, then, has marked recent idealism. The dissolution has been twofold: it is evident in the fissure between value and logic as indicative of two kinds of wholes which may be separate rather than integrated in the Absolute, and it is accentuated in the pulverization of the Absolute into a community of finite individuals. The long struggle in philosophy to grant finite individuals the status of reals, accompanied by the emasculation of the Absolute as regards values—in particular, the value of personality, has been paralleled by the rise of personalism.

Personalism is personal idealism; it is pluralistic and affirms that reality is composed of many persons—God and finite selves. Although personalism may be traced back to Leibniz, it came into its own in the nineteenth and twentieth centuries. Rudolf Hermann Lotze (1817–1881) in Germany, Charles Bernard Renouvier (1815–1903) in France, and F. C. S. Schiller (1864–1937) in England were personalists. In America, the leading personalists were Borden Parker Bowne (1847–1910), George Holmes Howison (1834–1916), Edgar Sheffield Brightman (1884–1953), and Ralph Tyler Flewelling (1871–1960) Today the leading exponents of personalism are W. H. Werkmeister and Peter Bertocci.

From the standpoint of speculative metaphysics, Brightman's thought illustrates personalism at its best.[175] Brightman defined metaphysics as "the mind's effort to view experience as a living whole";[176] consequently, he adhered to Hegel's basic intent, although he departed sharply from Hegel's conclusions. Brightman's metaphysics consists of four realms: the realm of essences, the realm of nature, the realm of values, and the realm of persons. Of the four realms, that of persons is ontologically primary; for all realms are concretely grounded in personal experience. Brightman defined a person as "a unity of complex conscious changes, including all its experiences—its memories, its purposes, its values, its powers, its activities, and its experienced interactions with its environment."[177] His definition underscores not only consciousness and experience, but also change, value, activity. A person, moreover, is one among many. God is a person; you are a person; and so am I. God, of course, is the highest person, the best person; but He is not infinite or omnipotent. Like us, God is a finite person engaged in moral struggle with his environment. According to Brightman, therefore, personalism is a pluralistic idealism of creative process. It is primarily a practical and secondarily a theoretical philosophy.

The story of idealism as a speculative philosophy is by no means over, although it is not as glorious at present as it has been in the past. With the pluralistic monadism of Leibniz on one side and the monistic absolutism of Hegel on the other, idealism encompasses a genuine diversity, even opposition, of doctrines. In between these poles stand the empirical idealism of Berkeley and the transcendental idealism of Kant, both fundamentally epistemological, yet both fecund with implications concerning the nature of reality. Whatever their particular biases—theoretical, practical, religious, idealists have variously employed such terms as "monad," "consciousness," "spirit," "transcendental ego," "will," "Absolute," "Whole," "Individual," "concrete universal," "system," "person," and their usages have been permeated with mentalistic connotations. However idealists may have disagreed on other issues, they have agreed on one—that reality is essentially mind. This principle of the primacy of mind has been in the past and remains today a nucleal idea inspiring speculative thought.

VI

PROCESS PHILOSOPHY

Today the most widely accepted type of speculative philosophy in America is process philosophy. Natural scientists, social scientists, humanists, theologians, and men of practical affairs in business and government seem to acknowledge, in their conduct if not in their theories, the reality of change, and measure their efforts and their achievements in terms of adaptation to and control of change. For them at least flux is king. In recent decades the term "process" has come to denote a type of philosophy. In *Science and the Modern World,* Whitehead has proclaimed: "The reality is the process." [1] And the major work of Whitehead's bears the title, *Process and Reality*. Although Whitehead himself chose to label his system "the philosophy of organism," [2] it has more readily been dubbed "process philosophy," a term which has gained wide currency and now embraces a variety of thinkers under its umbrella.[3]

HERACLITUS

Despite its contemporaneity, process philosophy is quite ancient. In the nineteenth century the term "flux," taken from the Latin *fluxus* derived from the verb *fluere,* meaning "to flow," denoted in philosophy a continuous succession of changes of condition, composition, or substance. It was applied to the philosophy of Heraclitus (fl. 500 B.C.). One of Heraclitus' fragments reads: "Nature likes to hide." [4] Considering the aphoristic style of Heraclitus, who was dubbed the Obscure in antiquity, it may be said that Heraclitus' meaning also likes to hide. But it is clear that Heraclitus did assemble a following who adhered to the doctrine of flux. One of these followers, Cratylus of Athens (circa 450–500 B.C.), inspired Plato to write a dialogue of the same name. Indeed, Plato originated, in *Cratylus,* the phrase that is the hallmark of process philosophy: πάντα ῥεί, "everything flows." Plato, of course, denigrated process philosophy when he inserted between the two words of its formula the phrase "like leaky pots."[5]

Heraclitus' advocacy of process philosophy is expressed in the obscure oracular aphorisms which are, in fragmentary form, his legacy. A selection of these aphorisms will serve to display his thought.

Fragment 49a: "In the same river, we both step and do not step, we are and we are not."

Fragment 91: "It is not possible to step twice in the same river."[6]

By Fragment 91, Heraclitus equated reality with a river which forever flows; flowing, reality changes, and changing, it ceases to be and becomes another. The flux, the process, the becoming, is neither being nor not-being, but a union of these opposites. Fragment 49a states Heraclitus' vision of the flux as being and not-being. Although the river remains self-same for the moment, retains its identity for a duration no matter how minute, the acting subject—stepping, not-stepping—is himself caught up in the flux; he ceases to be and becomes another before his action is completed. Extending Heraclitus' thought, Cratylus asserted that it is not possible to step once in the same river.

While Heraclitus compared reality to the flow of a river, he also interpreted its composition in terms of one of the four elements—fire.

Fragment 31: "The changes of fire: first, sea; and of sea, half is earth and half fiery water-spout. . . . Earth is liquified into sea."

Fragment 76: "Fire lives the death of earth, and air lives the death of fire; water lives the death of air, earth that of water."[7]

According to one line of interpretation, backed by the authority of Aristotle, Heraclitus is considered to have been a natural philosopher who, like the Milesians, sought to explain the plurality of phenomena as produced from a single basic element, and who selected fire as the basic element. Against this interpretation, however, recent scholarship takes its stand.[8] Heraclitus nowhere spoke of fire as a primary element from which other elements are derived. Rather he seems to have regarded fire as a standard by which all other elements and their transformations are measured. Thus he writes:

Fragment 66: "Fire, having come upon them, will judge and seize upon (condemn) all things."

Fragment 90: "There is an exchange: all things for Fire and Fire for all things, like goods for gold and gold for goods."[9]

In having chosen fire to serve as the standard of all things, Heraclitus made two points. First, he underscored the conception of reality as flux, since fire is constantly changing, thriving on the fuel it consumes. Second, he gave expression to the centrality of conflict in the flux, since fire best symbolizes conflict and opposition. As Heraclitus said:

Fragment 64: "The thunder-bolt (i.e. Fire) steers the universe."

Fragment 30: "The world was ever and is and shall be ever-living fire. . . ."[10]

The Heraclitean conception of the flux as a unity of opposites is not that of a bland harmony in which opposites are muted; instead, it projects a dynamic equilibrium made possible only because opposites oppose each other. For Heraclitus, conflict, war, is at the heart of reality, as several fragments proclaim.

Fragment 80: "One should know that war is general (*universal*) and jurisdiction is strife, and everything comes about by way of strife and necessity."

Fragment 53: "War is both king of all and father of all. . . ."

Fragment 8: "That which is in opposition is in concert, and from things that differ comes the most beautiful harmony."

Fragment 51: "They do not understand how that which differs with itself is in agreement: harmony consists of

> opposing tension, like that of the bow and the lyre."[11]

And in one fragment Heraclitus even suggested that the opposites which constitute the harmony by being opposites are also themselves identical.

> Fragment 60: "The way up and down is one and the same."[12]

W. K. C. Guthrie, who has made better sense of pre-Socratic philosophy than any of his predecessors, has summed up Heraclitus' thought in three principles: 1) that the harmony is of opposites, 2) that everything is in continuous motion and change, and 3) that the world is an ever-living Fire. These three principles, according to Guthrie, are focalized in the Heraclitean doctrine of the *logos*.[13] By declaration Heraclitus presented his works as the explanation of the logos. Universal law is the logos—"that which is common (*to all*)." This law, or truth, is not known to the majority of men; but it has been revealed to Heraclitus, and it is objective. As Heraclitus proclaimed:

> Fragment 1: "The Law (of the universe) is as here explained; but men are always incapable of understanding it, both before they hear it, and when they have heard it for the first time. For though all things come into being in accordance with this Law, men seem as if they had never met with it, when they meet with words (*theories*) and actions (*processes*) such as I expound, separating each thing according to its nature and explaining how it is made. As for the rest of mankind, they are unaware of what they are doing after they wake, just as they forget what they did while asleep."[14]

From Heraclitus' standpoint, the dumb majority triumphed over the *logos* in antiquity. Stoicism of course did incorporate the Heraclitean cosmology within its own philosophy, but Stoicism was primarily a practical tradition, the speculative disciplines of metaphysics and cosmology serving as appendages to its ethics and politics. Plato and Aristotle spoke for the speculative traditions. Plato found the flux philosophy untenable; indeed, he contended that it could be neither thought nor expressed. Thought requires stable concepts, and if everything flows, then thought, finding no static resting points upon which it can rest in the ongoing process, is impossible. Similarly, language consists of words which name things, and to be useful in communication, it demands that the things it names remain the same at least until the communication is completed; but this demand cannot be met if the flux is overwhelming. The thinker, before his thought is finished, would cease to be, and so would the object of thought. The subject of a statement would pass away before the predicate could be articulated. Plato adopted the Heraclitean doctrine of flux, but he restricted its application to the world of changing sensible particulars, erecting above this world another world of immutable intelligible universals. Aristotle followed in the footsteps of Plato in rejecting the flux philosophy. Aristotle formulated the law of thought known as the principle of non-contradiction. According to this principle, a subject cannot be said to have and to have not the same predicate in the same respect at the same time. The Heraclitean flux, conceived as a unity of opposites verging on identity, violates the principle. In fact, the principle itself would have to be both true and false. But as Aristotle would contend, to deny the principle significantly would involve tacit assumption of it, since if the principle is said to be false, then the principle cannot be said to be true in the same respect at the same time. And if the principle is true, it follows that flux to the point of identifying opposites cannot be thought or said. Aristotle, of course, refrained from following Plato with regard to the status of universals. For Aristotle, the forms of natural kinds are the specific essences that exist in the particular organisms. The immutable intelligible world that exists above nature is, according to Aristotle, populated with those pure acts or intelligible forms called the separate and unmoved movers.

Process came to be seen as an attribute of substance, rather than as a category of equal or superior status. Thus the Stoics, who revived the Heraclitean philosophy of flux, also resurrected a doctrine of categories, according to which material substance is first, and the three other categories are essential qualities, accidental qualities, and relations. Flux per se made little sense to thinkers except as the confined changes substance undergoes. It was not until the nineteenth century that flux itself again took precedence over enduring substance or static structure in the theories of philosophers. At first the recognition of the primacy of process occurred within the context of the substance philosophies themselves. Both dialectical materialism and dialectical idealism, as noted in Chapters IV and V, acknowledge the fundamental reality of change. Quite probably the political revolutions of the eighteenth century had prepared the intellectual atmosphere for the acceptance of change as the ground of new philosophies. But the direct stimulus to the rise of process philosophy was the acceptance of the theory of biological evolution in the nineteenth century as a scientific principle of the first magnitude.

EVOLUTION

The idea of evolution had a long and chequered career before it became scientifically respectable. As far back as Anaximander in the fifth century B.C. it had been suggested that the higher life-forms had originated in and evolved from more primitive forms.

A comprehensive theory of evolution presented in the context of biological science had, however, to wait upon the work of Chevalier de Lamarck (1744–1829). In the first place, Lamarck was a Deist. He believed that God created Nature; and he conceived Nature as a system of different material beings caught up in change subject to mechanical, natural laws. Science, then, could study Nature without any reference to God. Geological and paleontological evidence, moreover, had convinced Lamarck that the earth had existed for an immense period of time, and that the forms of animal life had undergone many changes. The fixity of the species was, he held, due to man's limited temporal perspective, not to any inherent stability. All species evolve, as individual organisms adapt to their environment. Having apprehended the basic fact of evolution, Lamarck nevertheless failed to grasp it in a coherently unified theory. He treated plants and animals as two independent lines of organic evolution which spring from two distinct types of spontaneous generation; and he divided the animal kingdom into two main classes: those animals that lack feeling; and those animals with feelings. To adapt to their environment, animals acquire habits and organs. Animals with feelings not only employ existing organs to satisfy felt needs; they also generate new organs when their needs are pressing and continuing. These newly generated organs, acquired through the efforts of individual organisms, are transmitted to the offspring. Lamarck's theory of evolution, initially devoid of systematic coherence, founders at last on the scientific evidence. Scientific research, far from confirming the Lamarckian hypothesis of the inheritance of acquired characteristics, has contradicted it. Yet credit is due Lamarck for having aroused researchers in the life sciences to seek the laws of change in the organic world.

Darwin succeeded where Lamarck, after pointing the way, had failed. He apprehended that all life-forms fall under the theory of evolution; and he backed his position with the weightiest masses of empirical evidence available. Thus Darwin's *Origin of Species* (1859) gave the theory of evolution scientific credibility. Of the three mechanisms that produce evolution: natural selection, sexual selection, and the inheritance of acquired characteristics, Darwin stressed the first. According to the theory of natural selection, variations in the species persist when these variations favor the survival of the organisms as they struggle with their environment; variations which are unfavorable disappear with the perishing of the organism.

This theory logically provokes several grave scientific and speculative questions. What causes the variations? Are they, as Darwin held, the products of mechanical causes? Or, to consider the suggestion of C. S. Peirce, are they random occurrences, evidence of a spontaneity or objective chance in nature? As regards the environment, is it indifferent to the organisms' efforts? Or is it hostile, imposing an authentic struggle for existence? Or does it cooperate, lending support to the organisms' endeavors? Indeed, is either the organism or the environment something which can be sharply distinguished from the other? As regards the change in the environment which stimulates the activity of the organism, is the change gradual? Is it sudden, and cataclysmic? Is it a mixture? Does evolution extend beyond the domain of living things to physical nature? Is it compatible in the physical world with the second law of thermodynamics? For while evolution projects the advancing diversification of life-forms, the second law of thermodynamics projects a dissipation of usable energy leading to a static deathlike state throughout the physical world. Is evolution applicable to values and social organization? Does it sift out and preserve the best? Or does it eliminate the morally superior? Or it is wholly indifferent to questions of values? Is man, his mind and all his values, irrevocably caught up in purely natural processes, having neither supernatural origin nor supernatural destiny?

The "influence of Darwin on philosophy" has been neatly assessed by John Dewey in a well-known essay by that title.[15] The very conjunction of the terms "origin" and "species" is, as Dewey noted, startling. For the Latin term "species," translated from the Greek term rendered "form" in English, denotes an immutable character, whereas the term "origin" signifies a beginning, a coming into being. To hold that species become, as the title of Darwin's famous book affirms, is to undermine the classic conception of a static nature where individual entities undergo extremely restricted change, directed by an end constitutive of the individual's very form, and where the forms, the species, are themselves fixed and eternal. In place of the concept of static nature, which restricts change to the individual's cycle of being born and passing away, there is derived from Darwin's theory the concept of an all-embracing change which, instead of being mere flux devoid of stable structure, is itself the source of all stable forms, however transient, and creates in the processes the norms which guide it, however fragmentarily. Mind and knowledge, caught up in the changing nature, are naturalized as instruments which enable the organism, not to seek eternal truth, but to cope with the ongoing problems of the everyday world. Knowledge, no longer regarded an abstract rational process with timeless being as its object, is seen to be a practical, experimental activity in which a highly developed organism engages to heighten its prospects of success in its struggle with its environment. Nature, ridden of the teleology of which the doctrine of fixed species was a part, is treated as a plastic subject-matter which invited men to utilize it for his own ends. Thus, according to Dewey, man as an active knowing being gains a freedom which the classic view had denied him. Dewey plainly exploited the pragmatist implications of Darwin's theory.

SPENCER

It would be wrong to suppose that Darwin's influence on philosophy was confined to the pragmatist development. Many philosophers, including Darwin's own contemporaries, appreciated the opportunities for systematic philosophical speculation afforded by the theory of evolution. Herbert Spencer (1820–1903) was the first thinker to consider evolution to be the key to a complete system of philosophy, embracing knowledge and the known. That Spencer simply expanded an otherwise sound scientific principle into a total and less sound philosophy has sometimes been charged. No doubt, Spencer's own reputation as a philosopher was inflated by the vogue of Darwin's scientific achievement.

The relationship of Spencer to Darwin merits passing comment. Although it is often held that Spencer derived his theory from Darwin, the evidence reveals that he came to the principle of evolution before the publication of Darwin's work. As a youth of twenty, Spencer, through a study of Lyell's *Principles of Geology,* which contains arguments against Lamarck, came to "a partial acceptance of Lamarck's view."[16] Thus the thesis that life conforms to a law of development according to which individual and social constitutions progressively adapt to environmental conditions was implicit in Spencer's earliest writings; it was stated with definiteness and consistency in *Social Statics* (1850). This thesis, called the development hypothesis, the law of evolution, and the law of progress, so excited Spencer's imagination that in January 1858 he projected, on its basis, a complete system of philosophy. Of Darwin's *Origin of Species,* Spencer said: "That reading it gave me great satisfaction may be safely inferred. Whether there was any set-off to this great satisfaction, I cannot now say; for I have quite forgotten the ideas and feelings I had." [17] Darwin did succeed, according to Spencer's own admission, in overturning Spencer's Lamarckian conviction that the inheritance of functionally produced modifications is the sole cause of organic evolution. Despite the annoyance of having one of his own beliefs overthrown, Spencer was by self-admission, "overwhelmed in the gratification . . . [he] felt at seeing the theory of evolution justified. To have the theory of organic evolution justified, was of course to get further support for that theory of evolution at large with which all . . . [his] conceptions were bound up." [18]

Spencer named his system "the synthetic philosophy." Within his system Spencer sought to include all scientific data; he also sought to employ the scientific method. Philosophy Spencer esteemed the widest system of knowledge. He declared: "Knowledge of the lowest kind is *un-unified* knowledge; Science is *partially-unified* knowledge; Philosophy is *completely-unified* knowledge." [19] As parts of the system he presented volumes on metaphysics, biology, psychology, sociology, and ethics. *First Principles* (1862) presents the basic theses of Spencer's metaphysics. It introduces the system of synthetic philosophy; and it is divided into two parts: Part I treats "The Unknowable," Part II "The Knowable."

In Part I, Spencer examined the conflict of religion and science as it appeared in nineteenth-century discussions. His aim was to find the grounds of reconciliation. Religions concur, he held, in the conviction that "the existence of the world with all it contains and all that surrounds it, is a mystery calling for interpretation"—that, in other words, "the Power which the Universe manifests to us is inscrutable." [20] Science employs the basic categories of Space, Time, Motion, Matter, Consciousness, but it, too, recognizes the incomprehensible. As Spencer said, "Ultimate Scientific Ideas are all representations of realities that cannot be comprehended." [21] Building on the philosophical conceptions of William Hamilton (1788–1856) and Henry Mansel (1820–1871), Spencer maintained that all knowledge is relative and, further, that the relativity of knowledge implies the existence of the non-relative. He wrote: "From the necessity of thinking in relation, it follows that the Relative is itself inconceivable, except as related to a real non-relative. Unless a real Non-relative or Absolute be postulated, the Relative itself becomes absolute, and so brings the argument to a contradiction."[22] The inscrutable power to which religions lead and the unknowable Absolute which science presupposes are, according to Spencer, identical. The reconciliation of science and religion centers on the fact that they both acknowledge the Unknowable Absolute.

The agnosticism of Part I of *First Principles* monopolized the attention of readers and critics, imparting a false emphasis to Spencer's thought and inducing the neglect of Part II, a neglect he deeply regretted. For, as Spencer later remarked in his *Autobiography,* he had written Part I merely to avoid the possible charge of being pure materialist. He explained:

> My expectation was that having duly recognized this repudiation of materialism, joined with the assertion that any explanation which may be reached of the order of phenomena as manifested to us throughout the Universe, must leave the Ultimate Mystery unsolved, readers, and by implication critics, would go on to consider the explanation proposed. To me it seemed manifest that the essential part of the book—the doctrine of Evolution—may be held without affirming any metaphysical or theological beliefs.[23]

In Part II, Spencer treated the knowable. The manifestations of the Unknowable, presented in Part I as the common point on which science and religion converge, make up the subject-matter of knowledge; these manifestations are termed "phenomena" or "appearances." It might be inferred that the Unknowable exclusively may be called "reality"; but this inference would be hasty and misleading. "By reality," Spencer said, "we mean *persistence* in consciousness. . . . The real, as we conceive it, is distinguished solely by the test of persistence."[24] Hence reality is found in the manifestations of the Unknowable, in phenomena or appearances. These phenomena are the data of science and philosophy. While science deals with specialized data, philosophy, which seeks the most general and inclusive system of knowledge, concentrates on those most universal data which promise the greatest measure of cohesion between the parts of knowledge.

The data of philosophy are the ultimate scientific ideas: space, time, matter, motion, and force. Spencer attempted to clarify each of these ideas construed as manifestations of what is intrinsically Unknowable. "Our consciousness of Space," he wrote, "is a consciousness of co-existent positions."[25] Similarly, our consciousness of Time is a consciousness of sequence. As Spencer said: "The abstract of all sequences is Time. The abstract of all co-existence is Space."[26] The idea of Matter is "that of coexistent positions that offer resistance."[27] The idea of Motion involves Space, Time, and Matter: for Motion is "a something perceived; a series of positions occupied by it in succession; and a group of co-existent positions united in thought with the successive ones."[28] For Spencer the most fundamental scientific idea is that of Force; Spencer called it "the ultimate of ultimates."[29] From our experiences of Force all our other basic ideas are built up. Spencer's empirical method traces the origin of our ideas of Space, Time, Matter, and Motion, back to "the primordial experiences of Force."[30] Each of these ideas, of course, is the effect of a Cause which is Unknowable. As Spencer explained: "Force, as we know it, can be regarded only as a conditioned effect of the Unconditioned Cause—as the relative reality indicating to us an Absolute Reality by which it is immediately produced."[31]

After examining the ultimate scientific ideas, Spencer considered the scientific truths which transcend the limits of the particular sciences and which qualify as topics of philosophy because of their generality. These truths express the indestructiblity of matter, the continuity of motion, the persistence of force, and the persistence of relations among forces. These truths, however, do not furnish—separately or jointly—"an idea of the Cosmos: meaning by that word the totality of the manifestations of the Unknowable."[32] Spencer imputed their failure to do so to their analytical character. Whereas the fundamental scientific truths are analytical, breaking the phenomena down into the component elements, philosophy for Spencer seeks as the ultimate interpretation of the Cosmos "a universal synthesis."[33] Philosophy seeks to display not the components of phenomena but the law of the composition. Representing the synthesis, this law is, Spencer reasoned, "the law of the continuous redistribution of matter and motion."[34]

Spencer identified the law of synthesis with the universal principle of evolution. His formula of this principle is noteworthy: *"Evolution is an integration of matter and concomitant dissipation of motion; during which the matter passes from an indefinite, incoherent homogeneity to a definite coherent homogeneity; and during which the retained motion undergoes a parallel transformation."*[35]

Evolution is evident in the facts at every level of existence: at the physico-chemical level, in the astronomical cosmos, in the variety of life-forms, in human psychology, and in society. The special sciences then treat the data which instantiate the law of evolution. But Spencer was not content simply to record the particulars of evolution; he wanted to present a full-scale interpretation. The crux of his interpretation consists in the thesis that "the phenomena of Evolution have to be deduced from the Persistence of Force."[36] Having defined Evolution in terms of matter and motion and having deduced it from the law of the persistence of force, Spencer subordinated it to the mechanical causation that prevails in the subject-matter studied by the science of physics.

Spencer's bias in physics, where force is paramount, is manifest in other features of his elucidation of evolution. He regarded evolution as a process whose elements are physical aggregates, physical motions, physical forces. The phases of evolution correlate with the phases of a dynamic physical system: 1) the instability of the homogeneous, 2) the multiplication of effects, 3) segregation, and 4) equilibration. Here, too, Spencer explained by resorting to the terms of physical aggregates, physical motions, physical forces. Evolution begins because of the condition Spencer named "the instability of the homogeneous." Instability resides in "the fact that the several parts of any homogeneous aggregate are exposed to different forces—forces which differ either in kind or amount; and are of necessity differently modified." [37] This condition, furthermore, is treated as a corollary of the Persistence of Force. Evolution continues through a process which Spencer called "the multiplication of effects." Acted upon by a given force, the homogeneous aggregate erupts into a multiplicity of effects, each fragment differing from the others and each a vehicle of force with a different quantity of direction. The homogeneous therefore becomes heterogeneous, the uniform multiform. The heterogeneity, the multiform, is not chaotic, however; it is orderly, its original indefiniteness rendered definite. For within the multiplicity, like parts collect the like parts so that groupings occur. At this stage evolution displays a phase in the process which Spencer called "segregation." Here, too, "the cause of that local integration which accompanies local differentiation—that gradually completed segregation of like units into a group, distinctly separated from neighbouring groups which are severally made up of other kinds of units" is found to consist in the way force operates.[38] Force exerts similar action on similar things, dissimilar action on dissimilar things, so that things as parts of aggregates separate. This process of separation, or segregation, would terminate in utter disintegration, were it not for that phase of evolution which Spencer called "equilibration." As Spencer amplified: "That universal co-existence of antagonist forces which . . . necessitates the universality of rhythm, and which . . . necessitates the decomposition of every force into divergent forces, at the same time necessitates the ultimate establishment of a balance. Every motion, being motion under resistance, is continually suffering deductions; and these unceasing deductions finally result in the cessation of the motion." [39]

When Spencer's philosophy is characterized as a process philosophy, or more strictly a philosophy of evolution, two things should be kept in mind: first, that the conception of process is itself rooted in a prior reality—namely, physical nature conceived as a mechanical system; and second, that the ultimate principle for Spencer is the principle of evolution *and* dissolution. Students and critics of Spencer's thought tend especially to neglect the second point, partly perhaps because Spencer himself did not dwell on dissolution since it lacked the various aspects of evolution which interested him. Nevertheless, Spencer did stress the significance of dissolution. He wrote:

> When Evolution has run its course—when an aggregate has reached that equilibrium in which its changes end, it therefore remains subject to all actions in its environment which may increase the quantity of motion it contains, and which in course of time are sure, either slowly or suddenly, to give its parts such excess of motion as will cause disintegration. According as its size, its nature, and its conditions determine, its dissolution may come quickly or may be indefinitely delayed—may occur in a few days or may be postponed for billions of years. But exposed as it is to the contingencies not simply of its immediate neighbourhood but of a Universe everywhere in motion, the time must at last come when, either alone or in company with surrounding aggregates, it has its parts dispersed.[40]

Dissolution, Spencer conceded, is the fate not only of all aggregates on the Earth but also of the Earth itself and the stars. However, whether dissolution is the fate of our entire Sidereal System, is a question which Spencer refrained from answering. He confessed: "While inferring that in many parts of the visible universe dissolution is following evolution, and that throughout these regions evolution will presently recommence, the question whether there is an alternation of evolution and dissolution in the totality of things is one which must be left unanswered as beyond the reach of human intelligence." [41]

BERGSON

Spencer's synthetic philosophy, which seemed to be the latest word in the scientific understanding of the cosmos, exerted a broad influence over nineteenth-century thought. Among the brilliant youths who fell under its spell was Henri Bergson. In the beginning, Bergson was committed to Spencer's point of view. Later, however, he noted Spencer's philosophy a failure on account of "the usual device of the Spencerian method," a device which "consists in reconstructing evolutions with fragments of the evolved."[42] In the early years, when Bergson pored over Spencer's books, he also studied the mathematics of natural science. This mix of preoccupations led him to abandon Spencer and to discover the new principle which was to inspire the philosophy of creative evolution. Mathematics, noted Bergson, could not express real time, for mathematics involves the superposition and/or juxtaposition of its elements, while real time flows. The question arose: What is real time? To find an answer, Bergson inspected consciousness, examining its immediate data. There, at last, he found "pure unadulterated inner continuity, continuity which was neither unity nor multiplicity, and which did not fit into any of our categories of thought."[43] "I was absorbed," he said, "by the vision of duration."[44]

Bergson's vision of duration rescued the principle of evolution from Spencer's mechanistic interpretation, and prepared the way for a metaphysics of creative process, of freedom, of novelty. The scientific deterministic materialism toward which the philosophy of evolution had edged in the thought of Spencer and to which it had collapsed in that of Haeckel was once and for all pierced by the realization that evolution could have a different, a more liberating import. Bergson was not alone in his discovery. Charles Sanders Peirce and William James moved in Bergson's direction.

Peirce—Evolution, according to Peirce, displays itself in three types: (1) *tychasm,* evolution by fortuitous chance; 2) *anancasm,* evolution by mechanical necessity; and 3) *agapasm,* evolution by creative love.[45] Peirce, moreover, favored *agapasm* as the climactic and synthesizing mode of evolution. Guided by this interpretation of evolution, he inferred from the facts and theories of all the special sciences a general theory of the cosmos. The correct "Cosmogonic Philosophy," Peirce speculated,

> would suppose that in the beginning—indefinitely remote—there was a chaos of impersonalized feeling, which being without connection or regularity would properly be without existence. This feeling, sporting here and there in pure arbitrariness, would have started the germ of a generalizing tendency. Its other sportings would be evanescent, but

> this would have a growing virtue. Thus, the tendency to habit would be started: and from this, with other principles of evolution, all the regularities of the universe would be evolved. At any time, however, an element of pure chance survives and will remain until the world becomes an absolutely perfect, rational, and symmetrical system, in which mind is at last crystallized in the infinitely distant future.[46]

James—Peirce, who failed to win a wide audience for his views, nevertheless influenced the more popular William James. It is well known that James thought, perhaps wrongly, that he had derived the doctrine of pragmatism from Peirce. Less well known is the fact that James, when he turned his attention to the problem of speculative metaphysics in *A Pluralistic Universe,* cited and elucidated in a separate appendix the basic principles of Peirce's cosmogonic philosophy, explicitly as an expression of the new philosophy of process and creativity that was in the making in the early twentieth century.[47] Peirce, of course, had fallen short of a systematic presentation of his views; James, too, had failed in this respect. In contrast, Bergson, upon whom James lavished praise,[48] succeeded in furnishing a comprehensive rationale for the philosophy of creative process.

Bergsonian Duration—The key to Bergson's philosophy is the concept of real time, or duration. What did Bergson mean by duration? To answer this question, it is helpful to consider Bergson's main points about duration: first, it is qualitative and intensive, rather than quantitative and extensive; second, it is process; third, it is continuous; fourth, it is cumulative; fifth, it is creative; and sixth, it is authentic existence. Each of these points needs clarification.

First, duration is intensive rather than extensive, qualitative rather than quantitative. In his first book, *Time and Free Will* (1885), Bergson defined duration in the context of the qualitative flux of intensive consciousness: "the duration in which it [a feeling] develops is a duration whose elements permeate one another."[49] A melody illustrates pure duration, "each [moment] permeating the other and organizing themselves like the notes of a tune, so as to form what we shall call a continuous or qualitative multiplicity with no resemblance to number."[50] As Bergson said, "We can thus conceive succession without distinction, and think of it as a mutual penetration, an interconnexion and organization of elements, each one of which represents the whole, and cannot be distinguished or isolated from it except by abstract thought."[51] Time is marked off from Space by virtue of this difference: Time is a qualitative fusion of heterogeneous moments, whereas Space is a homogeneous field in which elements are juxtaposed in external relatedness. Mathematical time is a fiction which results when Space, the form of external phenomena, is applied to consciousness; it is "an unbounded and homogeneous medium [which] is nothing but the ghost of space haunting the reflective consciousness."[52] Real time, on the other hand, is properly the succession of qualitatively heterogeneous psychical states, all melting together in a unity which nonetheless discloses intensive multiplicity. It is "a real duration, the heterogeneous moments of which permeate one another."[53]

Second, duration is process, change, becoming. Here, indeed, Bergson's thought emerges as process philosophy *par excellence.* His works are thronged with passages in which reality is equated with real time or duration, and real time or duration is equated with change. Introspection of consciousness had detected "the element of real time" because, according to Bergson, "time is just the stuff it [consciousness] is made of."[54] Bergson, at least in his early writings, seemed to maintain an extreme dualism, with duration the essence of consciousness and space that of matter. He wrote: "Outside us, mutual externality without succession; within us, succession without externality."[55] Later, however, he allowed that "the material universe itself, defined as a totality of images, is a kind of consciousness . . . ,"[56] and attributed to it qualities, each of which "consists of a succession of elementary movements."[57] In his mature system, *Creative Evolution,* Bergson declared: "The flux of time is the reality itself, and the things which we study are the things which flow."[58]

The equation of reality with process rules out the suppositions that there are things which undergo and make change or that there is a substrate underlying change. "There are changes, but there are underneath the change no things which change: change has no need of a support. There are movements, but there is no inert or invariable object which moves: movement does not imply a mobile." [59] Stable things emerge when intelligence and perception, bent on practical ends, attend to the flux and segregate parts of it, grouping qualities together into quasi-permanent entities upon which action may be exerted. Whereas all things actually blend together in one field of diversified becoming, man tends to take snapshots of the flux, to combine and order segments of it, and so to erect a world of things more stable than the flux.

Third, duration is continuous. The past exists in the present, as does the present in the future. Bergson wrote:

> What I call "my present" has one foot in my past and another in my future. In my past, first, because "the moment in which I am speaking is already far from me"; in my future, next, because this moment is impending over the future: it is to the future that I am tending, and could I fix this indivisible present, this infinitesimal element of the curve of time, it is the direction of the future that it would indicate.[60]

Accordingly, the moments of time are "saddle-backs," epochal quanta, and the razor-edge present is specious. The continuity of time, of change, of reality, moreover, is the basis of Bergson's solution of Zeno's famous paradoxes of motion. The motions of bodies are observed as real; each motion constitutes a duration; and each duration is an indivisible continuity of change. Zeno's paradoxes depend upon the division of motion into discrete units; they are resolved once it is recognized that "every movement, inasmuch as it is a passage from rest to rest, is absolutely indivisible." [61]

Fourth, duration is cumulative. The cumulativeness of duration is implicated in its continuity. At first this aspect of duration is expressed as a paradox: change and permanence are one. Many statements, distributed throughout Bergson's works, articulate the paradox: "A moving continuity is given to us, in which everything changes and yet remains." [62] "There is no essential difference between passing from one state to another and persisting in the same state." [63] The paradox is, of course, two-sided. On one side, it simply means that "the permanence of substance" is "a continuity of change." [64] That is to say, a process which is continuous is what is marked off as a thing. On the other side, it signifies that duration itself is tantamount to enduring. Thus, for example, "the universe *endures*," [65] or "the organism which lives is a thing that *endures*." [66] In any case, the cumulativeness of duration involves the prolongation of the past into the present. This prolongation is the work of memory, which has a cosmic—in addition to a biological and psychological—function. As Bergson said, "There is no consciousness without memory, no continuation of a state without the addition, in the present feeling, of the memory of past moments. . . . Inner duration is the continuous life of a memory which prolongs the past with the present." [67] Nothing that happens is forgotten or lost. "Duration is the continuous progress of the past which gnaws into the future and which swells as it advances." [68]

Fifth, duration is creative. "Time," said Bergson, "is what is happening, and more than that, it is what causes everything to happen." [69] Real time, or duration, is in the first place causally efficacious. Its efficacy is most directly operative in consciousness, where the passage of time makes radical differences in the quality of life. Even an act repeated or an event remembered differs from the original because of the flow of time. Less obviously but no less definitely time makes a causal difference in physical nature. Although, for example, it is possible to predict some physical events years in advance—as in astronomy, still the time must transpire before the events can occur. The efficacy of duration is most conspicuous in biology. For in life, there is not merely the consideration that maturation, which merely takes time, is crucial. There is the further consideration that evolution prevails among the life-forms.

Evolution, according to Bergson, implies "a real persistence of the past in the present, a duration which is, as it were, a hyphen, a connecting link." [70] Unless the past is prolonged by the preservation of its gains into existing organic forms, evolutionary advance would be impossible. "Duration," Bergson promised, "will be revealed as it really is—unceasing creation, the uninterrupted up-surge of novelty." [71] Evolution, then, is creative; its principle is the celebrated *élan vital,* the vital impulse. Bergson has compared the evolution of life-forms to the explosion of a rocket; the fire shooting up and out is life, and the shell casing falling out and down in fragments is materiality.[72] Creativity pervades the continuity of becoming, evolving into a myriad of organic forms that populate nature. It is like a jet of steam which rises in the air until it condenses and falls down.[73] Creative evolution is the expression of this vital impulse, a cosmic duration, which pushes onward in novelty, its condensations crystallizing in the multifarious organic species. There is in Bergson's thought a dualism: the upward thrust of the vital impulse toward more bountiful and higher forms of life and the downward fall of rigid forms as materiality are counterposed. Bergson identified God with the creative process. God, he declared, "has nothing of the already made; He is unceasing life, action, freedom." [74]

Sixth, duration is authentic existence. Bergson, in the first paragraph of the first page of *Creative Evolution,* discussed existence. Like Descartes before him, Bergson held that "the existence of which we are most assured and which we know best is unquestionably our own, for every other object we have notions which may be considered external and superficial, whereas, of ourselves, our perception is internal and profound." [75] Upon an analogy between the forms of conscious existence and the world Bergson, like Whitehead after him, constructed a vast cosmology, construing the world in terms of the qualitative intensities of psychical life. For Bergson exploited the privileged position of internal perception to inquire into the nature of existence. What he discovered was the flow of duration: "we find that, for a conscious being, to exist is to change, to change is to mature, to mature is to go on creating oneself endlessly." [76]

The starting point of Bergson's philosophy in the psychological disclosure of the fundamental life of consciousness is emphatically clear in his first book. In *Time and Free Will* Bergson distinguished two forms of consciousness—the superficial self and the fundamental self. Whereas the former is caught up in homogeneous time and space, its psychical states separated and spread out, the latter exists as duration. "Pure duration is the form which the succession of our conscious states assumes when our ego lets itself *live,* when it refrains from separating its present state from its former states."[77] Duration is the form of "the deep-seated self which ponders and decides, which heats and blazes up, . . . a self whose states and changes permeate one another and undergo a deep alteration as soon as we separate them from one another in order to set them out in space."[78] Freedom is a basic feature of the fundamental self in its action; it is a certain shade of quality of the action itself,[79] and it "consists in a dynamic progress in which the self and its motives, like real living beings, are in a constant state of becoming. The self, infallible when it affirms its immediate experience, feels itself free and says so."[80] The fundamental self in its freedom cannot be expressed in language; it cannot be analyzed; its action cannot be spread out in Space or homogeneous time and explained. Determinism, according to Bergson, is the only philosophical doctrine which can be derived from attempts to explain human action in rational language. Denying freedom, determinism is untrue to the immediate experience of the fundamental self in the process of living and action. As Bergson said:

> Freedom is the relation of the concrete self to the act which it performs. This relation is indefinable, just because we *are* free. For we can analyze a thing, but not a process: we can break up extensity, but not duration.[81]

Hence, for Bergson, duration is the authentic existence of the self and freedom belongs to its essence.

Bergson's version of process philosophy was the dominant mode of philosophical thought in the early twentieth century. However, its distrust of reason and its reliance upon intuition of the immediate experience of duration contributed to its decline in Bergson's own lifetime. Speculative philosophy seeks systematic formulation; and it employs language. Intuition is unsystematic, and eschewing language, it resorts to the ineffable. Although each of the six characteristics of duration discussed above furnishes an insight into the nature of time and of reality, it is difficult to see how they can be combined as the essential features of time conceived as the stuff of reality. This difficulty concerning the rational coherence of Bergson's thought is complemented by a difficulty with its applicability. The exclusion of the entire material world of spatialized objects from reality is philosophically respectable only if there is argument to explain its dependency on some more ultimate reality or at least how it arises as illusion. Such argument is absent from Bergson's philosophy. Rather Bergson concentrated on duration, and imposed upon it the total burden of accounting for all creation, a view of unsurpassed optimism since he believed the creative advance to greater and higher novelty endless. But no sooner had Bergson succeeded in proposing the erection of a cosmology on a radical distinction of Space from Duration (real time) than practitioners of the abstruse science of mathematical physics welded Space and Time together. The post-Bergsonian phase of process philosophy had to reckon with, not only the reality of external matter, but the reality of Space-Time as well. Bergson appreciated the threat to his philosophy posed by relativity physics with its field theory of mathematically expressible Space-Time; he even wrote a book to demonstrate that relativity theory did not bear on duration, or real time.[82] But Bergson's book went unheeded.

S. ALEXANDER

Process philosophy entered a new period of development. The initial impetus it had gained from Darwin's discovery of evolution in biology in the middle of the nineteenth century was joined by the challenge of Einstein's relativity physics in the second decade of the twentieth century. Samuel Alexander (1859–1938) proposed, in

Space, Time, and Deity (1920), a system of process philosophy which seemed, when it appeared, to be abreast of the altered scientific situation.

Realism—Alexander's philosophy marks the intersection of realism and process philosophy. Although he would gladly have abandoned the terms "idealism" and "realism," they did denote for him a real difference in the spirit of inquiry. According to idealism, "mind is the measure of things and the starting-point of inquiry," and according to realism, "mind has no privileged place except in perfection." [83] The realist theory of mind, Alexander held, may be established in two ways. The first way is "to begin by examining in detail the relation of mind to its objects, always on the empirical method of analysing that relation in our experience of it; and to draw from thence what indications are legitimate as to the general nature of things, and of their categorial features." [84] The second way is "to examine in their order the various categorial features of existence and to exhibit the relation of mind to its objects in its proper place in the system of finite empirical existences." [85]

Alexander followed the first way first, and consequently he was led into epistemological realism. Influenced by G. E. Moore, Alexander analyzed experience into two distinct elements and the relation between them: 1) the act of the mind or the awareness, 2) the object of which it is aware, and 3) the relation between them—i.e., compresence.

Alexander subsumed mental acts under the general name "consciousness" or "mind." They are various: sensing, perceiving, remembering, thinking, and so forth. The most fundamental distinction among mental acts, however, is the distinction between enjoyment and contemplation.[86] Enjoyment is an interior and reflexive act of the mind, relating the mind to itself and to nothing else. Thus no mind can enjoy an object or another mind. Contemplation, by contrast, relates a mind to its object. Alexander entertained the possibility that one mind may even contemplate another mind, but in that case, he observed, the contemplating mind would have to be a divine or angelic mind.

Compresence is the relation of mind and object. Alexander held that "our compresence with physical things, in virtue of which we are conscious of them, is a situation of the same sort as the compresence of two physical things with one another."[87] He amplified: "The relation of mind and object is comparable to that between table and floor, and the cognitive relation . . . is merely the simplest and most universal relation between finite things in the Universe."[88] This relation, Alexander insisted, should not be confused with dependence.

> When A is dependent on B, we mean at least that without B, A would not have qualities for which it is said to be dependent on B. Thus when we speak of a very dependent person, we mean that he can do nothing without the help of someone else. To be independent in any respect is for A to have these qualities in the absence of B. Now the object is clearly dependent on the mind for being known. But it is, as the mind itself declares in the experience, not dependent upon the mind for the qualities which make it what it is. The mind is indispensable to blue in so far as it is sensed, but not for its blueness.[89]

The objects of mind are independent of the mind in respect to the qualities they possess, except for the fact of being known. On the other hand, mind may be said to be dependent on objects, in that "in the order of creation, minds are strictly the issue, and the causal issue, of the physical order of things."[90]

Alexander's thought moved from epistemological realism into the region of speculative metaphysics. Mind, he inferred, "is a new quality of existence, and that which has mind is a new creature, existing at a higher level than physical or even living things."[91] The object, he further inferred, "is known for what it is, not necessarily as it is in its real nature, for there may be illusion, but at its face value, as blue or square or table or the number 2 or the law of gravitation."[92] Mind, he maintained, is not the whole of reality; nor is its object the whole; rather, both are fragments, fragments which enter into relations with one another. Aware of the expanding metaphysical context of his thought, Alexander undertook to make plain the whole of which mind and its objects are parts, to delineate its categories and its levels of empirical existence, and to explain the place of mind within the general scheme of things. This is the second way he sought to establish the realist theory of mind.

Space and Time—Alexander's *Space, Time, and Deity,* one of the historic monuments of process philosophy, provides the full-scale metaphysics which buttresses his realist theory of mind. The work is divided into four books. In the first book, Alexander investigated Space and Time, and their relation to one another. In the second book, he considered the categories of metaphysics and their relations to Space and Time. In the third book, he examined the various types of existents—Matter, Life, Mind, Deity—and exhibited their relations to one another within Space and Time. In the final book, Alexander discussed "what can be known as to the nature of deity, consistently with the whole scheme of things which we know, and with the sentiment of worship which is directed to God." [93] Let us consider the main theses of each book in turn.

Alexander assumed that Space and Time are real in their own right; consequently, he sought to ascertain the kind of reality they have. Space and Time, as presented in ordinary experience, "are commonly known as extension and duration." [94] In ordinary experience, moreover, we apprehend not Space and Time, but the bodies that occupy Space and the events that occur in Time. Sensible things come first; their spatial and temporal characteristics are secondary. Thus, Space and Time appear to be constructs from the secondary characteristics of the sensible things, suggesting that indeed Space and Time are merely relational, Space consisting in the co-existence of things and Time in the succession of events. Alexander, however, rejected the relational view of Space and Time. Relation, he remarked, is "the vaguest word in the philosophical vocabulary." [95] Upon examination, the relational theory of Space and Time is deemed a failure because spatial and temporal relations "are the same stuff as their terms;" relations between bits of Space are also spaces and the same may be said of Time.[96] While a critical assessment of the relational theory of Space and Time leads to the repudiation of this theory, a special mode of sense apprehension—what Alexander called "intuition"—enables us to think of Space and Time for themselves. This immediate experience of Space and Time, revealing their independence of things and events, suggests "that Space and Time . . . are, as it were, the stuff or matrix (or matrices) out of which things or events are made, the medium in which they are precipitated and crystallized; that the finites are in some sense complexes of space and time. In the language familiar from the seventeenth-century philosophy, things and events are 'modes' of these 'substances,' extension and duration." [97]

Alexander based his substantialist metaphysics of Space-Time on immediate experience. Empirically Space is presented as physical extension—i.e., "as something within which bodies are placed and move, which contains distinguishable parts but is continuous, so that the parts are not presented as having a separate existence, and which is infinite." [98] Time is experienced as duration—"as a duration of the successive; it is continuous, so that its distinguishable parts are not isolated but connected; . . . its parts are successive, and, like Space, it is infinite." [99] The continuity and infinitude of Space and Time are thus experienced facts. Intellectual analysis and construction are requisite to divide Space into points and Time into instants. For points and instants are conceptual constructions, useful when we try to understand Space and Time—particularly, in mathematical terms.

Reflection on our immediate experience of Space and Time further confirms their interdependence. As Alexander said, "there neither is Space without Time nor Time without Space; any more than life exists without a body or a body which can function as a living body exists without life; . . . . Space is in its very nature temporal and Time spatial." [100] The succession of the moments of Time means that when the present moment is, the past and the future are not. Time thus breaks down into a mere now. Successiveness seems, then, to contradict continuity, unless somehow the different moments of Time may be brought together. As Alexander said: "If . . . the past instant is not to be lost as it otherwise would be, or rather since this is not the case in fact, there needs must be some continuum other than Time which can secure and sustain the togetherness of past and present, of earlier and later. . . . This other form of being is Space."[101] In its turn, Space cannot be without Time. Taken by itself in its distinctive character of a whole of coexistence, Space has no distinct parts; without distinguishable elements, it is a blank and, therefore, not a continuum at all. As Alexander concluded,

> . . . the empirical continuity or totalness of Space turns out to be incompatible with the other empirical feature of Space, that it contains distinctness of parts. That distinctness is not supplied by the characteristic altogetherness of Space. There must therefore be some form of existence, some entity not itself spatial which disinguishes and separates the parts of Space. This other form of existence is Time.[102]

Space and Time, therefore, are shown to be interdependent, and for different reasons. As Alexander said:

> Without Space there would be no connection in Time. Without Time, there would be no points to connect. It is the two different aspects of continuity which compel us in turn to see that each of the two, Space and Time, is vital to the existence of the other.[103]

Alexander's conception of Space-Time as the ultimate substance affords a dynamic rather than a static interpretation of reality. "The physical universe," he declared, "is through and through historical, the scene of motion."[104] Since, for Alexander, Time is "the source of movement," Space "must . . . be regarded as generated in Time, or, if the expression be preferred, by Time."[105]

While Alexander stressed the dynamic character of Space-Time, he also emphasized that it is a formally structured whole. He wrote: "Space may then be imaged as the trail of Time, as long as it is remembered that there could be no Time without a Space in which its trail is left."[106] Space-Time, viewed metaphysically, is a plenum. Point-instants may be distinguished in the plenum; and lines may be drawn to connect each with all the other point-instants in the plenum. Each point-instant, moreover, constitutes a singular perspective on the whole. In combining process and structure in a single conception of Space-Time, Alexander offered an original theory. The originality may be appreciated best by a comparison with other recent theories.

Alexander, like Bergson, saw the world in terms of process; and like Bergson, too, he construed the process as continuous. But Bergson distinguished real time or duration from mathematical time, and held that intuition grasps real time, whereas the intellect distorts it when the intellect seeks to spatialize it, producing instead mathematical time. On the contrary, Alexander maintained that "the spatialising of . . . Time, which . . . Bergson regarded as a common and natural vice, is in fact of the essence of Time."[107] For Alexander, "Time is really laid out in Space, and is intrinsically spatial."[108]

Alexander admitted that his theory of Space-Time is "in essence and spirit identical" with that of Hermann Minkowski (1864–1909).[109] Minkowski represented the physical universe in a four-dimensional mathematical matrix, of which three dimensions are spatial and the fourth temporal. Alexander adopted this basic point. However, Alexander expressed misgivings over the fact that Minkowski tended to regard Time as an additional dimension set over against the three dimensions of Space and, consequently, neglected the mutual implication of Space and Time. Alexander wrote:

> For not only are Space and Time indispensable to one another . . . , but Time with its distinctive features corresponds to the three dimensions of Space, and is not additional to them. To use a violent phrase, it is, spatially, not temporally, voluminous. Metaphysically, (though perhaps mathematically), it is not therefore a fourth dimension in the universe, but repeats the other three. Space, even to be Space, must be temporal.[110]

Alexander then could accept Minkowski's mathematics but not his metaphysics.

Albert Einstein, when formulating his special theory of relativity, also utilized Minkowski's mathematics of Space-Time. Alexander agreed with Einstein that spatio-temporal measurements vary from the different perspectives of different observers; but he denied that Space-Time is wholly relative. Space-Time, according to Alexander, is a complete system which embraces all perspectives; each point-instant may be absolutely located within it. Indeed, Alexander was tempted to call Space-Time absolute, but because of the historical associations with Newton's doctrine, he refrained from doing so. Instead, he called Space-Time Total, for the purpose of indicating that it is "the synthesis of all partial space-times or perspectives of Space-Time."[111]

For Alexander, there is but one Space-Time; all spaces and times are parts of it. This total Space-Time is physical, or better, metaphysical. The coexistence and succession of elements, images, and states which consciousness enjoys constitute mental space-time; but mental space-time is characteristically the same as Space-Time which consciousness contemplates. It is in fact a part of Space-Time, as mathematical space-time is, too. For mathematical space-time is an abstraction, a partial selection of, the structures inherent in Space-Time. Hence Space-Time is the ultimate matrix or substance of which all things and events are modes. It "takes for us," Alexander admitted, "the place of what is called the Absolute in idealistic systems," but he was quick to add that it is "an experiential absolute."[112]

Space-Time as an experiential absolute contains some characters that are pervasive and some that are not. The nonpervasive are the variable qualities that belong to different existents. The pervasive characters are categories that belong to all existents.

Categories—Alexander defined categories as the "pervasive characters of existents;" they are "a priori or non-empirical characters;" nonetheless, they are "the essential and universal constituents of whatever is experienced, and in the wider sense of that term are therefore empirical."[113] Alexander's theory of the categories, moreover, is realistic: the categories belong primarily to reality, and to mind only because mind is itself a part—an existent or level of existence—within reality. "The categories are for us expressions of the nature of Space-Time itself." [114]

Alexander's categories are identity, diversity, existence; universal, particular, individual; relation; order; substance, causality, reciprocity; quantity, intensity; whole, parts, number; and motion. There is a nice question as to whether Space-Time is a category. As the infinite matrix of all finite beings, Space-Time is plainly not a category; but Space and Time, pervasive characters of all things, are just as plainly categorial. Space-Time, of course, is the principle in terms of which each of the categories is defined. A few of Alexander's definitions may be cited to illustrate his procedure. Identity is the numerical self-identity of a thing; it consists in the occupation of a space-time. Diversity consists in the occupation of another space-time. Existence, or determinate being, consists in "the occupation of any space-time, that is self-identity, in distinction from any other space-time." [115]

Alexander also ranked his categories in three grades. He wrote:

> The major categories are the first four—existence, universality, relation, and order. These communicate with each other. . . . Existence is different from other existence. As universal a thing is of the same sort as other particulars and different from another sort of particulars. Relation exists and has in turn universality, in the same sense as a thing is universal. The next group of categories—substance, quantity, number, etc.—communicate with each other and with the major group, but the major group do not communicate with them. Thus a substance is in a relation of causality with other substance, and it exists. But existence is not a substance, nor is relation necessarily causal, it may be a relation of number. . . . Motion forms the last or third group of categories. It presupposes the other categories and communicates with them. But they do not communicate with it. Even substance is not itself motion, though every *thing* besides being substance is motion. Substance represents motion only in respect of its persistent occupation of space through a lapse of time; but it does not include quantity, nor intensity, nor number. Whereas in motion the full tale of the fundamental determinations of Space-Time is told and motion is consequently the totality of what can be affirmed of every space-time.[116]

Qualities—Of qualities Alexander offered neither a definition nor an explanation. "Qualities," he asserted, "are to be noted and registered without the pretense of accounting for them."[117] The existence of qualities is "miraculous," although "it is at least a miracle which pervades the world of things."[118]

To clarify, if not to explain, the existence of qualities, Alexander used the term "emergence." He borrowed it from Lloyd Morgan (1852–1936), who in turn had borrowed it from George Lewes (1817–1878).[119] By virtue of Alexander's use of the concept of emergence, his system is regarded as the most comprehensive statement of the philosophy of emergent evolution. A few sentences quoted from the text will serve to present the position.

> New orders of finites come into existence in Time; the world actually or historically develops from its first or elementary condition of Space-Time, which possesses no quality except what we agreed to call the spatio-temporal quality of motion. But as in the course of Time new complexity of motions come into existence, a new quality emerges, that is, a new complex possesses as a matter of observed empirical fact a new or emergent quality. . . . The emergence of a new quality from any level of existence means that at that level there comes into being a certain constellation or collocation of the motions belonging to that level, and possessing the quality appropriate to it, and this collocation possesses a new quality distinctive of the higher complex.[120]

Constellation, or *collocation,* is the key to the emergence of a new quality, according to Alexander. Motions, changes, processes at one level of existence form a constellation or collocation. This constellation or collocation unifies the motions, changes, processes; its unity is indeed a new quality. The new quality signals a new level of existence. Motions, changes, processes of course occur at this new level of existence.

Qualities emerge inexplicably. Although some philosophers have been inclined to say that the emergence of qualities is to be noted under the compulsion of brute empirical facts, Alexander preferred to say "in less harsh terms [that it is] to be accepted with the 'natural piety' of the investigator. It admits of no explanation."[121] Clearly by "explanation" what Alexander meant was the assignment of an antecedent cause, and such an assignment is impossible with regard to the emergent. For the emergent is novel being in regard either to form or content or both; it is not merely a reorganizing of preexisting content.[122] Emergent evolution opens the world up for novelty and for freedom. As Alexander remarked: "A calculator given the state of the universe at a certain number of instants or at one instant with the law of its change could, given sufficient powers, calculate what the spatio-temporal conditions of the world would be at any given later instant. But he could not on our interpretation predict what qualities would be evoked by the complexes in Space-Time, unless he lived to observe them." [123]

Mind—Roughly speaking, the levels of existence listed in the order of their emergence are motions, matter as physical (or mechanical), matter with secondary qualities, life, mind.[124] According to Alexander, mind is a constellation of the neural processes in the physical brain of the living organism. Body-Mind seemed to him to be analogous to Space-Time, as when he said: "Time is the mind of Space and Space the body of Time." [125] But he was wary lest we imagine ourselves to be models of the universe at large. On the contrary, the universe is the model for ourselves. He wrote:

> Rather than hold that Time is a form of mind, we must say that mind is a form of Time . . . mind is mind and Time is Time. I mean that in the matrix of all existence, Space-Time, there is an element Time which performs the same function in respect of its bodily equivalent. The points of Space have no consciousness in any shape or form, but their instants perform to them the office of consciousness to our brains.[126]

Although mind has its place in the evolution of nature, it is in no wise privileged. Mind does not cap the process of evolution once and for all. As Alexander observed:

> Within the all-embracing stuff of Space-Time, the universe exhibits an emergence in Time of successive levels of finite existences, each with its characteristic empirical quality. The highest of these empirical qualities known to us is mind or consciousness. Deity is the next higher empirical quality to the highest we know.[127]

God—Alexander's naturalism, manifest in his treatment of mind, is triumphant in his theory of God. Deity, as the previous quotation reveals, is an empirical quality, an emergent. Though willing to concede that religious sentiment, which has God as its object, is valid, or sincere, Alexander insisted that God, as known by science and philosophy, "must be defined as the being, if any, which possessess deity or the divine quality; or, if there are more Gods than one, the beings which possess deity."[128] Thus Alexander focused on the quality of deity. Viewing the universe of Space-Time as an evolving hierarchy of emergent and emerging empirical qualities, he saw deity as "the next higher empirical quality" for any level of existence. "It is therefore a variable quality, and, as the world grows in time, deity changes with it. On each level a new quality looms ahead awfully, which plays to it the part of deity."[129] Mind, before emerging, appeared as deity to life, but once emergent, it faces a yet-to-emerge quality which for it is deity. Hence deity is a quality which is by stipulation never reached, but always emerging ahead. As Alexander pointedly said: "Deity is a nisus and not an accomplishment."[130] "Deity is some quality not realized but in process of realization, is future and not present."[131] Nevertheless, Alexander denied that the quality of deity is a value. He sought, by his denial, to buttress the objectivity of deity. Deity, he wrote,

> is not itself a value, for values are human inventions and deity is ultra-human. Deity belongs to the order of perfection and not to that of value. . . . The order of empirical qualities is one of perfection, and values are evolved within the level of mind, and indeed with proper qualifications within every level.[132]

Alexander's theory of God contains some special doctrines which are noteworthy. As life is the basis of mind, so mind is the basis of deity; but since there are many finite minds, it is possible that there are many finite beings possessing deity. Whether many such finite gods exist, Alexander confessed, cannot be ascertained. Whether infinite deity exists can, however, be determined. As Alexander said: "the world in its infinity tends towards infinite deity, or is pregnant with it, but that infinite deity does not exist; and we may now add that if it did, God—the actual world possessing infinite deity—would cease to be infinite God and break up into a multiplicity of finite gods, which would be merely a higher race of creatures than ourselves with a God beyond." [133] Furthermore, on Alexander's theory, God's nature is dual. By analogy, God has as his body the entire universe of empirical existences in Space-Time and as his mind the emerging quality of deity. As the body of the universe, God is immanent; as the deity toward which the universe evolves, he is transcendent. God, then, is not timeless, but involved in the temporal processes of evolution. Nor is God the creator in the ordinary sense of the word; but he is creative. Alexander wrote:

> . . . as being the whole universe God is creative, but his distinctive character is not creative but created. As embracing the whole of Space-Time he is creative; because Time is the moving principle that brings out that constant redistribution in the matrix which is equivalent to the birth of finite forms. Even then it is, properly speaking, Space-Time itself which is creator and not God.[134]
>
> God himself, that is the universe as leading to deity, is creative only of deity. On the other hand, deity owes its being to the pre-existing finites with their empirical qualities, and is their outcome. God then, like all things in the universe—for Space-Time itself is not in the universe, whereas God, since his deity is a part of the universe, is in it—is in the strictest sense not a creator but a creature. . . . He is an infinite creature of the universe of Space-Time.[135]

Alexander's cosmology of emergent evolution, like Bergson's metaphysics of creative evolution, projected an unending linear advance of novelty. Both Alexander and Bergson construed real time—the creative process—as a kind of Absolute, with a fixed past, an actual present, and an open future. Alexander, unlike Bergson, emphasized an essential link between Space and Time, and though he did not wish to call Space-Time absolute, the absolutist meanings hovered over his conceptions. Einstein's physics also posited linked Space-Time; but it stressed a relativity which would be accommodated in Alexander's theory only with ambiguity.

G. H. MEAD

Process philosophy, which had gained immeasurably from Darwin's scientific theory of evolution, was confronted with a major adjustment as a consequence of Einstein's relativity physics. If temporal distinctions are relative, events in the past, present, and future lack fixity with respect to one another, and are all relative as regards temporal location. Then the concept of evolution, of change from an earlier to a later state or condition, is altered, since linear advance or progress is itself relative. Time's arrow, it would appear, is not irreversible. Naturally, philosophers turned their attention to resolving the seeming conflict between evolution and relativity. None has surpassed George Herbert Mead (1863–1931) in proposing an original theory of time.

Mead's theory of time is a philosophy of the present. As he affirmed: "Reality exists in a present."[136] A present, moreover, is itself an emergent event. Each present yields novelty in its actual being. Citing a flash of a meteor as an example of a present, Mead said, "That which marks a present is its becoming and its disappearing."[137] The structure of time is based, for Mead, on the emergent event as present. Future and past both spread out from the present. Although Mead never asserted that the past is a pure invention of the present, his type of theory has been charged with the allegation of, to borrow a witty phrase of A. O. Lovejoy (1873–1962), "the futurity of yesterday."[138] It is clear, however, that Mead repudiated the view, shared by Minkowski, Alexander, and many historians, that the past exists in itself as a scroll of elapsed presents independent of and unaffected by what is going on at present.[139] For Mead the scroll concept of time is inconsistent with the actual procedures of scientists and historians. No historian can find such a past; he reconstructs the past from evidences found in the present. At the same time Mead rejected Bergson's view that the present somehow accumulates all the past. "The present," he said, "does not carry any such burden with it."[140] There is, instead of total accumulation, some past somehow in the present, operating as a condition of the present. As a condition of the present, the past lies within the present and is no external fixity. Temporal continuity from past to present prevails, with the present its fulcrum. As Mead wrote: "The actual passage of reality is in the passage of one present into another, where alone is reality, and a present which has merged in another is not a past. Its reality is always that of a present."[141]

Mead never provided in complete formulation the cosmological system which his theory of the present seemed to imply. His failure to do so may be attributed partly to his methodological preoccupations, partly to his distrust of metaphysics, and partly to the fact that his life was cut short when, like William James, he appeared to be facing the requirement of systematically expressing the basic principles of his philosophy. At any rate, Mead's posthumously published *Philosophy of the Act* suggests a philosophy of organism which interprets the basic categories—space, time, cause—by reference to the relation of the organism interacting with its environment.[142] Later John Dewey was to introduce the term "transaction" to denote this crucial relation or situation.[143]

A. N. WHITEHEAD

Transactional metaphysics, perhaps because of its concentration on experience, lacks the comprehensive sweep of traditional speculative thought. It obscures the cosmic background by focusing on the human foreground. To Alfred North Whitehead belongs credit for furnishing in his masterwork, *Process and Reality* (1929), the as yet unsurpassed systematic presentation of process philosophy. What Mead, who appreciated the early contributions of Alfred North Whitehead to process philosophy, would have said of Whitehead's *Process and Reality,* we do not know. We do know, however, that Samuel Alexander came to believe in the last decade of his life that Whitehead had excelled him.[144]

Whitehead's speculative philosophy is, as the title of his major work displays, a process philosophy. The examination of his conception of speculative philosophy in Chapter I should have made plain, however, that Whitehead was thoroughly immersed in the great traditions of philosophy, and that he had as high a respect for logic and formal thought as for process and experience. While process philosophers like Bergson had been disdainful of the intellectualistic distinctions fostered by abstract logic, Whitehead was inclined to resort to such distinctions. In Chapter II, Part I, of *Process and Reality,* Whitehead sketched his categorial scheme. The remaining five hundred pages of the book, of course, flesh it out, just as the entire body of his works illuminates and even revises it. Necessarily condensed, the sketch contains no fewer than forty-five categories: one category of the ultimate, eight categories of existence, twenty-seven categories of explanation, and nine categorial obligations. Add to these what Whitehead modestly called in the next chapter "some derivative notions," which include, among other concepts, that of God, and the performance may well dishearten the most sympathetic student.[145]

Basic Categories—Here it is useful to consider, in brief, his central notions. Whitehead himself has lightened the task by singling out four notions for special consideration: "that of an 'actual entity,' that of a 'prehension' that of a 'nexus,' and that of the 'ontological principle.' "[146] They underscore, by Whitehead's own assertion, his endeavor "to base philosophical thought upon the most concrete elements in our experience."[147]

The category of actual entity is a category of existence. Whitehead defined "actual entities," also termed "actual occasions," as "the final real things of which the world is made up."[148] Nothing is more real than actual entities. They are, he continued, "drops of experience, complex and interdependent."[149] An actual entity is conspicuously what Whitehead has called "a complete fact." The similarity between Whitehead's metaphysical endeavor and Aristotle's is manifest here, in that the pluralism of actual entities parallels Aristotle's pluralism of individual substances.[150] But the differences are also remarkable. The actual entity is no entity recognized by common sense and ordinary observation; it is microscopic. Nor does the actual entity endure in time: its existence is atomic;

it perishes the moment it becomes. Moreover, the actual entity is qualitative; it is a drop of experience. Further, actual entities are not separate, independent entities; they are related and interdependent. Finally, every actual entity is objectively immortal; it is "felt" by all subsequent actual entities.

The ontological principle is a category of explanation. It reinforces Whitehead's pluralism in its demand that only actual entities serve as reasons for what is. As Whitehead said: "According to the ontological principle there is nothing which floats into the world from nowhere. Everything in the actual world is referable to some actual entity."[151] In sum the principle maintains: "no actual entity, then no reason."[152] The demand for a reason is, however, not reducible to a demand for an efficient cause alone, since speculative reason for Whitehead, as previously noted, seeks final causes. Hence Whitehead readily termed the ontological principle the "principle of efficient, and final causation," adding that this "means that actual entities are the only *reasons;* so that to search for a *reason* is to search for one or more actual entities."[153]

The notion of "prehension," another category of existence, comes into play when the actual entity is analyzed. While various modes of analysis are available, Whitehead chose analysis in terms of prehension as that mode "which exhibits the most concrete elements in the nature of actual entities."[154] Prehensions not only denote the internal qualities of an entity being brought to unity; they are also—indeed, essentially—"concrete facts of relatedness,"[155] involving that entity in a complex of relations to other things. "A prehension," Whitehead amplified, "reproduces in itself the general characteristics of an actual entity: it is referent to an external world, and in this sense will be said to have a 'vector character'; it involves emotion, and purpose, and valuation, and causation."[156] In stressing the role of prehension in constituting the actual entity, Whitehead in effect attributed *feeling* to all actual entities.

Every actual entity prehends all past actual entities, and is in turn prehended by all future ones. The prehension within an actual entity involves at least assimilation of the data furnished it; but it includes as well an internal form which imparts unity to the complexity. This internal, or subjective, form points forward, toward a satisfaction attainable within the entity itself. Having attained its satisfaction, the entity perishes, to be in turn prehended by later actual entities. In this way, prehensions are facts of relatedness, and actual entities are immortal.

Thus the fourth notion central to Whitehead's metaphysics looms into view—the notion of "nexus." A nexus is "a particular fact of togetherness among actual entities." [157] Common words for "nexus" are "society" or "organized group." Since actual entities are for Whitehead microscopic, whether identified as electrically charged particles in physics or as drops of experience in psychology, they are elements component in the objects of common sense and ordinary experience. These latter objects are nexūs of actual entities, societies of occasions.

Whitehead singled out those four notions not simply because of their centrality to his system, but also "by reason of the fact that they involve some divergence from antecedent philosophical thought." [158] For a balanced understanding of his system, therefore, it is necessary to consider three additional notions: creativity, eternal objects, and God.

Creativity is "the category of the ultimate." [159] Describing it as "the universal of universals characterizing ultimate matter of fact," Whitehead wrote: "It is that ultimate principle by which the many, which are the universe disjunctively, become the one actual occasion, which is the universe conjunctively." [160] He continued: "'Creativity' is the principle of *novelty*. An actual occasion is a novel entity diverse from any entity in the 'many' which it unifies." [161] By applying the ultimate category of creativity in the interpretation of the cosmos, Whitehead, like Bergson with the *élan vital,* viewed the world process as a "creative advance." [162]

The notion of "eternal object" is that category of existence which stands out in contrast with the category of actual entities—with, in Whitehead's words, "a certain extreme finality." [163] Eternal objects designate "Pure Potentials for Specific Determination of Fact, or Forms of Definiteness." [164] Their function in Whitehead's system is reminiscent of Plato's Ideas—the forms or universals. In his presystematic writings on nature and modern science Whitehead had appealed to this type of being when he contended that objects "ingressed" into events.[165] The inclusion of the notion in the mature system has, however, troubled many commentators. Some have objected on the grounds that the category of *eternal* objects does violence to the process character of Whitehead's system; others that it allows too immense a domain of pure possibility.[166] Whatever the outcome of these objections, the doctrine of eternal objects is clearly a major factor in the theme of permanence which Whitehead accepted as the counterpart of the theme of flux. Eternal objects are ideals. Like past actual entities, they are prehended by the present actual entity, although they are timeless. Whereas the prehension of actual entities by a present actual entity is physical prehension, the prehension of eternal objects is conceptual prehension. Every actual entity is dipolar, physically prehending past entities and conceptually prehending timeless ideals. Hence every actual entity intersects lines of efficient and of final causation.

Finally, Whitehead's notion of "God" is worthy of consideration. In *Process and Reality* the notion of "God" is a derivative one, at least by explicit statement. For Whitehead maintained that "God is an actual entity, and so is the most trivial puff of existence in far-off empty space."[167] As creativity is the category of the ultimate, it follows that "God is its primordial, non-temporal accident."[168] Among the commentators on Whitehead, William A. Christian has elaborated most consistently the side of Whitehead's doctrine according to which God is an actual entity and, therefore, *not* a person, since a person is definitionally a nexus of actual entities.[169] On the other hand Charles Hartshorne, conceiving God to be a central and not a derivative notion, has construed the Whiteheadian God as a unique personal order.[170] Indeed, Hartshorne has reported that once in private conversation Whitehead had described God "as a 'society of occasions' (with personal order)."[171] Victor Lowe, also discussing the problem of God in Whitehead's philosophy, has suggested that it is "impossible to specify the exact logical structure of Whitehead's metaphysical position."[172] Nevertheless, the major outlines of Whitehead's doctrine of God are discernible. God as a cosmological principle has a dual nature: primordial and consequent. In his primordial nature God prehends the eternal objects; in his consequent nature he prehends all actual entities. Thus he determines the relevance of permanent but possible ideals to the flux of actual entities; and further, he assures objective immortality to every actual entity. Whitehead's theory of God, more so perhaps than the other major categories of his metaphysics, has served to baffle and to inspire other philosophers.

Whitehead's influence on the development of speculative philosophy in America has been considerable.[173] Two contemporaries, in particular, have developed original speculative philosophies which exhibit the profound impact of Whitehead: Paul Weiss[174] and Charles Hartshorne.[175] Their systems recognize categories which transcend process, as of course does Whitehead's.

Process—Whitehead was no ordinary process thinker. Consider the term "process," which he used interchangeably with the term "flux." However much other thinkers inclined to blur together flux, process, motion, becoming, and change into a single vague concept, Whitehead sought to draw distinctions. William A. Christian has indicated that in Whitehead's systematic work process has two meanings: 1) concrescence—i.e., "growth or internal change;" and 2) transition—i.e., "change of status in relation to other things."[176] Further, change is different from becoming. Strictly (systematically) speaking, concrescence is not change; it is becoming. The fundamental entities in Whitehead's system do not change; "they merely *become*."[177] Change denotes the sequence of differences between the fundamental entities which make up an event, or it designates the adventures of universal characteristics in the evolving universe of actual things. Moreover, process is not the same as motion. "An actual entity never moves; it is where it is and what it is."[178] This leads to the paradox that, for Whitehead, the becoming of an actual entity is its perishing. "The ancient doctrine that 'no one crosses the same river twice' is extended. No thinker thinks twice; and, to put the matter more generally, no subject experiences twice."[179] The first paradox is joined by yet another paradox: for Whitehead the perpetual perishing of the fundamental entities is tantamount to what he has called their "objective immortality."[180] The entities become data for all subsequent entities.

This introduces another feature marking Whitehead's philosophy off from the typical process philosophy. For Whitehead, process is not the sole theme of metaphysics. To formulate "the complete problem of metaphysics" in *Process and Reality,* Whitehead cited two lines of a famous hymn:

> Abide with me!
> Fast falls the eventide. . . .

He proceeded to comment: "Here the first line expresses the permanences, 'abide,' 'me' and the 'Being' addressed; and the second line sets these permanences amid the inescapable flux. . . . Those philosophers who start with the first line have given us the metaphysics of 'substance'; and those who start with the second line have developed the metaphysics of 'flux.' But, in truth, the two lines cannot be torn apart in this way."[181] No doubt, according to Whitehead, "the flux of things is one ultimate generalization around which we must weave our philosophical system,"[182] but as Victor Lowe has observed, even italicizing the word "one" when he quoted the line above, the other "ultimate generalization" for Whitehead is the idea of permanence.[183] Resuming the commentary on the lines of the hymn almost two hundred pages later, Whitehead said: "In the inescapable flux, there is something that abides; in the overwhelming permanence, there is an element that escapes into the flux. Permanence can be snatched only out of the flux; and the passing moment can find its adequate intensity only by its submission to permanence. Those who would disjoin the two elements can find no interpretation of patent facts."[184]

TEILHARD DE CHARDIN

Whitehead's philosophy then, may be seen as one which converted process to accept parity with permanence. It contrasts with the philosophy of Pierre Teilhard de Chardin (1881–1955), who stressed the primacy of process within the context of a traditional system of substantialist permanence. Teilhard was a Roman Catholic priest of French nationality. An adherent to Bergson's evolutionism, he was expelled from his teaching position at the Catholic Institute in Paris in 1926, and exiled to China. He engaged in paleontological researches in China, participating in the discovery of Peking man. When he returned to the West in 1946, he was an internationally recognized scientist, and he also had in hand the manuscript of his major work, *The Phenomenon of Man* (1955). Teilhard was refused permission to publish this work by the Vatican during his lifetime. Posthumously published, it created a considerable stir in France, England, and the United States. Despite the opposition not only of orthodox Catholic thinkers but also of scientists, Teilhard's philosophy has fired the imagination of many who seek to interpret the scientific theory of evolution within the context of concern for humanistic and religious values. Teilhard's system is lacking in categorial precision, but it is strong in poetic expression. No survey of process philosophy today would be adequate if it neglected to consider Teilhard's thought.

Teilhard stressed the speculative side of his work when in the Foreword to *The Phenomenon of Man* he declared: "My only aim, and my only vantage-ground in these pages, is to try to see."[185] Speculation for Teilhard, however, is in the service of philosophical anthropology. His aim, he added, was "to try to develop a *homogeneous* and *coherent* perspective of our general extended experience of man. A *whole* which unfolds."[186] But the speculative grasp of the whole in which man is central is cosmic. Teilhard traced the processes of evolution back in the world before the advent of life, then within life in the world until thought is born, marking the emergence of man, next in humanity as civilized society develops, and finally beyond humanity, culminating in the Omega point.

The material world according to science is, as Teilhard says in imagery reminiscent of Bergson, "a rocket rising in the wake of time's arrow, that only bursts to be extinguished; an eddy rising on the bosom of a descending current."[187] But science pictures things only from without; it is incomplete. According to Teilhard, "co-extensive with their Without, there is a Within to things."[188] The Without is Matter; the Within, Mind. Spiritual energy pervades the Within of things; physical energy, the Without. For Teilhard, moreover, "all energy is psychic."[189] Thus spiritual and physical energies are somehow unified in a single cosmic energy. Despite the scientific laws of the conservation of energy and of entropy, furthermore, cosmic energy is constantly increasing.

For Teilhard evolution prevails. It operates in the two-leveled field of energy. Consequently it is displayed in two ways. First, the universe, regarded sidereally, expands endlessly in space from the infinitesimal to the immense. Second, the universe exhibits involution; it develops from the extremely simple to the extremely complex, a process which is accompanied by an increase in interiorization—i.e., of consciousness. Hence evolution is a process of increasing complexification and interiorization.

Life, according to Teilhard, is no eruption nor emergent quality in a totally alien physical world; it is instead a natural issue of a cosmic process. Each kind of living thing has a "cosmic embryogenesis" as well as a "historic birth." Living things, once born, collectively produce "the amazing profusion of organic matter whose matted complexity come to form the last (or rather the last but one) of the envelopes of our planet: the *biosphere*."[190] Furthermore, living things evolve psychologically—a process which Teilhard termed "psychogenesis." With man thought arrives in nature. Man occurs as a phenomenon within the biosphere. For man's superiority over the other animals consists in reflection. As Teilhard said, ". . . reflection is . . . the power acquired by a consciousness to turn in upon itself, to take possession of itself *as an object* endowed with its own particular consistence and value; no longer merely to know, but to know oneself; no longer merely to know, but to know that one knows."[191] Man's "individualization of himself in the depths of himself" enables him to constitute himself "a *centre* in the form of a point at which all the impressions and experiences knit themselves together and fuse into a unity that is conscious of its own organization."[192] A transformation takes place. "The being who is the object of his own reflection, in consequence of that very doubling back upon himself, becomes in a flash able to raise himself into a new sphere. In reality, another world is born."[193] Man is, Teilhard asserted, "nothing else than evolution become conscious of itself."[194]

The phenomenon of man subjects the world to a new evolutionary process—a process which Teilhard called "hominisation." This process has a dual meaning; it embraces not only "the individual and instantaneous leap from instinct to thought," but also "the progessive phyletic spiritualisation in human civilization of all the forces contained in the animal world."[195] Another name for hominisation is noogenesis. For this is the process by which mind is born; and mind constitutes another world or layer of the world.

"Noosphere" is Teilhard's term for the world of mind. Teilhard, in remarkable fashion, sought to locate the noosphere in nature as studied by empirical science. Geology, he noted, teaches that the earth is composed of four zones or layers which radiate from the center outward. These four layers are 1) the barysphere, which is the central metallic core; 2) the lithosphere, which is the rocky layer; 3) the hydrosphere; and 4) the atmosphere. The last two layers are made up of the fluids—liquid or gaseous—which surround the second layer. The four layers are surrounded by a fifth—the biosphere, which is the living membrane of fauna and flora. With the advent of thought, a sixth layer is discernible, according to Teilhard's argument—the noosphere. "Much more coherent and just as extensive as any preceding layer, it is really a new layer, the 'thinking layer,' which . . . has spread over and above the world of plants and animals."[196] With the noosphere, as Teilhard observed, "The earth 'gets a new skin.' Better still, it finds its soul."[197]

The noosphere, moreover, culminates in what Teilhard called the "Soul of souls."[198] Another name he used to denote this climactic mode of evolution is the term "the Omega point." Teilhard was led to posit the Omega point for two reasons: the reason of love and the reason of survival. By love, Omega initiates and maintains the unanimity of the particles—the particular minds—in the noosphere; it functions as a kind of final cause. But it is not merely ideal: it is "a real and present centre . . . supremely present."[199] For the reason of survival, Omega is "independent of the collapse of the forces with which evolution is woven."[200] Omega, then, is not dissipated in time; rather it transcends temporal process and time. As Teilhard said: "In Omega we have in the first place the principle we needed to explain both the persistent march of things toward greater consciousness, and the paradoxical solidity of what is most fragile."[201]

Viewed in the perspective of the history of philosophy, Teilhard's system seems to be a syncretic construction, striving to fuse the systems of Plotinus and of Bergson. Teilhard's system with its levels of matter, biosphere, noosphere, and Omega corresponds to Plotinus' system of matter and of the three hypostases: soul, mind, and the One. But Teilhard, unlike Plotinus and like Bergson, stresses temporal process, and the evolution of the higher levels from the lower. In attempting to incorporate both eternalistic monism and temporalistic evolutionism within a coherent system, Teilhard illustrates the latest phase in the development of process—the quest for an eternity in time, an absolute within relativity. Whitehead before him had resorted to the most exacting sort of categorial scheme to effectuate this aim. Teilhard, after sketching crudely the phases of the process, as revealed by the sciences, followed the path of his predecessors, Plotinus and Bergson—the path of mysticism. Plotinus intuited the One beyond time and all distinctions; Bergson duration, wholly temporal; and Teilhard? His mysticism caps a procedure which attends to science, its methods, its facts, its theories; and it is reserved for the apprehension of the Omega point.

Unfortunately, mystical intuition of the Omega point once achieved, Teilhard's system remains a topic which is susceptible to doubt. He undertook to present his thought as Christian. But is Omega identical with the Christian God? Analytic understanding of Omega gives rise to two rival interpretations: either it is the not yet achieved goal of evolution—akin to Alexander's emergent deity; or it is the teleological structure that pervades and guides the entire evolutionary process—akin to Whitehead's dipolar God. The first interpretation is too naturalistic, the second too pantheistic, to suit orthodox Christian theology with its eternal transcendent God. Teilhard's persistence in regarding his system as Christian has only served to strain the meanings of his terms and statements.

Nevertheless, an object lesson concerning process philosophy has been learned. Few process philosophers have ever been satisfied with the primacy of change exclusive of permanence. From Heraclitus' *logos* to Teilhard's Omega they have sought instead to reconcile process with eternal principles. Their various endeavors, however unsuccessful, indicate a challenge for philosophical speculation which remains urgent.

VII

THE USES OF SPECULATIVE PHILOSOPHY

Despite the traditional concern of philosophers with realism, materialism, idealism, and process philosophy, recent thinkers have been suspicious of and hostile to speculative philosophy. In an influential essay, "Critical and Speculative Philosophy," C. D. Broad has drawn a distinction between these two kinds of philosophizing in a fashion which favors the critical over the speculative. Critical philosophy, he said, tries "to analyze and define the concepts which are used in daily life and in the special sciences."[1] It also examines the fundamental propositions we assume in our reasoning. The "business" of speculative philosophy, on the other hand, "is to take over all aspects of human experience, to reflect upon them, and to try to think out a view of Reality as a whole which shall do justice to all of them."[2] Broad acknowledged that "it is certainly held to be the function of a philosopher to discuss the nature of Reality as a whole, and to consider the position and prospects of men in it."[3] And he was quick to admit that the critical philosopher had perforce to assume "a certain view on this question."[4] But if Broad implied that the critical philosopher presupposes speculative philosophy, he emphatically held that the speculative philosopher ought to be critical. As he said, "it is perfectly useless to take over the scientific, social, ethical, aesthetic, and religious experiences of mankind in their crude, unanalyzed form. We do not know what they mean or what weight to attach to various parts of the whole mass till we have submitted them to a critical analytic investigation."[5] From these considerations, Broad adduced two conclusions: "(i)

We cannot admit the claim of any system of Speculative Philosophy to be the final truth, as it will be subject to modification as more facts are known, and as known facts become more and more fully analyzed and criticized. (ii) We must always admit the possibility that Critical Philosophy has not yet been carried far enough to make any attempt at Speculative Philosophy profitable." [6]

The force of Broad's conclusions prevails among the majority of contemporary Anglo-American philosophers. Nowadays thinkers go beyond admitting the possibility that critical philosophy is not sufficiently advanced to permit speculation; they despair of speculative philosophy altogether. In fact, it has become fashionable to distinguish the philosopher, who is nearly always an analyst, from the sage, who performs the speculative function of constructing a vast system of thought.[7] Truth, according to the distinction, is won by the philosopher not by the sage, if it is won at all. The term "speculation" is retained mainly in the sense of conjectural thinking, as, for instance, when John Passmore, who employs the distinction between philosopher and sage, writes that metaphysics "is speculation controlled by rational criticism, just as science is speculation controlled by experiment and mathematics is speculation controlled by proof." [8] John Wisdom epitomized the dominant Anglo-American position *vis-à-vis* philosophy when he wrote: "To philosophize is to analyze." [9] Wisdom, however, must have felt misgivings about his neat formula. To it he added the footnote: "Apart from speculative philosophy, which is the deductive study of the existence of God and the immortality of the soul." [10] It is doubtful that any speculative philosophers were reassured by Wisdom's afterthought.

The disenchantment with speculative philosophy is not confined to Great Britain, the United States, and—one might add—Canada, Australia, New Zealand, and the Scandinavian countries, where analytic philosophy is strong. On the contrary, the distrust of speculative philosophy extends to Europe and Latin America, where thinkers disclaim the theoretical endeavor to frame ultimate and comprehensive systems of categories. Describing human experience phenomenologically, these thinkers have abandoned speculative systems of thought to focus on the uniqueness of human existence and the social, moral, and religious predicaments of men. Jean-Paul Sartre, in his remarkable essay on engaged literature, has eloquently expressed this existentialist standpoint. "Metaphysics," he wrote, "is not a sterile discussion on abstract notions unrelated to experience; it is a living effort to grasp from the inside the human condition in its totality."[11]

Although it is not inherent in speculative philosophy that it avoid analysis, or that it engage in sterile discussion on abstract notions, it has suffered from the hostility of both analysts and existentialists, themselves entangled in hostility. Young philosophers tend to neglect the field. After surveying the course of metaphysics in the United States from 1930 to 1960, Manley Thompson prophesies a dim future for speculation. While he is unwilling to assert that "speculative metaphysics in the grand manner . . . will disappear altogether," he deems it "safe to say" that such enterprises "have about run their course."[12] Of course Manley Thompson may be proved a false prophet. At any rate, he seems correct in his extrapolation from tendencies in the 1960s. For the speculative philosopher, when he appears, finds a miniscule audience or none at all. Too often, without so much as a cursory study of the products of speculation, it is concluded that the speculative philosopher has been insufficiently critical and analytical, or that he has evaded the concrete problems of human experience for a mere play of empty concepts. The upshot is deplorable, because speculative philosophy has its uses. Without deciding between rival speculative philosophies, it is in order here to explore these uses.

COGNITIVE USE

The most obvious use of speculative philosophy is its theoretical or cognitive use. Speculative philosophers promise to provide knowledge, or wisdom. Just at this point, however, a grave question arises concerning the knowledge allegedly afforded by speculative philosophy. As regards factual content and the principles and methods germane to such content, speculation is no longer considered reliable. Empirical science and experimental method are too entrenched at present to permit speculative thought to originate cognitions which have factual claims. Of course, speculative philosophy has historically been the source from which whole sciences have sprung. Nevertheless, it is customary today for individual thinkers to reverse the course of historical evolution, and to look to the sciences for the construction of speculative systems rather than to philosophical speculation for the initiation of new sciences.

C. S. Peirce, in his essay, "The Architecture of Theories," represents the current view on the matter.[13] Peirce canvassed each of the sciences to elicit the basic principles and key conceptions upon which to build an original speculative cosmology. Yet if speculative philosophy does not provide knowledge in the sense of empirical content, what does it provide? So far as any thinker accepts the question, his answer seems to be: structure. Accordingly, the speculative philosopher brings order to otherwise divergent empirical sciences. Instead of arranging topics as an encyclopedia does in an alphabetical order, the philosopher contrives a system with a logical structure of elements. This system exhibits, in Kant's terminology, architectonic. It achieves, in the language of Herbert Spencer (1820–1903), synthesis.

However, in the twentieth century the cognitive claims of speculative philosophy have been vigorously challenged. The most damaging assaults have been launched by the logical positivists. In the aphoristic statement which closes the *Tractatus Logico-Philosophicus* (1921), Ludwig Wittgenstein (1889–1951) asserted: "Whereof one cannot speak, thereof one must be silent."[14] However much Wittgenstein himself may have deviated from the position of the logical positivists, he was a source of inspiration for them. Silence was the sentence they passed on philosophical speculation, and they justified this sentence with a theory of knowledge which excluded speculative metaphysics. Knowledge, they said, is a system of statements, some of which are logically true, the others of which are empirically true. The statements of logic and mathematics are logically true; that is, they are true by virtue of the rules of the language in which they are made. Such statements are tautologous; they assert nothing of the domain of facts which lie outside the language. The statements of the natural sciences are empirically true; that is, they are true by virtue of their verification through observation of, and experimentation with, the facts of experience.

Where, according to this theory, do the statements of speculative philosophy fall? If these statements are warrantable by the rules of language, then they are logically true, and, asserting nothing of reality, belong to logic and mathematics. If they are testable in experience, then they belong to the empirical sciences. The statements of speculative philosophy which resist classification as logical or empirical turn out, on further analysis, to be confused statements. Rudolf Carnap has classified these statements as pseudo-object sentences.[15] Carnap's point requires amplification. Statements fall into three classes: object sentences, syntactical sentences, and pseudo-object sentences. Object sentences are statements which refer to entities outside language; their mode of speech is material. For example: "Babylon was a big town." Syntactical sentences are statements which refer to words and sentences; their mode of speech is formal. For example: " 'Five' is a number-word." Pseudo-object sentences are statements which seem to refer to entities outside language but really refer to words and sentences; their mode of speech is material. For example: "Five is not a thing, but a number." In classifying philosophical statements as pseudo-object sentences, Carnap regarded them as linguistically confused and confusing. Only when these statements are translated into the formal mode of speech, he held, can they be salvaged.[16] He said: "Translatability into the formal mode of speech constitutes the touchstone for all philosophical sentences . . ."[17] By this touchstone Carnap expected to eliminate speculative metaphysics. Either a metaphysical statement is translatable into a syntactical sentence in the formal mode, or it is discarded as utter nonsense produced by the violations of linguistic rules.

Carnap's employment of his touchstone for the elimination of metaphysics has resulted in his historic confrontation with the thought of Martin Heidegger.[18] In *Was ist Metaphysik* (1929) [19] Heidegger had launched his famous discussion of "Nothing," which contains the startling formula "Das Nichts nichtet"—viz., "Nothing nots." Carnap subjected Heidegger's statements to logical analysis, and he found these statements to be wrongly constructed, with Heidegger using the word "Nothing" as noun and as verb when it is simply a logical sign for a negative statement. Heidegger's doctrine of "Nothing," despite its appeal to existentialists, is dismissed as meaningless because, according to Carnap, it violates the syntactical rules of the language in which it is expressed.

When Carnap and his followers used logical analysis to disclose linguistic confusions with the intention of eliminating speculative metaphysics, they were convinced that philosophical speculation had no valid cognitive function. For them, the proper aim of logical analysis was to remedy the confusions of language which had misled human intelligence into nonsense rather than knowledge. Henceforth sound philosophical activity would be therapy. At least this is what the logical positivists in the 1930s and the 1940s expected. But subsequent developments in the history of thought betrayed their expectation. The logical positivist theory of knowledge involved ontological assumptions about, e.g., the nature of fact, of logical structure, of meaning, of truth, which not only failed to gain widespread acceptance, but which also stimulated prolonged discussion and abstruse polemics conspicuously speculative in character.

Thus analytic philosophers who shared the logical positivist belief that the statements of the speculative metaphysicians embody linguistic confusions, nevertheless, began to maintain that these statements do serve a cognitive function. As John Wisdom had observed: "Philosophical theories are illuminating . . . when they suggest or draw attention to a terminology which reveals likenesses and differences concealed by ordinary language." [20] According to Wisdom, the statements of the speculative metaphysicians should not be dismissed as nonsense; rather they should be respected as paradoxes which "draw attention, though often in a confused way, to some imperfectly recognized features of the procedure characteristic of a class of statements or questions."[21] "A paradox," wrote Wisdom, "is a flag which declares a discovery—not a new continent nor a cure for pneumonia but a discovery in the familiar. . . ."[22] Hence Wisdom took issue with Wittgenstein upon whom he leans so heavily. Wittgenstein, he says, too much represented the statements of speculative philosophers "as merely symptoms of linguistic confusion. I wish to represent them as also symptoms of linguistic penetration."[23] Of course Wittgenstein, as evident from a recently published lecture he delivered at Cambridge in 1929 or 1930, deeply respected the tendency of speculative thinkers to ask those ultimate questions which he considered non-sensical.[24] Wisdom carried the issue further. His essay, "Philosophical Perplexity," ends with the excusably smart remark: "Philosophers should be continually trying to say what cannot be said."[25]

To follow Wisdom's recommendation is to assume that there is a realm about which nothing can be said and that it may somehow be illuminated by futile efforts to say something about it. Here is a paradox, indeed. Yet it does concede that speculative philosophy, for all its non-sense, has a cognitive function. And this function is performed even when the philosophers disagree. In fact, lack of agreement among speculative metaphysicians, instead of being a mark of the impotence of their enterprise to advance human knowledge, appears as a positive merit. The worst fate philosophy could suffer would be the adoption once and for all of a single philosophical system. In his essay, "Philosophy, Anxiety, and Novelty," Wisdom has stated the point superbly:

> *It is not because it's bad that the old system won't do, but because it's old. As we all know but* won't remember, any classificatory system is a net spread on the blessed manifold of the individual and blinding us not to all but to too many of its varieties and continuities. A new system will do the same but not in just the same ways. So that in accepting *all* the systems their blinding power is broken, their re-

vealing power becomes acceptable; the individual is restored to us, not in a box as when language mastered us, but in "creation's chorus." [26]

The cognitive function of speculative philosophy is therefore best performed through the introduction of novelty into various categorial schemes. The price that must be paid is disagreement among the philosophers. But if incessant controversy haunts speculative philosophy, does this mean that there can be no progress in the field? Unquestionably lack of progress has been charged against speculative metaphysics. Yet equally unquestionably Brand Blanshard has nailed this charge down and refuted it. The charge, according to Blanshard, involves three theses: 1) that lack of agreement signifies lack of progress, 2) that science alone sets the rate of advance by reference to which progress in metaphysics should be measured, and 3) that "it is time the whole enterprise be turned over to science." [27]

Let us review Blanshard's devastating responses to each of these theses. First, Blanshard contends that there are other evidences of progress besides agreement, such as (a) "the sealing off of blind alleys" for future inquirers—e.g., proving the immortality of the soul in the manner of Socrates; (b) the elimination of crackpot theories; (c) the sharper definition of problems; and (d) the increased subtlety and sophistication with which a theory is advanced.[28] Second, Blanshard denies that the rate of advance in science should be the standard to measure philosophical problems. His denial is supported by several reasons: (a) scientific questions may be answered piecemeal and in isolation, while philosophical questions must be solved together because of the systematic character of the field; (b) the scientist proceeds without worrying about his assumptions, whereas "the march of metaphysics is always open to attack from the rear"; and finally, (c) the problems with which speculative metaphysicians deal are simply the most difficult.[29] Third, Blanshard argues that it will hardly do to dismiss philosophy and to rely exclusively on science. For science needs philosophy, and at both ends of its undertakings. As Blanshard says: "Critical philosophy precedes science in the sense that it deals with the ideas and assumptions that the scientist brings to his work. Speculative philosophy comes after science, in the sense that it attempts to put the results of the various disciplines into a consistent view of the world."[30] Further, man himself, by his very nature, has need of speculative metaphysics. Blanshard writes:

> Men know that, lurking behind the cosmic curtain, there are answers to their questions about where they came from, about their place in the strange world of stars and atoms, about their destiny. While they know that this treasure is there, they can no more forget about it than Arthur's knights could forget their grail. Seek it they must. Their interest is too much a part of their human nature to die out.[31]

Speculative philosophy, then, is an unavoidable human enterprise. And so its cognitive function should be respected even though its cognitive results fall short of all that is hoped for. In addition to the origination of sciences, speculative philosophy offers, according to traditional conceptions, a kind of knowledge which the special sciences do not provide. Speculative philosophy is said to study being *qua* being, or the first causes, or the basic principles of logic and of knowledge, or the divine, or the transcendental conditions of experience and knowledge, or the systematic structure of the cosmos, of freedom, of the destiny of man beyond nature. Despite the differences of opinion among speculative philosophers, there is considerable agreement that speculative philosophy is general since all the special sciences are founded upon it, yet is specific since it alone can attain the kind of knowledge sought. After all, speculative philosophy promises knowledge about matters which, though of the utmost importance to men, nevertheless lie beyond the reach of their other methods of investigation. However speculative philosophy may fare in its cognitive function as regards science, it has been adopted as an instrument of knowledge as regards religion. For speculative philosophy has a religious use.

RELIGIOUS USE

In the nineteenth century, speculative philosophy was subjected to one of its most severe assaults from the standpoint of religion.

With Hegel and the Hegelians in mind, Søren Kierkegaard (1813–1855) launched an attack on speculative philosophy within the framework of Christianity, although other philosophical systems and other religions could be substituted. According to Kierkegaard, the speculative philosophers had evaded the crucial issue of faith vs. doubt; they had assumed "Christianity . . . as given." [32] They consequently regard religion as an object, as a historical phenomenon, which they undertake to embrace in a system of categories. But religion, above all, is subjective; it relates to the concrete individual's concern for his eternal happiness. Therefore, religion and speculative philosophy are fundamentally opposed. As Kierkegaard wrote: "The subject [as religious] is in passion infinitely interested in his eternal happiness, and is now supposed to receive assistance from speculation, i.e., by himself philosophizing. But in order to philosophize he must proceed in precisely the opposite direction, giving himself up and losing himself in objectivity, thus vanishing from himself." [33] Kierkegaard expatiated on the inability of philosophical systems to penetrate and to comprehend the concrete and the existential. "An existential system," he declared, "is impossible." [34] This means, he continued, that an existential system, though it may be real, cannot be formulated. "Reality itself is a system—for God; but it cannot be a system for any existing [changing, temporal] spirit. System and finality correspond to one another, but existence is precisely the opposite of finality." [35]

Here, then, are the basic elements of Kierkegaard's attack on speculative philosophy from the standpoint of religion. These elements are the opposition between subjectivity and objectivity, existence and logic, religion and philosophy. As soon as the speculative philosopher attempts to explain religion, he mutilated it, glossing over the existential but illogical character of its demands and its promises. In sum, Kierkegaard asserted: "Speculative philosophy achieves the triumph of understanding Christianity entire; but it is to be noted that it does not understand it in a Christian manner, but speculatively, which is precisely a misunderstanding, since Christianity is the very opposite of speculation." [36]

Despite the vigor with which it was prosecuted, Kierkegaard's gravamen against speculative philosophy proved less than devastating. Not only did it presuppose a baggage of concepts—subjectivity/objectivity, existence/logic, and so forth—which revealed an implicit metaphysics; it also scored its points against a particular kind of speculative philosophy, one which equated existence and thought and which dogmatically claimed finality. Surely it is possible to distinguish speculative philosophy from religion, and simultaneously to maintain that speculative philosophy, besides its cognitive use, has a religious use.

Although religious men point to a singular experience, or to a particular institution, or to a special revelation, in order to justify their faith and to deepen their worship, speculative philosophy may be used to clarify the experience, to rationalize the institution, and to elucidate the revelation. To participate in the experience, to adhere to the institution, to acknowledge the revelation, some men need speculative philosophy. Hence speculative philosophers have performed a considerable service to religion. No doubt, speculative proofs for the existence of God, originating at a time when philosophy was the handmaiden of religion and theology the queen of the sciences, remain as permanent achievements of human culture, whether or not they are correct. Further, speculative philosophy may not only be used in the service of religion; but also in some cases it is used as religion. For some men, for example, knowing God through intellectual proofs of His existence is tantamount to a religious experience with Him.

AESTHETIC USE

Mention has been made of the fact that, regardless of their truth or validity, proofs of the existence of God are part of man's permanent cultural heritage. All the major systems of philosophy may be similarly esteemed. At least the values which these speculative philosophies add to human civilization are aesthetic. This was admitted even by the logical positivists, who held that metaphysical statements, though linguistically confused and non-sensical from the standpoint of knowledge, do express emotive meaning. As

Carnap said, these statements "have no logical content, but are only expressions of feeling which in their turn stimulate feelings and volitional tendencies on the part of the hearer."[37] Yet the logical positivist concession is extremely grudging. It betrays insensitivity to the aesthetic values of philosophical systems, as when Carnap remarked: "Metaphysicians are musicians without musical ability."[38] And it is also oblivious to the kinds of knowledge works of art convey. W. H. Walsh's observations are pertinent here: "We need to enter into the thought of a metaphysician as we enter into that of a writer of imaginative literature; we can derive enrichment and illumination from the first as much as from the second. A person who has succeeded in mastering the thought of a major metaphysician sees the world with fresh eyes; whether he accepts the point of view urged or not, the possibilities of experience have been multiplied for him."[39]

A generation earlier, W. P. Montague (1873–1953) advanced a similar line of argument, consistently formulating its implications. He proposed that philosophy should abandon inquiry into the domain of the actual and should concentrate on inquiry into the domain of the possible. The justification of a philosophy, he argued, is the vision it furnishes.[40] But if thinkers like W. H. Walsh and W. P. Montague have demonstrated the cognitive function of speculative systems conceived as artistic creations of the imagination, consideration of the aesthetic dimension proper to these systems has fallen to Stephen Pepper, the leading American academic aesthetician. In his recently published article, "An Essay on the Essay: An Aesthetic Appreciation," Pepper maintains that the essay is the purest form of literature.[41] Occupying a lowly place in literature in comparison with the drama, the novel, and the lyric, the essay has for its material ideas, the most abstract of which Pepper terms concepts, and these ideas have intrinsic aesthetic worth. Pepper finds the great essays in the works of the philosophers, the scientists, and the mathematicians. Of course Pepper's case is not restricted to the systems of speculative philosophy, but obviously it embraces them.

Speculative systems furnish each a uniqueness and a wholeness of experience akin to the enjoyment of the masterpieces of poetry, painting, music, architecture, sculpture, and drama. It is no overstretched imagination that compares a system of speculative philosophy to a masterpiece of architecture. Just as beauty is discernible in the physical structure, so it may be expected and appreciated in the intellectual. Although the philosopher may himself deem such beauty as a fortunate by-product irrelevant to his intended design, the beauty is there to be enjoyed. Happy are those students who can suspend their critical search for truth sufficiently to savor the aesthetic values the systems of philosophy contain! Sometimes philosophies win their adherents as much, if not more, by virtue of the aesthetic power of their language and their architectonic as by the truths they express. An interesting but false doctrine, because of its aesthetic delightfulness, often wins out over a true but dull one. A. N. Whitehead once asserted: "It is more important that a proposition be interesting than that it be true."[42] At any rate, speculative philosophers enrich mankind with art objects of inestimable worth; their systems appear as symbols congealing values independently of their reference. Hence speculative philosophy has its aesthetic use.

MORAL USE

However, if the aesthetic use of speculative philosophy be deemed frivolous, there is compensation in considering its moral use. Yet to hold that speculative philosophy has a moral use is to go against the major trend in recent Anglo-American theories of ethics. This trend exhibits, as Iris Murdoch has said, "the elimination of metaphysics from ethics."[43] It is, moreover, sustained by the convergence of three arguments. The first argument is the pervasive "anti-metaphysical" posture of contemporary thought, resulting from the critique and the analysis of language and of knowledge. Then there are two arguments which stem specifically from recent developments in philosophical ethics. One argument is "the antinaturalistic argument" originated by G. E. Moore (1873–1958); it denies that the "ought" can be derived from the "is," that "goodness" is a natural property, that value is based on fact.[44] The other argument is a complex of moral reasons justifying the refusal to ground ethics on metaphysics. Dogmatism is the product of efforts to base ethics on metaphysics, and dogmatism weakens the entire fabric of morality by undermining the essential element—namely, the responsibility of the individual to make a free choice. According to Miss Murdoch's analysis, then, the current view of the relation between ethics and metaphysics favored by Anglo-American thinkers holds, first, that it is theoretically impossible to base ethics on metaphysics and, second, that, if it were theoretically possible, it would be morally wrong to do so.

Now Miss Murdoch is careful to indicate that "the elimination of metaphysics from ethics" operates primarily in the context of philosophical empiricism and moral individualism. She writes: "Nothing, we tend to assume, can *contain* the individual, except possibly his habits and his traditions, and these are merely facts like other ones, and capable of being reflectively examined." [45] And this, she is quick to add, is "only one way . . . of conceiving morality." [46] Another way, which she calls the "Natural Law" morality, and which Thomists, Hegelians, and Marxists follow, regards the individual "as held in a framework which transcends him, where what is important and valuable is the framework, and the individual only has importance or even reality, in so far as he belongs to the framework." [47] At last Miss Murdoch touches the sensitive juncture of ethics and metaphysics.

The synoptic vision of the whole and the penetration to the depths of being which speculative philosophers promise have moral bearings. Even a pragmatist detects differences between speculative idealism, with its assurances concerning the durability of values, and speculative materialism, with its suspicions concerning the mutability and contingency of values; and it is not necessary to be a pragmatist to appreciate the moral import of these differences. Plain men and moral philosophers from Plato to Kant have appealed to speculative metaphysics to provide the postulates necessary for morality. True, theories of morality often stand without speculative doctrines concerning God, freedom, and immortality, and men behave morally without giving much thought to these topics. Still, many philosophers and nonphilosophical persons share the conviction that what is right and what is good, whether defined or rather considered indefinable, are ultimately related—logically, ontologically, cosmologically—with what is, with what must be, and with what may be, and so speculative philosophy is required. For these men, then, speculative philosophy performs an important moral function in supplying the foundations, or the framework, of morality.

SOCIAL USE

Next to the moral use of speculative philosophy is its social use. This use, however, cannot be easily spelled out, since the relation of philosophy to society is complex and obscure. When Sidney Hook, America's leading social philosopher, denied a necessary logical connection "between a theory of being or becoming and any particular theory of ethics or politics,"[48] his line of reasoning seemed to extend from ethics to politics the process of eliminating metaphysics. However, what Hook denied is strictly a logical connection, for he did concede that "there is a definite historical connection between the social movements of any period and its dominant metaphysical teachings."[49]

Hook's admission of a historical connection between metaphysics and politics is consonant with the historicist attitude of many contemporary students of the social sciences. As Karl Mannheim (1893–1947) has said, historicism "epitomizes our *Weltanschauung*."[50] It treats philosophy, along with science, art, religion, and all economic, political, and social institutions, as part of the cultural configuration in a given epoch in history. And it reduces the truth claim of a philosophical theory to a relative claim, its truth holding only for a limited period of time. When historicism propounds this total view of culture, however, it is easily elevated into a speculative system in its own right. But then it is impugned by a peculiar defect; it is refuted by self-reference, by applying its tenets to itself. For the claim that all truth is historically relative must itself be treated as historically relative.

Another approach to the question concerning the relation of

philosophy and society harks back to Karl Marx (1818–1883) and Frederick Engels (1820–1895). For the orthodox Marxist, a philosophy merely reflects the society in which it dwells. Thus the British Marxist, Maurice Cornforth, writes, "in every epoch the ways of thinking characteristic of the philosophers do reflect the character of the economic development and social relations of that epoch."[51] Cornforth, moreover, traces philosophy to the class structure of society. "Philosophy," he says, "has always expressed and could not but express a class standpoint."[52] Philosophy is, in the Marxist sense of the term, ideology. As Engels stated: "Ideology is a process accomplished by the so-called thinker consciously but with false consciousness. The real motives impelling him remain unknown to him, otherwise it would not be an ideological process."[53] Hence the orthodox Marxist view dialectically produces a contradiction. First, it maintains that a philosophy reveals the society of which it is a part. Second, it maintains that, since the consciousness of the philosopher is false, a philosophy conceals its society. The contradiction is further aggravated by the consideration that Marxism itself propounds a philosophy of dialectical materialism. Despite its being self-styled "scientific," it is basically speculative. And dialectical materialism is more than a passive mirror of natural and historical reality: rather it is used by the Marxists as a revolutionary instrument to transform societies.

The development of a society may well be shaped by speculative systems. Among contemporary American philosophers, F. S. C. Northrop and James K. Feibleman have recognized that philosophies are causally efficacious in the formation of human cultures. According to Northrop, the various national cultures in the West were shaped by rival philosophies which converge in conceding formal concepts central importance in knowledge, the cultures in the East are imbued with a philosophy which places paramount emphasis on the aesthetic continuum enjoyed in human experience, and it is possible to establish international understanding by reconciling, without suppressing, these differences.[54] According to Feibleman, postulate sets of fundamental beliefs about knowledge, reality, and value determine the nature and careers of entire cultures.[55]

Sometimes coherent, yet sometimes entailing inconsistent practices, these beliefs nonetheless control action. Since they usually operate without men being aware of them, and since they pertain to what men esteem to be really real, Feibleman names a set of these beliefs "the implicit dominant ontology" of a culture. A major task of the philosopher in a time of social troubles, Feibleman contends, is to make explicit these implicit dominant ontologies for purposes of criticism and reconstruction.

Differences of opinion among the historicists, the Marxists, Sidney Hook, F. S. C. Northrop, and James K. Feibleman notwithstanding, agreement on one point emerges: How a people behaves and evaluates its behavior is due, in some measure, to how it conceives the world and its place in the world. Although the line of causation between speculative idea and actual conduct is obscure, so intimate a link is believed to hold that some societies devote a large part of their intellectual energies articulating their philosophies, formulating doctrines and dogmas concerning the ultimate substance of reality, the patterns of development in nature and history, the destiny of man, the being or non-being of God. Speculative philosophy then hardens into ideology, and political leaders take firm measures to protect orthodoxy and to suppress nonconformity. No doubt, these societies lose in flexibility and freedom what they gain in cohesiveness and conscious purposefulness. But they do point up the social use of speculative philosophy, and if free societies were to address themselves to the task of self-consciously stating their ideologies, they would gain enlightenment concerning instruments and goals, means and ends. Making explicit what is implicit sharpens and deepens what is believed; it also purges away inconsistent and undesirable elements and enhances the genuine values. Here speculative philosophy has a social use the benefits of which are incalculable.

PSYCHOLOGICAL USE

Just as speculative philosophy may be used socially to impart cohesiveness and purposefulness, it may also be used psychologically. Since ancient times the speculative philosopher has been the butt of raillery for the plain man of practical affairs. He has been regarded as an eccentric in flight from the actual world. Alexander Herzberg has argued that, by comparison with conventional standards of psychological normalcy, philosophers appear to be abnormal.[56] From examining the life careers of thirty-one historically important philosophers, Herzberg concluded that "philosophers were men of unusually strong impulses," that they suffered inhibitions which were "more than normally intense," that they exhibited "unsuitableness for practical life," that they tended to "poetical expression," and that they were "predisposed to neuroses."[57] The suspicion mounts that theories born in the minds of such men might not pass the scrutiny of more level-headed thinkers.

A favored method of coping with philosophical theories has been to appeal to common sense. In recent thought G. E. Moore has been the unrivalled exponent of the method of common sense in philosophy. G. E. Moore has said: "I am one of those philosophers who have held that the 'Common Sense view of the world' is, in certain fundamental features, wholly true."[58] But as Moore added, all philosophers concur in subscribing to the beliefs that comprise the commonsense view of the world; however, they disagree about the logical analyses of these beliefs. Sometimes these logical analyses are internally inconsistent, sometimes they are inconsistent with the ordinary meanings of the commonsense beliefs, sometimes they cannot be logically supported by the commonsense beliefs. In such cases, according to Moore, the philosopher should, by using common sense as his touchstone, discard the discredited logical analyses. Thus idealism, in all its varieties, deserves dismissal. Nevertheless, Moore admitted that the appeal to common sense does not resolve all philosophical questions; in fact, he concluded his important essay, "A Defense of Common Sense," in perplexity over the logical analyses of such commonsense beliefs as "There are and have been material things" and "There are and have been many Selves."[59]

Philosophical speculation is more deeply rooted than errant wandering from common sense; it persists even after a return to common sense has occurred. Immanuel Kant was, no doubt, correct when he insisted that metaphysical speculation is inevitable. He went on to ground it in the very nature of human reason, although he qualified it not only as inevitable but as illusion. Arthur Schopenhauer (1788–1860) imparted to Kant's theory a pessimistic twist. Man, said Schopenhauer, has a need for metaphysics: "It is wickedness, evil, and death that qualify and intensify the philosophical astonishment. Not merely that the world exists, but still more that it is such a world, is the *punctum pruriens* of metaphysics, the problem which awakens in mankind an unrest that cannot be quieted by scepticism nor yet by criticism."[60] More specifically, man's awareness of death instigates his venture into metaphysical speculation, as he seeks a transcendent justification of a world in which he finds himself doomed.[61] Fundamentally, Schopenhauer furnished the basic elements for a psychoanalytic theory of speculative metaphysics.

Deepened and expanded by the work of Sigmund Freud (1856–1939), psychoanalytic theory has been applied to speculative metaphysics with heightened sophistication by the linguistic philosophers, John Wisdom* and Morris Lazerowitz. A "verbal dream" is Morris Lazerowitz's term for a metaphysical theory. Although constructed out of words during waking life, a metaphysical theory resembles a dream in that it is "a production of the unconscious and has both sense and motivation."[62] Further, Lazerowitz points to two layers in the structure of metaphysical theories. The uppermost, or conscious layer, is "the *illusion* of a theory about the nature or real existence of a phenomenon, the illusion, that is to say, that a metaphysical sentence states a view of some sort about reality;" and the "deeper and less accessible layer" contains the "realities" to which the sentences of the uppermost layer refer—realities, however, which "are subjective, the unconscious contents of our minds, not the physical world."[63] For example, a metaphysician propounds a theory which reduces change to recurrent trans-

* Not to be confused with John O. Wisdom, who also uses psychoanalysis to explain philosophical doctrines and who is the author of *The Unconscious Origin of Berkeley's Philosophy* (London, 1953).

formations of unchanging substances; he seems to be saying something about the real world, but actually he is expressing a basic dread of change.[64] So far Lazerowitz's conception of metaphysics illustrates the viewpoint of so-called therapeutic positivism. Metaphysicians, because of deep-seated and unconscious impulses, are concocters of cognitive nonsense; they need to be cured to be saved from their fantasies.

Lazerowitz's intention is, however, not exclusively therapeutic. He recognizes still a third layer or aspect of metaphysical theories. John Wisdom, let us recall, refused to dismiss metaphysical theories as mere instances of linguistic confusion; he stressed that they are examples of linguistic penetration as well. Hence, for Wisdom, metaphysical theories also serve the cognitive purpose of disclosing the features of language or of thought or reality which had been concealed in the familiar formulas. Lazerowitz follows Wisdom up to a point in appreciating the positive value of metaphysics; but by contrast, he finds these values in the noncognitive purposes of metaphysical theories. Lazerowitz writes: "A metaphysical sentence, which causes, at the conscious level of our minds, the erroneous idea that it states the existence or non-existence of a phenomenon or that the phenomenon has or lacks a certain property, is itself a pre-conscious re-edition of a familiar term and expresses one or more unconsciously held beliefs, the purpose of which is to satisfy a repressed longing or to ward off a repressed fear."[65] Thus the metaphysician introduces a linguistic innovation not for the sake of knowledge, but rather because it gives "him and others pleasure."[66]

The psychoanalytic approach permits, therefore, a positive appreciation of speculative metaphysics. Alexander Herzberg, whose remarks on the psychology of the philosophers have been unflattering, has nonetheless written of the threefold "biological value of philosophy." (The term "psychological" could well be substituted for the term "biological.") According to Herzberg, first, philosophy "serves as a substitute for practical action in the discharge of excess impulse-energies—secondly, it creates, in the place of harsh and intractable and therefore unsatisfying reality, a painless and therefore satisfying world—and thirdly, it leads, by means of a detour, to the real satisfaction of powerful interests. And in all three ways it serves to maintain mental health: its value lies in the realm of psychic hygiene."[67] Hence speculative philosophy, in meeting the needs of the poorly adjusted or the mentally ill, has a psychological use.

Of course, the psychoanalytic approach misrepresents the needs the philosophers themselves have felt when they engaged in speculation. What these philosophers, men of learning and intellectual achievement, have sought is ultimacy and coherence and comprehensiveness in their thoughts. The need is manifest in some degree in all thinking; in speculative philosophy it grows into an insistent demand. Only speculative philosophy promises to satisfy this need, and it continues to promise even when it fails. Hence speculative philosophy has a psychological use, and if the world is so constructed that reality actually answers to this demand of thought, then speculative philosophy in its psychological use culminates also in its cognitive use.

CONCLUDING REMARKS

Essentially, the justification of speculative philosophy in terms of its uses is pragmatic. Now the connection of metaphysics and pragmatism was clear to William James. After all, he defined pragmatism as "primarily a method of settling metaphysical disputes that otherwise might be interminable,"[68] and he compared it to a hotel corridor onto which rooms open where different residents are elaborating diverse metaphysical theories. Suppose the occurrence of disputes over whether the world is one or many, fated or free, materialistic or theistic. Then the pragmatic method, according to James, proposes "to interpret each notion by tracing its respective practical consequences. What difference would it practically make to any one if this notion rather than that notion were true?"[69] Where there is no difference, James decided, the dispute is idle. Where there is a difference, James decided in favor of the hypothesis with the more desirable practical results. In this way, James accepted the hypotheses of pluralism, of freedom, and of theism.

After William James, John Dewey led the pragmatist movement in American philosophy. Unlike James's posture with regard to speculative metaphysics, Dewey's is openly hostile. Calling upon philosophers to attend to the problems of men, Dewey sought to eliminate traditional metaphysics altogether. Dewey presented his position on the issue in two well-known books: *Reconstruction in Philosophy* (1920) and *The Quest for Certainty* (1929). His condemnation of traditional speculative philosophy amalgamates psychological and sociological modes of explanation.

According to Dewey, the cognitive function of intelligence is to guide action. However, action is caught up in all sorts of contingencies and conditions which involve insecurity. To escape from these insecurities, men indulge in imaginative constructions which, like the great religions, promise a transcendent certainty beyond nature and human experience. The inherent yearning for certainty—the desire to "escape from peril"—is one causative principle in the development of traditional speculative metaphysics.[70] The other principle, according to Dewey, is social. The class structure of society in the ancient world had liberated one group from the requirements of work, the inequitable social arrangement being justified by custom. In time, custom, including traditional religion, crumbled under the pressures of criticism. The leisure class, which indulged in cultural pursuits, then turned to philosophy to fill the breach. By dialectical means the speculative philosophers had constructed systems of concepts which promised men the absolute certainty they could not find in experience. Further, they delineated the structure of the cosmos in terms favorable to their own class interests. They placed reason above experience, thought above action, being above change. As Dewey put the matter, "that which had rested upon custom was to be restored, resting no longer upon the habits of the past, but upon the very metaphysics of Being and the Universe. Metaphysics is a substitute for custom as the source and guarantor of higher moral and social values."[71]

As in the examination of the charge that there is no progress in philosophy, here, too, Brand Blanshard may serve as guide. For

Blanshard has done a superb job of refuting Dewey. First, consider Dewey's claim that speculative metaphysics is essentially conservative, an indulgence of a leisure class to defend the *status quo*. As Blanshard says, "The suggestion that speculative thinking is confined to one social class, that it has favored conservatism rather than change, and that it is committed to the advantage of any one social class or political faction falls down very quickly before a little historical inquiry."[72] Secondly, Blanshard faults Dewey's pragmatic thesis that the purpose of thought is to guide action as an incorrect analysis of the nature of thought. According to Blanshard, Dewey confounded a crucial distinction, one not only operative in ordinary thinking, but also of paramount significance for the possibility of speculative metaphysics. This distinciton is the difference between the kind of satisfaction a man finds in successful action and the kind of satisfaction he finds in understanding. As Blanshard says:

> When we puzzle over such questions as whether space has a limit, or whether our choices are determined, or whether the universe was created at some point in past time, we are not trying to decide how *to act*. We are trying, however fumblingly, to find out the truth about something, and . . . this interest in knowing is stubbornly irreducible to the interest in doing things. . . . The ordering of behavior is one aim of thought, but it is not its distinctive or primary aim. That primary aim is to know; and in the past, the thought of the metaphysician has been regarded as the purest expression of this aim.[73]

In summary, the uses of speculative philosophy are many: cognitive, religious, aesthetic, moral, social, and psychological. While each use may be considered in isolation from the others, they are intimately related. Perhaps, indeed, they are mutually implicated, but this suggestion must here remain *mere* suggestion. True, each of these uses is found in other activities and instruments, and possibly all the higher cultural activities of man, religion, art, science, as well as speculative philosophy, have an equally wide range of multiple uses. These considerations, however, do not detract from the uses of speculative philosophy. For speculative philosophy not only has these uses; it has them in its own distinctive ways. Reflection on the uses of speculative philosophy should, for those who think, constitute an exhortation to speculate. If today speculative philosophy is scorned as useless, it is no fault of speculative philosophy; it is rather the fault of those who, ignorant of its uses, do not speculate.

NOTES

INTRODUCTION

[1] A. N. Whitehead, *The Function of Reason* (Princeton, N.J.: Princeton University Press, 1929; Beacon Press paperback, 1958), p. 10.

[2] Ibid., p. 12. [3] Ibid., p. 9. [4] Ibid., pp. 37–38. [5] Ibid., p. 65.

[6] Ibid.

[7] See Andrew J. Reck, "Contemporary American Speculative Philosophy," to be published in the *Revue internationale de philosophie.*

[8] Roderick M. Chisholm, Herbert Feigl, William K. Frankena, John Passmore, Manley Thompson, *Philosophy* (Englewood Cliffs, N.J.: Prentice Hall, 1964), p. 231.

[9] For the history of this society, see Paul G. Kuntz, *The Metaphysical Society of America 1950–1970,* 18 mimeographed pages.

[10] Paul Weiss, "The Four-Fold Art of Avoiding Questions," in "Notes and Observations," *Review of Metaphysics,* vol. IV (1950), pp. 133–34.

[11] Ibid. [12] Ibid., p. 135.

[13] A. N. Whitehead, *Science and the Modern World* (New York: Macmillan, 1925), pp. 299–300.

CHAPTER I

[1] Plato, *Republic,* V, 475, in *The Dialogues of Plato,* trans. by B. Jowett (New York: Random House, 1937), vol. I, p. 739. All citations are to this edition.

[2] Ibid., VI, 484, in *The Dialogues of Plato,* vol. I, p. 744.

[3] *Oxford English Dictionary,* vol. X, p. 558.

[4] James Mark Baldwin, ed., *Dictionary of Philosophy and Psychology,* vol. II, p. 568. Paul Edwards, *Encyclopedia of Philosophy* (New York: Macmillan, 1967), has no entry for "speculation" or "speculative philosophy."

[5] See P. F. Strawson, *Individuals* (London: Methuen, 1959).

[6] H. P. Grice, D. F. Pears, and P. F. Strawson, "Metaphysics," *The Nature of Metaphysics,* ed. D. F. Pears (London and New York: Macmillan and St. Martin's Press, 1957), p. 21.

[7] Aristotle, *Metaphysics,* bk. IV, ch. 1, l. 1003a, in *The Basic Works of Aristotle,* Richard McKeon, ed. (New York: Random House, 1941), p. 731.

[8] See Werner Jaeger, *Aristotle,* 2nd ed. (Oxford: Clarendon Press, 1934), p. 192; and W. D. Ross, *Aristotle,* 3rd ed. (London: Methuen, 1937), p. 157.

[9] Plotinus, *Enneads,* VI, ch. ix, sec. 11, in *The Philosophy of Plotinus,* Joseph Katz, trans. (New York: Appleton-Century-Crofts Inc., 1950), p. 158.

[10] Descartes, *Discourse on Method,* Part II, in *Descartes Selections,* Ralph M. Eaton, ed. (New York: Scribner's, 1927), pp. 16–17.

[11] *Œuvres de Descartes,* Charles Adam and Paul Tannery, eds. (Paris: Cerf, 1897–1913), vol. IX, Part 2, p. 14. (Translation my own.)

[12] Ibid.

[13] Spinoza, *Ethics* (1677), V. Prop. xlii, Scholium, in *Spinoza Selections,* ed. by John Wild (New York: Charles Scribner's Sons, 1930), p. 400.

[14] John Locke, *Essay Concerning Human Understanding,* ed. by A. C. Fraser (New York: Dover paperback 1959), vol. I, p. 14.

[15] Ibid., p. 26. [16] Ibid., p. 31. [17] Ibid.

[18] David Hume, *An Enquiry Concerning the Human Understanding* (1748), in *The Philosophy of David Hume,* Vere Chappell, ed. (New York: Modern Library, 1963), p. 391. All citations are to this edition.

[19] Christian Wolff, *Preliminary Discourse on Philosophy in General,* trans. and Introduction by Richard J. Blackwell (Indianapolis: Bobbs-Merrill, 1963), p. 17.

[20] Ibid., p. 41. [21] Ibid., p. 39.

[22] Immanuel Kant, *Critique of Pure Reason,* trans. by N. K. Smith (London: Macmillan, 1933), p. 300.

[23] Immanuel Kant, "Solution," *Prolegomena to Any Future Metaphysics,* trans. by Lewis W. Beck (New York: Library of Liberal Arts, 1950), p. 114.

[24] R. G. Collingwood, *An Essay in Metaphysics* (Oxford: Clarendon Press, 1940), p. 40.

[25] Ibid., p. 41. [26] Ibid., p. 47. [27] Ibid., p. 246. [28] Ibid., p. 49.

[29] William Wallace, trans., *The Logic of Hegel* (Oxford: Clarendon Press, 1892), p. 16.

[30] F. H. Bradley, *Appearance and Reality* (Oxford: Clarendon Press, 1946), p. xii.

[31] A. E. Taylor, *Elements of Metaphysics* (New York: Barnes and Noble paperback, 1961), p. 4.

[32] Ibid., p. 39.

[33] Henri Bergson, "Introduction to Metaphysics," *The Creative Mind,* trans. by M. L. Andison (New York: Philosophical Library, 1946), p. 221.

[34] Ibid. [35] Ibid.

[36] See Andrew J. Reck, *Introduction to William James* (Bloomington: Indiana University Press, 1967), pp. 57–68.

[37] See John Dewey, *Experience and Nature* (New York: Dover paperback, 1958), pp. 1a–39.

[38] Alfred North Whitehead, *Process and Reality* (New York: Macmillan, 1929), p. 4.

[39] Ibid., p. 5. [40] Ibid. [41] Ibid., p. 6. [42] Ibid., p. 4.

[43] Ibid., p. 6. [44] Ibid., pp. 15–16. [45] Ibid., p. 6. [46] Ibid., p. 7.

[47] Ibid., p. 8. [48] Ibid. [49] Ibid., p. 12. [50] Ibid. [51] Ibid., p. 13.

[52] W. Mays, *The Philosophy of Whitehead* (London: Allen and Unwin, 1959), p. 51.

[53] Alfred North Whitehead, *Adventures of Ideas* (New York: Macmillan, 1933), p. 286.

[54] Ibid., p. 184. [55] Ibid., p. 187. [56] Ibid., p. 286.

[57] Whitehead, *Process and Reality,* p. 6.
[58] Ibid., p. 32.

CHAPTER II

[1] Josiah Royce, *The World and the Individual* (New York: Macmillan, 1899), vol. I, p. 12. Both volumes of this work are now available as Dover paperbacks.
[2] Ibid., p. 53. [3] Ibid. [4] Ibid., p. 54. [5] Ibid., p. 56.
[6] Ibid., vol. II, p. 335. [7] Ibid., vol. I, pp. 16–17. [8] Ibid., p. 61.
[9] Ibid., p. 137. [10] Ibid., p. 179. [11] Ibid., p. 61. [12] Ibid., p. 186.
[13] Ibid., p. 177. [14] Ibid., p. 180. [15] Ibid., p. 202. [16] Ibid., p. 240.
[17] Ibid., pp. 244, 251. [18] Ibid., p. 356. [19] Ibid., p. 61.
[20] Ibid., p. 37. [21] Ibid., p. 23.
[22] Edward Gleason Spaulding, *The New Rationalism, the Development of a Constructive Realism upon the Basis of Modern Logic and Science, and Through the Criticism of Opposed Philosophical Systems* (New York: Henry Holt and Co., 1918), p. 364.
[23] Ibid., p. 177. [24] Ibid. [25] Ibid.
[26] William Ernest Hocking, *Types of Philosophy* (London: Scribner's, 1929), pp. 420–21.
[27] Ibid., pp. 434–35. [28] Ibid., p. 437. [29] Ibid., p. 441.
[30] Wilmon H. Sheldon, *The Strife of Systems and Productive Duality* (Cambridge, Mass.: Harvard University Press, 1918), p. 33.
[31] Wilmon H. Sheldon, *God and Polarity: A Synthesis of Philosophies* (New Haven: Yale University Press, 1954), p. 157.
[32] Ibid., p. 158. [33] Ibid., p. 140.
[34] Sheldon, *The Strife of Systems,* p. 423.
[35] Ibid., p. 415. [36] Ibid., p. 417. [37] Ibid., pp. 471–72.
[38] Ibid., pp. 524–25. [39] Ibid., p. iv.
[40] Sheldon, *God and Polarity,* p. 674.
[41] Ibid., p. 424. [42] Ibid., p. 441. [43] Ibid., p. 502. [44] Ibid., p. 500.
[45] Wilmon H. Sheldon, *America's Progressive Philosophy* (New Haven: Yale University Press, 1942).
[46] See Andrew J. Reck, "Wilmon H. Sheldon's Philosophy of Philosophy," *Tulane Studies in Philosophy,* vol. VII (1958), pp. 111–28.
[47] Stephen C. Pepper, *World Hypotheses, a Study in Evidence* (Berkeley and Los Angeles: University of California Press, 1948), p. 104.
[48] Ibid., pp. 112–13.
[49] Stephen C. Pepper, *Concept and Quality, A World Hypothesis* (La Salle, Ill.: Open Court Publishing Co., 1967), p. 27.
[50] Ibid., p. 18.
[51] Newton P. Stallknecht and Robert S. Brumbaugh, *The Compass of Philosophy* (New York, London, Toronto: Longmans, Green and Co., 1954), p. 11.
[52] Ibid., p. 21. [53] Ibid., p. 89–90. [54] Ibid., p. 229.
[55] Jacques Maritain, *A Preface to Metaphysics, Seven Lectures on Being* (London: Sheed and Ward, 1939), p. 46.
[56] Alfred North Whitehead, *Process and Reality* (New York: Macmillan, 1929), p. 4.

[57] Everett W. Hall, *Philosophical Systems, A Categorial Analysis* (Chicago: University of Chicago Press, 1960), p. 31.

CHAPTER III

[1] A. O. Lovejoy, *The Revolt against Dualism* (La Salle, Ill.: Open Court Publishing Co., 1930), p. 3.

[2] Plato, *Republic*, bk. VI, 509e–11e, in *The Dialogues of Plato*, trans. by B. Jowett (New York: Random House, 1937), vol. I, pp. 771–73. All citations of Plato are to this edition.

[3] Plato, *Timaeus*, 29, vol. II, p. 13.

[4] Ibid., 48–49, vol. II, p. 29.

[5] Plato, *Parmenides*, 130, vol. II, p. 91.

[6] Plato, *Phaedo*, 100, vol. I, p. 485.

[7] Plato, *Parmenides*, 131, vol. II, p. 91.

[8] Plato, *Republic*, VI, 508–09, vol. II, pp. 770–71.

[9] Plato, *Sophist*, 251–53, vol. II, pp. 260–61.

[10] Plato, *Timaeus*, 28–29, vol. II, pp. 12–13.

[11] Aristotle, *Metaphysics*, bk. I, ch. 3, 938a–b in *Basic Works of Aristotle*, Richard McKeon, ed. (New York: Random House, 1941), p. 693. All citations of Aristotle are to this edition.

[12] Ibid., ch. 10, 933a, ll. 14–16, p. 711.

[13] Aristotle, *Categories*, ch. 4, 1b, ll. 25ff, p. 8.

[14] Ibid., ch. 5, 2a, ll. 10–15, p. 9.

[15] Aristotle, *Metaphysics*, bk. VII, ch. 3, 1028b, ll. 34–36, pp. 784–85.

[16] Aristotle, *Categories*, ch. 5, 2b, ll. 15–18, p. 9.

[17] Ibid., 3b, l. 10, p. 12. [18] Ibid., l. 33, p. 12.

[19] Ibid., 4a, ll. 10–18, p. 13. [20] Ibid., 2b, l. 5, p. 9.

[21] Aristotle, *Metaphysics*, bk. VII, ch. 13, 1038b–39a, pp. 804–06.

[22] Ibid., ch. 4, 1029b, ll. 14–15, p. 786.

[23] Ibid., bk. XII, ch. 7, 1072b, ll. 25–30, p. 880.

[24] Ibid., ch. 9, 1074b, ll. 25–35, p. 885.

[25] *The Confessions of Saint Augustine*, trans. by Edward B. Pusey (New York: Modern Library, 1949), bk. VII, p. 140.

[26] See Willard Van Orman Quine, *From a Logical Point of View*, 2nd ed. (Cambridge, Mass.: Harvard University Press, 1961), pp. 9–18. Quine has mitigated his nominalism somewhat, in that in his book—*Word and Object* (Cambridge: Massachusetts Institute of Technology Press, 1960)—he has come to admit the reality of classes.

[27] For a lively account of their famous controversy, see Henry Adams, *Mont Saint-Michel and Chartres* (Boston: Houghton Mifflin Co., 1905), pp. 286–300.

[28] Frederick Copleston, S.J., *A History of Philosophy*, vol. II (London: Burns Oates and Wasbourne, Ltd., 1950), pp. 147–48.

[29] Ibid., p. 150. [30] Ibid., pp. 154–55. [31] Ibid., p. 330.

[32] Ibid., p. 512. [33] Ibid., p. 513. [34] Ibid., vol. III, pp. 56–59.

[35] Ludwig Wittgenstein, *The Blue and Brown Books* (Oxford: Basil Blackwell, 1958), pp. 1ff.

[36] See Renford Bambrough, "Universals and Family Resemblances," *Proceedings of the Aristotelian Society,* N.S., 61 (1961), pp. 215–22.

[37] *St. Augustine on the Teacher* in *Medieval Philosophy,* Herman Shapiro, ed. (New York: Modern Library, 1964), pp. 34, 35, 40–41.

[38] St. Anselm, *Proslogium,* ch. II, in Shapiro, op. cit., pp. 110–11.

[39] See Charles Hartshorne, *The Logic of Perfection and Other Essays in Neoclassical Metaphysics* (La Salle, Ill.: Open Court Publishing Co., 1961), pp. 50–51. See also Charles Hartshorne, *Anselm's Discovery: A Re-examination of the Ontological Argument for God's Existence* (La Salle, Ill.: Open Court Publishing Co., 1965).

[40] Gaunilon, *In Behalf of the Fool,* in Shapiro, op. cit., pp. 113–19.

[41] St. Thomas Aquinas, *Summa Theologica,* Part I, Question 2, Article 1, in *Introduction to St. Thomas Aquinas,* Anton C. Pegis, ed. (New York: Random House, 1948), p. 22. All citations of St. Thomas Aquinas are to this edition.

[42] Ibid., Article 3, p. 25. [43] Ibid., p. 26. [44] Ibid.

[45] Ibid. [46] Ibid., p. 27. [47] Ibid.

[48] See A. O. Lovejoy, *The Great Chain of Being* (Cambridge, Mass.: Harvard University Press, 1936).

[49] René Descartes, *Meditations,* in *Descartes Selections,* Ralph M. Eaton, ed. (New York: Scribner's, 1927), p. 97. All citations of Descartes are to this edition.

[50] Ibid., p. 113. [51] Ibid., p. 118. [52] Ibid., p. 122. [53] Ibid., p. 140.

[54] Ibid., p. 100. [55] Ibid., p. 137. [56] Ibid., p. 160.

[57] Spinoza, *Ethics,* First Part, Definition III, in *Spinoza Selections,* John Wild, ed. (New York: Scribner's, 1930), p. 94. All citations of Spinoza are to this edition.

[58] Ibid., Definition VI, p. 95.

[59] Ibid., Definition IV, p. 94.

[60] Ibid., Second Part, Prop. I, p. 145.

[61] Ibid., Prop. II, p. 146.

[62] Ibid., First Part, Prop V, p. 94.

[63] For discussions of American realism and realists, see Herbert Schneider, *Sources of Contemporary Philosophical Realism in America* (New York: Bobbs-Merrill, 1964); Andrew J. Reck, *Recent American Philosophy* (New York: Pantheon Books, 1964); and Andrew J. Reck, *The New American Philosophers* (Baton Rouge: Louisiana State University Press, 1968).

[64] George Santayana, *Scepticism and Animal Faith* (New York: Dover, 1955), p. 15.

[65] Ibid., pp. 33ff. [66] Ibid., p. 42. [67] Ibid., pp. 9, 30, 103.

[68] Ibid., p. 164.

[69] George Santayana, *Realms of Being* (New York: Scribner's, 1942), p. 18.

[70] Ibid., p. 21. [71] Ibid., p. 155. [72] Ibid., p. 202. [73] Ibid., p. 233.

[74] Ibid., p. 331. [75] Ibid., p. 404. [76] Ibid., p. 549.

CHAPTER IV

[1] *Epicurus to Herodotus,* 55–56, in Cyril Bailey, *Epicurus: The Extant Remains* (Oxford: Clarendon Press, 1926), p. 33. All citations of Epicurus are to this edition unless otherwise indicated.

[2] Aristotle, *Generation and Corruption,* 325a, 23, quoted in W. K. C. Guthrie,

A History of Greek Philosophy (Cambridge: Cambridge University Press, 1965), II, p. 390.

[3] *Epicurus to Herodotus,* 72–73, pp. 44–47.

[4] Guthrie, *op. cit.,* p. 400.

[5] Lucretius, *De Rerum Natura,* ii, ll. 62–332.

[6] Fragment 2 in *Ancilla to the Pre-Socratic Philosophers,* Kathleen Freeman (Oxford: Basil Blackwell, 1948), p. 91.

[7] Fragment 9 in ibid., p. 93.

[8] Frederick Albert Lange, *The History of Materialism* (London and New York: Kegan Paul, Trench, Trubner and Co., Ltd., and Harcourt, Brace and Co., 1925), 3rd ed., vol. I, p. 37.

[9] Epicurus, *Principal Doctrines,* II, 139, p. 95.

[10] *Epicurus to Herodotus,* 77, pp. 48–49.

[11] Epicurus, *Principal Doctrines,* I, 139, p. 95.

[12] See G. S. Brett, *The Philosophy of Gassendi* (London: Macmillan, 1908).

[13] René Descartes, *Principles of Philosophy,* Part II, Principle 1, in *The Philosophical Works of Descartes,* trans. by E. S. Haldane and G. R. T. Ross (Cambridge: Cambridge University Press, 1934), II, p. 254. Page references to Descartes' *Principles of Philosophy* are to Volume II of the Haldane and Ross edition.

[14] *Principles of Philosophy,* Part II, Principle 16, p. 262.

[15] Ibid., Principle 20, p. 264.

[16] "The Third Set of Objections," in Haldane and Ross edition, II, p. 62.

[17] Ibid., p. 61. [18] Ibid., p. 62. [19] Ibid., p. 70.

[20] *Elements of Philosophy,* in *The English Works of Thomas Hobbes,* William Molesworth, ed. (London: John Bohn, 1839), Part I, ch. 1, no. 2, p. 1. Page references to Hobbes's *Elements of Philosophy* are to vol. I of the Molesworth edition.

[21] Ibid., no. 3, p. 3. [22] Ibid., no. 6, p. 7. [23] Ibid., ch. 6, no. 1, p. 66.

[24] Ibid., ch. 1, no. 8, p. 10. [25] Ibid. [26] Ibid., no. 9, p. 11.

[27] Ibid., ch. 6, no. 4, p. 68. [28] Ibid., no. 5, pp. 69–70.

[29] Ibid., no. 6, pp. 70–71. [30] Ibid. [31] Ibid., p. 72. [32] Ibid.

[33] Ibid., no. 7. p. 73. [34] Ibid., Part II, ch. 7, no. 2, p. 94.

[35] Ibid., no. 3, p. 95. [36] Ibid., ch. 8, no. 10, p. 109.

[37] Ibid., ch. 9, no. 3, pp. 121–22. [38] Ibid., ch. 8, no. 1, p. 102.

[39] Ibid., no. 2, p. 104. [40] Ibid., no. 3, p. 104. [41] Ibid.

[42] Ibid., Part IV, ch. 25, no. 3, pp. 391–92. [43] Ibid., no. 26, p. 415.

[44] Ibid., no. 3, p. 417.

[45] Hobbes, *Leviathan, or the Matter, Forms and Power of a Commonwealth Ecclesiastical and Civil,* ed. by Michael Oakeshott (Oxford: Basil Blackwell, 1946), Part I, ch. 6, p. 32.

[46] Ibid., p. 37. [47] Ibid., p. 38. [48] Ibid., Introduction, p. 5.

[49] Ibid., Part I, ch. 12, p. 68.

[50] C. D. Broad, *The Mind and Its Place in Nature* (London: Routledge and Kegan Paul, Ltd., 1925), ch. II.

[51] See Leonora Cohen Rosenfield, *From Beast-Machine to Man-Machine* (New York: Oxford University Press, 1941).

[52] Descartes, *Discourse on Method*, Part V, in *The Philosophical Works of Descartes.* vol. I, pp. 115–17.

[53] Gilbert Ryle, *The Concept of Mind* (London: Hutchinson's University Library, 1949), pp. 15–16.

[54] Aram Vartanian, *La Mettrie's L'homme machine* (Princeton, N.J.: Princeton Univesity Press, 1960), p. 152. All citations are to this edition. (Translation my own.)

[55] Ibid., p. 154. [56] Ibid., p. 163. [57] Ibid., p. 166. [58] Ibid., p. 179.

[59] Ibid., p. 180. [60] Ibid., p. 186.

[61] Baron d'Holbach, *The System of Nature; or, the Laws of the Moral and Physical World* (London: E. Truelove, 1884), Part I, ch. 1, p. 8.

[62] Ibid., ch. 2, p. 12. [63] Ibid., p. 20. [64] Ibid., ch. 1, p. 8.

[65] Ibid., ch. 5, pp. 44–45. [66] Ibid., ch. 1, p. 8. [67] Ibid.

[68] Ibid. [69] Ibid., ch. 6, p. 52. [70] Ibid., ch. 7, p. 64. [71] Ibid., p. 66.

[72] Ibid. [73] Ibid., ch. 1, p. 2. [74] Ibid., ch. 11, p. 123.

[75] Ibid., p. 144.

[76] John Dalton, *New System of Chemical Philosophy,* 2nd ed. (London: J. Weale, 1842), p. 213.

[77] Michael Faraday, "A Speculation touching Electric Conduction and the Nature of Matter," *Philosophical Magazine,* vol. XXIV (1844), pp. 136–44.

[78] Ernest Haeckel, *The Riddle of the Universe,* trans. by Joseph McCabe (London: Watts and Co., 1950), p. 12.

[79] Louis Büchner, *Force and Matter,* ed. and trans. by Frederick Collingwood, 2nd English ed. (London: 1870), p. 2.

[80] Ibid., p. 25. [81] Ibid., p. 2. [82] Ibid., p. 4. [83] Ibid., p. 135.

[84] Ibid., p. 136. [85] Ibid., p. 137. [86] Haeckel, op. cit., p. 173.

[87] Ibid., p. 177. [88] Ibid., p. 106. [89] Ibid., p. 155. [90] Ibid., p. 236.

[91] Ibid., p. 238. [92] Ibid.

[93] William James, *Essays in Radical Empiricism* (London and New York: Longmans, Green and Co., 1912), pp. 3–4.

[94] Bertrand Russell, *The Analysis of Mind* (London and New York: Allen and Unwin, and Macmillan, 1921), pp. 24–25.

[95] Ibid., p. 6.

[96] Bertrand Russell, *The Analysis of Matter* (London and New York: Kegan Paul, Trench, Trubner and Co., Ltd., and Harcourt, Brace and Co., 1927), p. 246.

[97] Ibid., p. 385. [98] Ibid., p. 382. [99] Ibid., p. 384. [100] Ibid., p. 387.

[101] Ibid., p. 388.

[102] Paul K. Feyerabend, "Materialism and the Mind-Body Problem," *Review of Metaphysics,* vol. XVII (1963), pp. 49–66; J. J. C. Smart, "Sensations and Brain Processes," *Philosophical Review,* vol. LXVIII (1959), pp. 141–56; and Herbert Feigl, "The 'Mental' and the 'Physical,'" in *Minnesota Studies in Philosophy of Science,* Herbert Feigl et al., eds. vol. II (Minneapolis: University of Minnesota Press, 1958), pp. 370–497.

[103] See, for example, J. J. C. Smart, *Philosophy and Scientific Realism* (New York: Humanities Press, 1963).

[104] Karl Marx, *A Contribution to the Critique of Political Economy,* trans. from

2nd rev. ed. by N. I. Stone (New York and London: The International Library Publishing Co., and Kegan Paul, Trench, Trubner and Co., Ltd., 1904), pp. 11–12.

[105] Frederick Engels, *Ludwig Feuerbach and the Outcome of Classical German Philosophy* (London: Martin Lawrence, n.d.), p. 15.

[106] Ibid., pp. 73–75.

[107] In addition to the work by Engels cited above, the following works by him are also pertinent landmarks in the development of dialectical materialism: *Dialectics of Nature,* trans. and ed. by Clemens Dutt (London: Lawrence and Wishart, Ltd., 1949); *Anti-Duhring, Herr Eugen Duhring's Revolution in Science* (Moscow: Foreign Languages Publishing House, 1954).

[108] V. I. Lenin, *Materialism and Empirio-Criticism* (Moscow: Foreign Languages Publishing House, 1947).

[109] J. Stalin, *Dialectical and Historical Materialism* (London: Lawrence and Wishart, Ltd., 1941).

[110] Ibid., p. 5. [111] Ibid., p. 6. [112] Ibid. [113] Ibid., p. 7.

[114] Ibid [115] Ibid. [116] Ibid., p. 9. [117] Ibid.

[118] Ibid., p. 11. [119] Ibid., p. 12. [120] Ibid., p. 13.

[121] Richard T. De George, *Patterns of Soviet Thought* (Ann Arbor: University of Michigan Press, 1966), p. 211.

[122] Roy Wood Sellars, "Reflections on Dialectical Materialism," *Philosophy and Phenomenological Research,* vol. V (1944–45), 157–79.

CHAPTER V

[1] Ralph Barton Perry, *Present Philosophical Tendencies* (London: Longmans, Green and Co., 1912), p. 114.

[2] Leibniz, *Monadology,* no. 3, in *Leibniz Selections,* Philip P. Wiener, ed. (New York: Scribners Student Library, 1951), p. 533. All citations of Leibniz are to this edition.

[3] Ibid., no. 8, p. 534. [4] Ibid., no. 7, p. 534.

[5] Leibniz, *Principles of Nature and Grace,* no. 1, p. 522.

[6] Ibid., no. 2, p. 523. [7] Ibid., no. 4, p. 523.

[8] Leibniz, *Monadology,* no. 18, p. 536.

[9] Ibid., no. 20, p. 537. [10] Ibid., no. 21, p. 537.

[11] Leibniz, *Principles of Nature and Grace,* no. 3, pp. 523–24.

[12] Leibniz, *Monadology,* no. 19, p. 537.

[13] Leibniz, *Principles of Nature and Grace,* no. 4, p. 524.

[14] Ibid.

[15] Leibniz, *Monadology,* no. 29, p. 539.

[16] Ibid., no. 30, p. 539.

[17] Leibniz, *Principles of Nature and Grace,* no. 15, p. 531.

[18] Leibniz, *Monadology,* no. 40, pp. 540–41.

[19] Leibniz, *New System of Nature* (1695), no. 11, p. 112.

[20] Ibid.

[21] Leibniz, "Second Explanation of the System of the Communication of Substances," (1696), p. 118.

[22] Ibid. [23] Ibid. [24] Ibid., pp. 118–19.

[25] Leibniz, *Monadology,* no. 46, p. 542.
[26] John Locke, *An Essay Concerning Human Understanding,* vol. II, no. 1, p. xxiii.
[27] Ibid., no. 2, p. xxiii.
[28] George Berkeley, *The Principles of Human Knowledge,* in G. J. Warnock edition of *The Principles of Human Knowledge and Three Dialogues between Hylas and Philonous* (London: Collins, 1962), no. 1, p. 65. All citations are to this edition.
[29] Ibid., no. 2, p. 65. [30] Ibid., p. 66. [31] Ibid., no. 3, p. 66.
[32] Ibid., no. 7, p. 67. [33] Ibid., no. 23, p. 76.
[34] George Berkeley, *Philosophical Commentaries,* ed. by A. A. Luce (London: Thomas Nelson, 1944), p. 429; quoted in A. A. Luce, *Berkeley's Immaterialism* (London: Thomas Nelson, 1945), p. 61.
[35] Berkeley, *The Principles of Human Knowledge,* no. 7, p. 68.
[36] Ibid., no. 6, pp. 67–68.
[37] Berkeley, *Three Dialogues Between Hylas and Philonous,* p. 258.
[38] Bertrand Russell, *Our Knowledge of the External World,* rev. ed. (London: Allen and Unwin, 1926), pp. 96–97.
[39] Alfred Jules Ayer, *The Foundations of Empirical Knowledge* (London: Macmillan, 1940), p. 232.
[40] Berkeley, *The Principles of Human Knowledge,* no. 32, p. 79.
[41] Ibid., no. 98, p. 114. [42] Ibid., no. 116, p. 123. [43] Ibid., no. 9, p. 69.
[44] John Stuart Mill, *An Examination of Sir William Hamilton's Philosophy* (London: Longmans, Green and Co., 1865), p. 198.
[45] David Hume, *A Treatise on Human Nature,* ed. by L. A. Selby-Bigge (Oxford: Clarendon Press, 1896), bk. I, Part IV, ch. 2, p. 207.
[46] Berkeley, *The Principles of Human Knowledge,* no. 142, p. 142.
[47] Immanuel Kant, *Critique of Pure Reason,* trans. by Norman Kemp Smith (London: Macmillan, 1933), B274, p. 244. All citations are to this translation.
[48] G. E. Moore, "The Refutation of Idealism," *Mind,* vol. XII (October 1903), pp. 433–53; reprinted in *Philosophical Studies* (London: Routledge and Kegan Paul, Ltd., 1922).
[49] Ralph Barton Perry, "The Egocentric Predicament," *Journal of Philosophy, Psychology, and Scientific Methods,* vol. VII (1910), pp. 5–14.
[50] Walter T. Stace, "The Refutation of Realism," *Mind,* vol. XLIII (1934), pp. 145–55.
[51] Walter T. Stace, *The Theory of Knowledge and Existence* (Oxford: Clarendon Press, 1932), p. 443.
[52] Walter T. Stace, *The Nature of the World, An Essay in Phenomenalist Metaphysics* (Princeton, N.J.: Princeton University Press, 1940), p. 34.
[53] Ibid., p. 36. [54] Ibid., p. 244.
[55] Immanuel Kant, *Critique of Pure Reason,* A369, p. 345.
[56] P. F. Strawson, *The Bounds of Sense, an Essay on Kant's Critique of Pure Reason* (London: Methuen and Co., 1966), p. 15.
[57] Ibid., pp. 15–16. [58] Ibid., p. 32. [59] Ibid., p. 16.
[60] Immanuel Kant, *Prolegomena to any Future Metaphysics,* trans. with Introduction and Notes by Peter G. Lucas (Manchester: Manchester University Press, 1953), no. 36, p. 82.
[61] Ibid., p. 50.

[62] Immanuel Kant, *Critique of Pure Reason,* A79, B105, p. 113.
[63] Ibid., A95, p. 128. [64] Ibid., p. 160.
[65] Kant, *Prolegomena to any Future Metaphysics,* no. 39, p. 85.
[66] Immanuel Kant, *Critique of Pure Reason,* B159, p. 170.
[67] Strawson, op. cit., p. 24.
[68] Ibid., p. 25. [69] Ibid., p. 26.
[70] Immanuel Kant, *Critique of Pure Reason,* B131, p. 152.
[71] Ibid., Bxxx, p. 29.
[72] Arthur Schopenhauer, *The World as Will and Idea,* trans. by R. B. Haldane and John Kemp (London: Trubner and Co., 1886), vol. II, Supplement to Second Book, ch. XVIII, p. 405.
[73] Ibid., pp. 405–06. [74] Ibid., p. 407. [75] Ibid., vol. I, bk. IV, p. 354.
[76] Ibid., bk. II, p. 191. [77] Ibid., bk. IV, p. 402.
[78] Ibid., p. 398. [79] Ibid., p. 404. [80] Ibid., p. 402.
[81] W. T. Harris, Preface to J. G. Fichte, *The Science of Knowledge,* trans. by A. E. Kroeger (London: Trubner and Co., 1889), p. xix.
[82] Fichte, *The Science of Knowledge,* p. 63.
[83] Ibid., p. 72. [84] Ibid., p. 77. [85] Ibid., p. 78.
[86] Ibid., p. 84. [87] Ibid., p. 259. [88] Ibid., p. 265.
[89] John Watson, *Schelling's Transcendental Idealism, A Critical Exposition* (Chicago: S. C. Griggs and Co., 1882), p. 72.
[90] William Wallace, *The Logic of Hegel* (Oxford: Clarendon Press, 1892), 2nd ed., no. 42, p. 89.
[91] Ibid., p. 89. [92] Ibid., p. 90. [93] Ibid., no. 45, p. 93.
[94] Ibid., pp. 93–94. [95] Ibid., p. 94.
[96] Hegel, Preface to *Phenomenology of Mind,* trans. by J. B. Baillie, 2nd ed. (London: Allen and Unwin, 1931), p. 79.
[97] Wallace, op. cit., no. 85, p. 156.
[98] Ibid., p. 157.
[99] Hegel, op. cit., p. 80.
[100] Hegel, *Lectures on the History of Philosophy,* trans. by E. S. Haldane and F. H. Simson (London: K. Paul, Trench, Trubner and Co., 1892–1896), vol. III, p. 256.
[101] Ibid., pp. 257–58. [102] Ibid. [103] Ibid., pp. 285–86.
[104] Ibid., p. 287. [105] Ibid., p. 288.
[106] Thomas Hill Green, *Prolegomena to Ethics,* ed. by A. C. Bradley (Oxford: Clarendon Press, 1883), no. 13, p. 17.
[107] Ibid., no. 28, p. 31. [108] Ibid., no. 29, p. 32.
[109] G. Watts Cunningham, *The Idealistic Argument in Recent British and American Philosophy* (New York and London: The Century Company, 1933), ch. XVI, esp. pp. 382–407.
[110] F. H. Bradley, *The Principles of Logic,* 2nd ed. (London: Oxford University Press, 1922), vol. I, p. 13.
[111] Ibid., p. 10.(The bracketed adjective is supplied from note 11 to ch. I, p. 39.)
[112] Ibid., I. p. 10. [113] Ibid., p. 11. [114] Ibid., p. 46.
[115] F. H. Bradley, *Appearance and Reality,* 2nd ed. (Oxford: Clarendon Press, 1897), ch. III, no. 1, p. 20.
[116] Ibid., no. 2, p. 25. [117] Ibid. [118] Ibid., p. 26.

[119] Ibid. [120] Ibid., pp. 26, 27. [121] Ibid., no. 3, p. 27.
[122] Ibid., p. 120. [123] Ibid., p. 123. [124] Ibid., p. 125.
[125] Ibid., p. 126. [126] Ibid., p. 127. [127] Ibid., p. 128.
[128] Ibid., p. 129. [129] Ibid., p. 140.
[130] F. H. Bradley, *Essays on Truth and Reality* (Oxford: Clarendon Press, 1914), p. 188.
[131] Cunningham, op. cit., p. 400.
[132] B. Bosanquet, *The Principle of Individuality and Value* (London: Macmillan, 1912), p. v.
[133] Ibid., p. 68. [134] Ibid. [135] Ibid., p. 37. [136] Ibid., p. 38.
[137] Ibid., p. 283. [138] Ibid., p. 287. [139] Ibid., p. 69.
[140] Ibid., p. 320. [141] Ibid., p. 322. [142] Ibid., p. 378.
[143] See Andrew J. Reck, "Royce's Metaphysics," *Revue internationale de philosophie,* no. 79–80 (1967), pp. 8–21.
[144] Josiah Royce, *The Religious Aspect of Philosophy* (Boston: Houghton, Mifflin and Co., 1885), p. 141.
[145] Ibid., p. 423.
[146] See especially Royce's supplementary essay on individuality in *The Conception of God* (New York: Macmillan, 1897), pp. 135ff.
[147] Josiah Royce, *The World and the Individual* (New York: Macmillan, 1899), vol. II, pp. 507ff.
[148] Josiah Royce, *The Problem of Christianity* (New York: Macmillan, 1913), vol. II, pp. 272–73, 218–19.
[149] John McTaggart Ellis McTaggart, *Studies in Hegelian Cosmology* (Cambridge: University Press, 1918), no. 3, p. 3.
[150] Ibid., no. 42, p. 37. [151] Ibid., nos. 52–56, pp. 47–52.
[152] Ibid., no. 61, p. 57. [153] Ibid. [154] Ibid., no. 70, p. 68.
[155] Ibid., no. 86, p. 83. [156] Ibid., no. 87, p. 83. [157] Ibid., p. 84.
[158] John McTaggart Ellis McTaggart, *The Nature of Existence,* 2 vols. (Cambridge: Cambridge University Press, 1921, 1927). This work constitutes one of the high points of speculative metaphysics, on which Charles Dunbar Broad has written a two-volume commentary, *Examination of McTaggart's Philosophy* (Cambridge: Cambridge University Press, 1933, 1938). A study of both McTaggart's work and C. D. Broad's commentary affords perhaps the richest experience of metaphysics and analysis available to the contemporary student.
[159] McTaggart, *The Nature of Existence,* vol. I, no. 135, p. 147.
[160] Ibid., vol. II, no. 488, p. 176.
[161] Ibid., nos. 401–04, pp. 82–86; and no. 491, p. 178.
[162] Ibid., no. 492, p. 179.
[163] Ibid., no. 495, pp. 181–82.
[164] Ibid., ch. xxxiii; and McTaggart, "The Relation of Time and Eternity," *University of California Chronicle,* vol. X, no. 2 (1908), pp. 3–28.
[165] McTaggart, *The Nature of Existence,* vol. II, no. 329, p. 20.
[166] Ibid. [167] Ibid. [168] Ibid., vol. II, no. 331, p. 21. [169] Ibid.
[170] For criticisms of McTaggart's arguments concerning time, see Cunningham, op. cit., pp. 501–07; and Broad, op. cit., vol. II, pp. 313–17. Broad's criticism is especially caustic, charging that "McTaggart's main argument against the reality

of Time is a philosophical 'howler' of the same kind as the Ontological Argument for the Existence of God" (p. 16).

[171] McTaggart, *The Nature of Existence,* vol. II, no. 500, p. 185.

[172] Ibid., no. 501, p. 186.

[173] John McTaggart Ellis McTaggart, *The Further Determination of the Absolute* (privately printed, 1896?), p. 15; and McTaggart, *Studies in Hegelian Cosmology,* no. 271, p. 260.

[174] For discussion of the philosophies of Hocking, Boodin, and Urban, see Andrew J. Reck, *Recent American Philosophy* (New York: Pantheon Books, 1964), chs. 2, 4, 5. For a discussion of Blanshard's philosophy, see Andrew J. Reck, *The New American Philosophers* (Baton Rouge: Louisiana State University Press, 1968), ch. 3.

[175] For a full discussion of Brightman's philosophy, see Reck, *Recent American Philosophy,* ch. 10, pp. 311–36.

[176] Edgar Sheffield Brightman, *Person and Reality,* ed. by Peter A. Bertocci in collaboration with J. E. Newhall and R. S. Brightman (New York: The Ronald Press, 1958), p. 18.

[177] Edgar Sheffield Brightman, *Nature and Values* (New York: Abingdon Press, 1945), p. 56.

CHAPTER VI

[1] Alfred North Whitehead, *Science and the Modern World* (New York: Macmillan, 1925), p. 106.

[2] Alfred North Whitehead, *Process and Reality* (New York: Macmillan, 1929), p. v.

[3] Douglas Browning, ed., *Process Philosophy* (New York: Random House, 1966).

[4] Heraclitus, Fragment 123, *Ancilla to the Pre-Socratic Philosophers,* in Kathleen Freeman (Oxford: Basil Blackwell, 1948), p. 33.

[5] Plato, *Cratylus,* 440C. See Philip Wheelwright, *Heraclitus* (Princeton, N.J.: Princeton University Press, 1959), p. 138.

[6] Freeman, op. cit., pp. 28,31.

[7] Ibid., pp. 27,30.

[8] G. S. Kirk, *Heraclitus: The Cosmic Fragments* (Cambridge: Cambridge University Press, 1954), p. 319.

[9] Freeman, op. cit., pp. 29,31.

[10] Ibid., pp. 29,26. [11] Ibid., pp. 30,28,24,28. [12] Ibid., p. 29.

[13] W. K. C. Guthrie, *A History of Greek Philosophy* (Cambridge: Cambridge University Press, 1962), II, ch. vii, especially pp. 419ff.

[14] Freeman, op. cit., p. 24.

[15] John Dewey, *The Influence of Darwin on Philosophy and Other Essays in Contemporary Thought* (New York: Henry Holt and Co., 1911).

[16] Herbert Spencer, *An Autobiography* (New York: D. Appleton and Co., 1904), vol. II, p. 7.

[17] Ibid., p. 57. [18] Ibid., pp. 57–58.

[19] Herbert Spencer, *First Principles* (Akron, Ohio: D. Appleton and Co., 1900), 6th ed., p. 119.

[20] Ibid., pp. 27,39. [21] Ibid., p. 55. [22] Ibid., pp. 82–83.
[23] Spencer, *An Autobiography,* vol. II, p. 86.
[24] Spencer, *First Principles,* p. 143.
[25] Ibid., p. 147. [26] Ibid., p. 146. [27] Ibid., p. 148. [28] Ibid., p. 150.
[29] Ibid., p. 151. [30] Ibid. [31] Ibid., p. 152. [32] Ibid., p. 249.
[33] Ibid., p. 251. [34] Ibid., p. 252. [35] Ibid., p. 367. [36] Ibid., p. 369.
[37] Ibid., p. 374. [38] Ibid., p. 423. [39] Ibid., p. 447.
[40] Ibid., p. 475. [41] Ibid., p. 506.
[42] Henri Bergson, *Creative Evolution,* trans. by A. Mitchell (New York: Modern Library, 1944), p. 396.
[43] Henri Bergson, *The Creative Mind,* trans. by M. L. Andison (New York: Philosophical Library, 1946), p. 12.
[44] Ibid.
[45] Charles Sanders Peirce, "Evolutionary Love," originally published in *Monist,* vol. III (1893); reprinted in *Collected Works,* vol. VI, p. 302.
[46] Charles Sanders Peirce, "The Architecture of Theories," originally published in *Monist,* vol. I (1891); reprinted in *Collected Works,* vol. VI, p. 33.
[47] William James, *A Pluralistic Universe* (New York: Longmans, Green and Co., 1909), pp. 347–52.
[48] Ibid., pp. 225ff.
[49] Henri Bergson, *Time and Free Will, An Essay on the Immediate Data of Consciousness,* trans. by F. L. Pogson (London: Macmillan, 1913), p. 133.
[50] Ibid., p. 105. [51] Ibid., p. 101. [52] Ibid., p. 99. [53] Ibid., p. 110.
[54] Bergson, *Creative Evolution,* p. 6.
[55] Bergson, *Time and Free Will,* p. 227.
[56] Henri Bergson, *Matter and Memory,* trans. by N. Paul and W. S. Palmer (London: Macmillan, 1913), p. 313.
[57] Bergson, *Creative Evolution,* p. 328.
[58] Ibid.. p. 374.
[59] Bergson, *The Creative Mind,* p. 173.
[60] Bergson, *Matter and Memory,* p. 177.
[61] Ibid., p. 246. [62] Ibid., p. 260. [63] Ibid., p. 4.
[64] Bergson, *The Creative Mind,* p. 103.
[65] Bergson, *Creative Evolution,* p. 14.
[66] Ibid., p. 19.
[67] Bergson, *The Creative Mind,* p. 211.
[68] Bergson, *Creative Evolution,* p. 7.
[69] Bergson, *The Creative Mind,* p. 11.
[70] Bergson, *Creative Evolution,* p. 27.
[71] Bergson, *The Creative Mind,* p. 17.
[72] Bergson, *Creative Evolution,* p. 271.
[73] Ibid., pp. 269–70. [74] Ibid., p. 271. [75] Ibid., p. 3. [76] Ibid. p. 10.
[77] Bergson, *Time and Free Will,* p. 100.
[78] Ibid., p. 125. [79] Ibid., p. 182. [80] Ibid., p. 183. [81] Ibid., p. 219.
[82] Henri Bergson, *Durée et simultanéité* (Paris: F. Alcan, 1926).
[83] S. Alexander, *Space, Time, and Deity* (London: Macmillan, 1920), vol. I, p. 8.

[84] Ibid., pp. 10–11. [85] Ibid., p. 10.

[86] Alexander, "The Basis of Realism," *Proceedings of the British Academy* (1913–14), vol. VI, p. 285.

[87] Ibid., p. 284. [88] Ibid., p. 288. [89] Ibid., p. 302.

[90] Ibid., p. 304. [91] Ibid., p. 289. [92] Ibid., p. 292.

[93] Alexander, *Space, Time, and Deity,* vol. I, p. 31.

[94] Ibid., p. 37. [95] Ibid., p. 171. [96] Ibid., p. 166. [97] Ibid., p. 38.

[98] Ibid., p. 39. [99] Ibid., p. 40. [100] Ibid., p. 44. [101] Ibid., p. 46.

[102] Ibid., p. 47. [103] Ibid., p. 48. [104] Ibid., p. 65. [105] Ibid., p. 61.

[106] Ibid. [107] Ibid., p. 149. [108] Ibid., p. 143. [109] Ibid., p. 87.

[110] Ibid., p. 59. [111] Ibid., p. 76. [112] Ibid., p. 346. [113] Ibid., p. 185.

[114] Ibid., p. 191. [115] Ibid., p. 194. [116] Ibid., vol. II, p. 323.

[117] Ibid., p. 74. [118] Ibid., p. 142. [119] Ibid., p. 14.

[120] Ibid., p. 45. [121] Ibid., p. 47.

[122] A. O. Lovejoy, "The Meaning of 'Emergence' and Its Modes," *Proceedings of the Sixth International Congress of Philosophy* (New York: Longmans, Green and Co., 1927).

[123] Alexander, *Space, Time, and Deity,* vol. II, p. 73.

[124] Ibid., p. 52. [125] Ibid., p. 38. [126] Ibid., p. 44.

[127] Ibid., p. 345. [128] Ibid., p. 342. [129] Ibid., p. 348.

[130] Ibid., p. 364. [131] Ibid., p. 379. [132] Ibid., p. 410.

[133] Ibid., p. 396. [134] Ibid., p. 397. [135] Ibid., p. 398.

[136] George Herbert Mead, *The Philosophy of the Present* (La Salle, Ill.: Open Court Publishing Co., 1932), p. 1.

[137] Ibid.

[138] A. O. Lovejoy, "Time, Meaning and Transcendence," *Journal of Philosophy,* vol. XIX (1922), p. 505.

[139] Mead, op. cit., p. 9.

[140] George Herbert Mead, "The Nature of the Past," in *Selected Writings,* Andrew J. Reck, ed. (Indianapolis: Bobbs-Merrill, 1964), p. 349.

[141] Ibid., p. 345.

[142] George Herbert Mead, *The Philosophy of the Act,* edited with Introduction by Charles W. Morris (Chicago: University of Chicago Press, 1938). For a discussion of Mead's philosophy, see Andrew J. Reck, *Recent American Philosophy* (New York: Pantheon Books, 1964), ch. 3.

[143] John Dewey and Arthur Bentley, *Knowing and the Known* (Boston: Beacon Press, 1949), p. 123. For a recent example of transactional metaphysics, see John Herman Randall, *Nature and Historical Experience* (New York: Columbia University Press, 1958). For a discussion of Randall's philosophy, see Andrew J. Reck, *The New American Philosophers* (Baton Rouge: Louisiana State University Press, 1968), ch. IV.

[144] John Laird, "Samuel Alexander 1859–1938," *Proceedings of the British Academy,* vol. XXIV (1939), p. 15.

[145] For an excellent guide, see Donald W. Sherburne, *A Key to Whitehead's 'Process and Reality'* (New York: Macmillan, 1966).

[146] Whitehead, *Process and Reality,* p. 27.

[147] Ibid. [148] Ibid. [149] Ibid., p. 28.

[150] See Ivor Leclerc, *Whitehead's Metaphysics* (New York: Macmillan, 1958), p. 17.

[151] Whitehead, *Process and Reality,* p. 373.

[152] Ibid., p. 28. [153] Ibid., pp. 36–37. [154] Ibid., p. 28.

[155] Ibid., p. 32. [156] Ibid., p. 28. [157] Ibid., p. 30.

[158] Ibid., p. 27. [159] Ibid., p. 31. [160] Ibid. [161] Ibid.

[162] Ibid., p. 32. [163] Ibid., p. 33. [164] Ibid., p. 32.

[165] Alfred North Whitehead, *An Enquiry Concerning the Principles of Natural Knowledge* (Cambridge: Cambridge University Press, 1919); and Alfred North Whitehead, *The Concept of Nature* (Cambridge: Cambridge University Press, 1920).

[166] Even Whitehead's disciple, Victor Lowe, is troubled by the doctrine of eternal objects. He proposes to assign the role of eternal objects as potentials to Whitehead's category of propositions. See Victor Lowe, *Understanding Whitehead* (Baltimore: Johns Hopkins University Press, paperback, 1966), p. 260.

[167] Whitehead, *Process and Reality,* p. 28.

[168] Ibid., p. 11.

[169] William A. Christian, *An Interpretation of Whitehead's Metaphysics* (New Haven: Yale University Press, 1959), pp. 409ff.

[170] Charles Hartshorne, "Whitehead's Idea of God," *The Philosophy of Alfred North Whitehead,* ed. by Paul Arthur Schilpp ("The Library of Living Philosophers") (Evanston: Northwestern University Press, 1940), pp. 515–59.

[171] Charles Hartshorne, *The Divine Relativity* (New Haven: Yale University Press, 1948), pp. 30–31.

[172] Lowe, op. cit., p. 290.

[173] See Andrew J. Reck, "The Fox Alone is Death: Whitehead and Speculative Philosophy," *American Philosophy and the Future,* ed. by Michael Novak (New York: Scribner's, 1968), pp. 156–64.

[174] See especially Paul Weiss, *Modes of Being* (Carbondale: Southern Illinois University Press, 1958). For a discussion of Weiss's philosophy, see Reck, *The New American Philosophers,* ch. X.

[175] See especially Hartshorne, *The Divine Relativity.* For a discussion of Hartshorne's philosophy, see Reck, *The New American Philosophers,* ch. IX.

[176] Christian, op. cit., pp. 28–29.

[177] Whitehead, *Process and Reality,* p. 124.

[178] Ibid., p. 113. [179] Ibid., p. 43. [180] Ibid., p. 94.

[181] Ibid., p. 318. [182] Ibid., p. 314.

[183] Lowe, op. cit., p. 260.

[184] Whitehead, *Process and Reality,* p. 513.

[185] Pierre Teilhard de Chardin, *The Phenomenon of Man,* rev. Engl. ed. (New York: Harper and Row, 1965), p. 35.

[186] Ibid. [187] Ibid., p. 52. [188] Ibid., p. 56. [189] Ibid., p. 64.

[190] Ibid., p. 78. [191] Ibid., p. 165. [192] Ibid. [193] Ibid.

[194] Ibid., p. 221. [195] Ibid., p. 180. [196] Ibid., p. 182.

[197] Ibid., p. 183. [198] Ibid., p. 268. [199] Ibid., p. 269.

[200] Ibid., p. 270. [201] Ibid., p. 271.

CHAPTER VII

[1] C. D. Broad, "Critical and Speculative Philosophy," *Contemporary British Philosophy,* 1st Series, ed. by J. H. Muirhead (London and New York: Allen and Unwin, and Macmillan, 1924), p. 83.

[2] Ibid., p. 96. [3] Ibid. [4] Ibid. [5] Ibid. [6] Ibid., pp. 96–97.

[7] John Passmore, "The Place of Argument in Metaphysics," in *Metaphysics, Readings and Reappraisals,* ed. by W. E. Kennick and Morris Lazerowitz (Englewood Cliffs, N.J.: Prentice Hall, 1966), p. 358.

[8] Ibid.

[9] John Wisdom, "Ostentation," *Philosophy and Psychoanalysis* (New York: Philosophical Library, 1953), p. 3.

[10] Ibid., fn.

[11] Jean-Paul Sartre, "Qu'est ce que la littérature," *Situations,* vol. II (Paris: Gallimard, 1948), p. 251. (Translation my own.)

[12] Roderick M. Chisholm, Herbert Feigl, William K. Frankena, John Passmore, Manley Thompson, *Philosophy* (Englewood Cliffs, N.J.: Prentice Hall, 1964), p. 231.

[13] C. S. Peirce "The Architecture of Theories," *Collected Papers,* vol. VI, pp. 11–37.

[14] Ludwig Wittgenstein, *Tractatus Logico-Philosophicus* (London: Routledge and Kegan Paul, Ltd., 1960), p. 189.

[15] Rudolf Carnap, *The Logical Syntax of Language* (London: Routledge and Kegan Paul, Ltd., 1937), p. 286.

[16] Ibid., pp. 303–04. [17] Ibid., p. 313.

[18] Rudolf Carnap, "The Elimination of Metaphysics Through Logical Analysis of Language," trans. by Arthur Pap in *Logical Positivism,* ed. by A. J. Ayer (Glencoe, Ill.: The Free Press, 1959), pp. 69–73.

[19] Martin Heidegger, "What is Metaphysics?" trans. by R. F. C. Hall and Alan Crick in *Existence and Being,* ed. by W. Brock (Chicago: Regnery and Co., 1949).

[20] Wisdom, "Philosophical Perplexity," *Philosophy and Psychoanalysis,* p. 41.

[21] John Wisdom, *Paradox and Discovery* (New York: Philosophical Library, 1965), p. 165.

[22] Wisdom, *Philosophy and Psychoanalysis,* p. 178.

[23] Ibid., p. 41.

[24] Ludwig Wittgenstein, "A Lecture on Ethics," *Philosophical Review,* vol. LXXIV (1965).

[25] Wisdom, *Philosophy and Psychoanalysis,* p. 50.

[26] Ibid., p. 119.

[27] Brand Blanshard, "In Defense of Metaphysics," in *Metaphysics: Readings and Reappraisals,* op. cit., p. 334.

[28] Ibid., pp. 334–35. [29] Ibid., pp. 335–37.

[30] Ibid., p. 338. [31] Ibid., pp. 338–39.

[32] *Kierkegaard's Concluding Unscientific Postscript,* trans. by David L. Swenson and Walter Lowrie (Princeton, N.J.: Princeton University Press, 1941), p. 49.

[33] Ibid., p. 55. [34] Ibid., p. 107. [35] Ibid. [36] Ibid., p. 243.

[37] Carnap, *The Logical Syntax of Language,* p. 278.
[38] Carnap, "The Elimination of Metaphysics Through Logical Analysis of Language," op. cit., p. 80.
[39] W. H. Walsh, *Metaphysics* (New York: Harcourt, Brace and World, Inc., 1963), p. 18.
[40] William Pepperell Montague, *Great Visions of Philosophy* (La Salle, Ill.: Open Court Publishing Co., 1950), pp. 13–21.
[41] Stephen Pepper, "An Essay on the Essay: An Aesthetic Appreciation," *The New Scholasticism,* vol. XLI (1967), pp. 295–311.
[42] A. N. Whitehead, *Adventures of Ideas* (New York: Macmillan, 1949), p. 313.
[43] Iris Murdoch, "Metaphysics and Ethics," *The Nature of Metaphysics,* ed. by D. F. Pears (London and New York: Macmillan and St. Martin's Press, 1957), p. 104.
[44] G. E. Moore, *Principia Ethica* (Cambridge: Cambridge University Press, 1903).
[45] Murdoch, op. cit., pp. 114–15.
[46] Ibid., p. 115. [47] Ibid.
[48] Sidney Hook, *Political Power and Personal Freedom* (New York: Criterion Books, 1959), p. 44.
[49] Ibid.
[50] Karl Mannheim, "Historicism," *Essays on the Sociology of Knowledge,* ed. by Paul Kecskemeti (London: Routledge and Kegan Paul, Ltd., 1952), p. 84.
[51] Maurice Cornforth, *In Defense of Philosophy* (New York: International Publishers, 1950), p. 48.
[52] Ibid., p. 45.
[53] Ibid., p. 46. Frederick Engels' letter to F. Mehring, July 14, 1893, quoted by Cornforth.
[54] F. S. C. Northrop, *The Meeting of East and West* (New York: Macmillan, 1946).
[55] James K. Feibleman, *The Theory of Human Culture* (New York: Duell, Sloan and Pearce, 1946).
[56] Alexander Herzberg, *The Psychology of the Philosophers* (London and New York: Kegan Paul, Trench, Trubner and Co., Ltd., and Harcourt, Brace and Co., 1929).
[57] Ibid., p. 185.
[58] G. E. Moore, "A Defense of Common Sense," *Contemporary British Philosophy,* 2nd Series, ed. by J. H. Muirhead (London and New York: Allen and Unwin, Macmillan, n.d.), p. 207.
[59] Ibid., pp. 222–23.
[60] Arthur Schopenhauer, *The World as Will and Idea,* trans. by R. B. Haldane and J. Kemp (London: Routledge and Kegan Paul, Ltd., 1948), vol. II, p. 375.
[61] Ibid., pp. 359ff.
[62] Morris Lazerowitz, *The Structure of Metaphysics* (London: Routledge and Kegan Paul, Ltd., 1955), p. 26.
[63] Ibid., p. 66. [64] Ibid., pp. 69ff. [65] Ibid., p. 67. [66] Ibid.
[67] Herzberg, op. cit., p. 221.
[68] William James, *Pragmatism* (New York and London: Longmans, Green and Co., 1907), p. 45.
[69] Ibid.

[70] John Dewey, *The Quest for Certainty* (New York: Capicorn Books, 1960), ch. I.
[71] John Dewey, *Reconstruction in Philosophy* (New York: New American Library, 1950), p. 39.
[72] Blanshard, op. cit., p. 341.
[73] Ibid., p. 343.

INDEX